D1810913

# The Importance of Ideals

## Debating Their Relevance
## in Law, Morality, and Politics

P.I.E.-Peter Lang

Bruxelles · Bern · Berlin · Frankfurt/M · New York · Oxford · Wien

Wibren VAN DER BURG & Sanne TAEKEMA (eds.)

# The Importance of Ideals

# Debating Their Relevance in Law, Morality, and Politics

Series Philosophy & Politics
No.10

No part of this book may be reproduced in any form, by print, photocopy, microfilm or any other means, without prior written permission from the publisher. All rights reserved.

© P.I.E.-Peter Lang S.A.
PRESSES INTERUNIVERSITAIRES EUROPÉENNES
Brussels, 2004
1 avenue Maurice, 1050 Brussels, Belgium
info@peterlang.com; www.peterlang.net

ISSN 1376-0920
ISBN 90-5201-226-1
US ISBN 0-8204-6615-8
D/2004/5678/09
Printed in Belgium

*CIP available from the British Library, GB
and the Library of Congress, USA.*

Bibliographic information published by "Die Deutsche Bibliothek"

"Die Deutsche Bibliothek" lists this publication in the "Deutsche Nationalbibliografie"; detailed bibliographic data is available in the Internet at <http://dnb.ddb.de>.

# Table of Contents

# Preface

In the period 1997-2002, a group of some twenty researchers at Tilburg University has cooperated in a research programme entitled 'The Importance of Ideals in Law, Morality and Politics'. This research programme was partly funded by a PIONIER grant from the Netherlands Organisation for Scientific Research (NWO). Without the generous support of not only NWO, but also of Tilburg University and its Schoordijk Institute, the programme would not have been possible.

This volume of essays marks the conclusion of the project: here, the most important findings of the programme on the role of ideals have been brought together. It is a truly interdisciplinary study in which (as a result of the long cooperation within the research group) insights from different disciplines such as law, legal theory, political philosophy, ethics and social sciences are combined and confronted with each other.

The authors of the present volume all participated in the PIONIER programme, but its success also depended on the work done by the other participants: Frans Brom, Margreth de Bonth, Ernst Hirsch Ballin, Thijs Jansen, Sophie van Bijsterveld, Maarten van Dijck, Paul van Seters, Anton Vedder, and Bertjan Wolthuis. The programme as a whole has also benefited greatly from discussions with colleagues in both Dutch and international forums, and especially from the scholars who visited the group: Lior Barshack, Bernard Gert, Hans Joas, Jeff Johnson, David Luban, Philip Selznick, Brian Tamanaha, and Jeremy Waldron.

We would also like to thank Hildegard Penn for editing the manuscript and Tomas Roosenschoon and Luigi Corrias for their help in processing the manuscript.

the existence of ideals as an identifiable aspect of social practices may be doubted.

Moreover, there is another reason that justifies the attention paid to ideals. A description of ideals and the way they function can also be used for the critical assessment of normatively laden fields such as law and morality. The claim is then that an ideal-oriented theory is of more use for the evaluation of such fields: here, a descriptive theory of ideals is linked to a normative theory.

## Thesis 3: Ideal-orientation is fruitful for the evaluation and guidance of practices in law, morality and politics

This means that understanding the role of ideals can help to formulate criticism of the use made of ideals, of the way they are interpreted and of the extent to which they are neglected or overemphasized. By means of this critical perspective on the role of ideals, proposals can be made both for guidance in a problem area and for a better implementation of ideals. Explicating ideals involved in legal or political practice is necessary for a well-informed evaluation of such practices. It is, however, an approach that connects ideals to specific topics in the fields of law, politics and morality, and it is only in connection with these specific topics that evaluation can be meaningfully done. Thus, it is not wholesale ideological critique, an unmasking of the neglect of ideals across the board or anything of the kind that is proposed; it is in the combination of guiding ideals with particular problems and discussions that ideal orientation works for a normative theory.

This view of ideals and ideal-oriented theory is typical in its propositions of jurisprudence that is sociologically informed. Stressing the connection between ideals and social reality as well as the combination of descriptive and normative theory, it takes a large part of its inspiration from the 'jurisprudential sociology' of the Berkeley School in sociology, in particular from the work of Philip Selznick.[5] In the field of the philosophy of law, it has a close affinity with the work of Lon Fuller. These are two theorists who have stressed, first, the role of an aspirational element in law, and second, the place of law in society. Although their

---

[5]  The term 'jurisprudential sociology' is taken from the title of an article by Philippe Nonet, 'For Jurisprudential Sociology', *Law & Society Review* 10 (1976), 525-545, in which he explains what he calls the 'Berkeley Program'. Works by Selznick on the sociology of law include *Law, Society and Industrial Justice*, New York, Russell Sage Foundation, 1969, 'The Sociology of Law', in David Sills (ed.), *International Encyclopedia of the Social Sciences*, New York [etc.], MacMillan & the Free Press [etc.], 1968, and Nonet and Selznick, *Law and Society in Transition: Toward Responsive Law*, New York, Harper & Row, 1978.

views were mostly developed in connection with the domain of law, they are not restricted to it, and especially Selznick has always given his ideas wider scope.[6]

Selznick sees key social phenomena, such as democracy, parenthood and law, as governed by ideals.[7] Such a phenomenon is a system in which people's behaviour, the norms they adhere to and the problems they perceive can best be understood in relation to the ideal towards which the system is oriented. Participants criticize and applaud actions and arrangements in terms of the overarching ideal: an election that was not truly democratic, a father falling short of being a good parent. It is this fact of the ideal orientation of people involved in a normative practice that requires a theorist who seeks real understanding to include ideals. The argument for a social theory including ideals is, first of all, empirical: because ideal orientation can be observed to play a part in people's lives, a description of social reality is lacking if it ignores ideals. Without attention for motivating ideals human behaviour cannot really be understood, because the meaning of what a person does would remain obscure.[8] Second, there is a, less explicit, normative argument: if a theory is to contribute to the criticism and improvement of social phenomena, it needs to acknowledge the concerns of those involved in the phenomenon. Any effective normative position needs to be in touch with the internal point of view.[9]

A theory such as Selznick's blurs the distinction between fact and value in two ways. Most importantly, the ideal is seen as part of social reality: it is itself a fact, maybe not directly observable but out there in society nonetheless. Second, such ideals are a starting point for normative conclusions of the theorist: thus the boundary between the descrip-

---

[6] Fuller was not only interested in the connections between law and morality, see *The Morality of Law* (New Haven, Conn., Yale University Press, 1969), but also in the broader subject of mechanisms of social order; see Ken Winston (ed.), *The Principles of Social Order: Selected Essays of Lon L. Fuller*, Durham, N.C., Duke University Press, 1981. Selznick's largest work, *The Moral Commonwealth* (Berkeley, Cal., University of California Press, 1992), is on social theory in general, of which law and justice are but a small part.

[7] See Philip Selznick, 'Sociology and Natural Law', *Natural Law Forum* 6 (1961), 84-108. For a discussion of Selznick's work, see Sanne Taekema, *The Concept of Ideals in Legal Theory*, The Hague, Kluwer Law International, 2003.

[8] Selznick's arguments are directed especially against a behaviouristic social science; see the 'Rejoinder to Donald Black', *American Journal of Sociology* 78 (1973), 1266-1269.

[9] Cf. Dworkin, *Law's Empire*, pp. 13-14. For a discussion of the internal/external distinction, see Brian Tamanaha, *Realistic Socio-Legal Theory*, Oxford, Clarendon Press, 1997, pp. 153-195.

14

tive and the normative is blurred.[10] This is motivated by the idea that it is not enough to give a neutral description of a legal or political situation, but that a theorist should identify strengths and weaknesses and assess what is problematic and why.[11] Here we can recognize Selznick's background of pragmatist philosophy, more specifically, of John Dewey's philosophy. Theoretical distinctions, such as the one between fact and value, are to be assessed according to their contribution to understanding, they should never be treated as absolute dogmas. Theory cannot be viewed as separate from practical concerns: it is itself a practical enterprise and it should be connected to, and help solve, practical problems.[12]

Ideals, as Selznick says, are latent in reality.[13] They are rooted in existing situations as standards that accompany the development of any normative system. The ideal of good parenting arises naturally from the ties between a parent and a child: having a relationship with a child in a factual sense – feeding it, bathing it, attending to its needs – will cause a parent to value that relationship and to have a sense, however implicit, of what being a good parent means. Ideals are not added later on as a criterion of assessment, but are based in the practice to which they attach. Seeing ideals as internal standards that arise with the working of the system itself is an idea parallelled by the internal morality of law in Lon Fuller's thought.

Fuller saw law as a system governed by two sets of standards, internal morality and external morality. The internal morality of law is characterized by an inherent connection to the idea of a legal system itself: gross violation of the criteria of internal morality makes a system fail to be law. Thus, a legal system cannot exist as law without fulfilling the criteria of law's internal morality. What is especially interesting is that Fuller saw morality as a combination of the requirements of duty and aspiration. There is a minimal way of being moral, obeying baseline rules, and there is an optimizing way, trying to achieve the best.[14] Fuller

---

[10] A good example is Antonie Peters, 'Law as Critical Discussion', in Gunther Teubner (ed.), *Dilemmas of Law in the Welfare State*, Berlin/New York, De Gruyter, 1986, pp. 250-279.

[11] See Gertrude Jaeger and Philip Selznick, 'A Normative Theory of Culture', *American Sociological Review* 29 (1964), 653-669.

[12] See John Dewey, *The Quest for Certainty*, in Jo Ann Boydston (ed.), *The Later Works, 1925-1953, Vol. 4*, Carbondale [etc.], Southern Illinois University Press, 1984.

[13] Selznick, 'Sociology and Natural Law', p. 90.

[14] Cf. the distinction made by Karl Llewellyn between the bare-bones and the questing aspect of law-jobs: 'The Normative, the Legal, and the Law-Jobs: The Problem of Juristic Method', *Yale Law Journal* 49 (1940), 1355-1400.

applied this distinction between duty and aspiration both to external morality and to internal morality. The internal aspirational morality is on a par with Selznick's governing ideals. What Fuller made explicit was the connection between ideals and basic rules. These are on the same scale: complete neglect of an ideal constitutes the violation of a duty, and there is no precise point at which we can say it is only the failure to reach an aspirational aim. This depends on the way the rules are formulated in a given legal system. Like Selznick, Fuller is interested in what makes a legal system work, and in the continuity between minimal functioning and a full-blown, good system of law. In such a perspective, getting a grasp of the ideals at work in a social system is implied in understanding the functioning of the phenomenon in any meaningful way.[15]

In the philosophy of law, Fuller's theory did not receive the attention and assent it might have had, and the strictly rule-oriented theory of his contemporary H.L.A. Hart became the benchmark for serious legal philosophy. It was only when Ronald Dworkin attacked Hart's theory that the debate on the nature of law as a system of rules was really opened.[16] Dworkin's distinction between rules and principles showed that a normative system such as law consists of different categories, rules and principles having a different character and function. For Dworkin, the main point was the different logic involved in the application of rules and principles: rules have an all-or-nothing character, meaning they are either applicable or not, while principles have a dimension of weight that allows principles to be more or less important for a legal case. In addition, Dworkin argued that principles soften the boundaries of the legal system: because the validity of principles is not based on any formal recognition, but on their importance regardless of their source, principles are both legal and moral. Dworkin argued convincingly that law comprises different kinds of standards, but here we would like to take the categorization one step further by distinguishing principles from ideals.

This can be connected to Robert Alexy's work on principles.[17] Alexy, elaborating Dworkin's distinction between principles and rules,

---

[15] For more extensive discussions of Fuller, see Kenneth I. Winston, 'The Ideal Element in a Definition of Law', *Law and Philosophy* 5 (1986), 89-121]; the special issue of *Law and Philosophy* 13 (1994) 3, edited by Kenneth Winston; and Willem Witteveen and Wibren van der Burg (eds.), *Rediscovering Fuller: Essays on Implicit Law and Institutional Design*, Amsterdam, Amsterdam University Press, 1999.

[16] See, esp., *Taking Rights Seriously*, Cambridge, Mass., Harvard University Press, 1978, pp. 14-80.

[17] Robert Alexy, 'Rechtsregeln und Rechtsprinzipien', *ARSP Beiheft* 25 (1985), 13-29.

describes principles as having two aspects: a deontological aspect, functioning as a norm, and an axiological aspect, oriented towards a value. This leads him to define principles as *Optimierungsgebote*, norms requiring the optimal realization of a value. This definition makes room for a threefold set of standards, consisting of rules, principles and values or ideals.

Although principles have an open character compared to rules, they are still fairly specified norms of conduct within reach of those applying them. Such straightforward application is not possible in the case of ideals: these are even more open-ended and beyond immediate realization. Unlike principles, the meaning of ideals is not directly clear: they often remain implicit. In addition, we cannot grasp the meaning of ideals completely; there is always a surplus of meaning. These two characteristics, the unrealizability of ideals and the impossibility to formulate them completely, are the reason for including them as a third category of normative standards. It also means, however, that the role of such standards in practical pursuits is limited and should be seen in conjunction with principles or rules. This is clearest in legal examples: judicial decisions, for instance, have to be justified by reference to concrete elements of the legal system in order to be legitimate and to safeguard legal certainty. For judges, therefore, a direct reference to ideals in the motivation of their decision is usually uncalled for. This does not mean that they do not play a role in deliberation nor that they are absent from the implicit background of the decision. It does mean that they cannot stand alone as the justification for a judicial decision. Thus, ideals are better suited as tools to understand longer-term developments: they make it easier to see changes and continuities in, for instance, a legislative tradition or a political debate. It does not mean they are irrelevant to practical concerns: especially at times and in areas where new rules or principles still need to be developed, an ideal may serve to point in the right direction.

Going into the differences between ideals and principles has already brought out some of the characteristics of ideals.[18] We use the following

---

[18] We are interested in ideals as a conceptual category, not as a linguistic term. Although we prefer the term ideals, others have used terms such as purposes, values, virtues or aspirations to express similar ideals. For 'purpose', see W.A. Galston, *Liberal Purposes: Goods, Virtues, and Diversity in the Liberal State*, Cambridge, Cambridge University Press, 1991, and Nonet and Selznick, *Law and Society in Transition*; for 'value', see Selznick, *Moral Commonwealth*, and John Rawls, esp. in some of his later work such as 'Justice as Fairness: Political not Metaphysical', *Philosophy and Public Affairs* 14 (1985), 223-251; for 'virtue', see Alasdair MacIntyre, *After Virtue*, Notre Dame, Ind., University of Notre Dame Press, 1981, Dworkin, *Law's*

conception of ideals. Ideals are best understood as values that are usually not completely realizable. They are usually implicit in legal, moral and political practices and are often difficult to formulate exactly. They function as points of orientation for these practices and can thus play a role in motivating action and in justifying decisions and opinions.[19]

In normative theory, recognition of the role of ideals is basically recognition of room for improvement. In the ideas of Selznick and Fuller this is apparent; they argue for continuing clarification of the direction in which, for instance, a legal system should move. Selznick stresses the governance of law by the ideal of legality, the progressive reduction of arbitrariness, and thereby opposes a technocratic approach of law. The tendency in law and policy of focusing on specific regulations and the efficiency of their operation involves a blindness to the larger values involved.[20] Similarly, Fuller warns against the meagreness of seeing the internal standards of law simply as basic rules: it should not be forgotten that such standards keep pointing towards perfection, and our legal system will be a bare one if that impetus is overlooked.[21]

It is this aspect of ideal-oriented theory that connects with a strand in moral philosophy that takes up the subject of ideals. Nicholas Rescher, for instance, regards the following as the main function of ideals: the positive influence their pursuit has on human action; they motivate people to take an extra step.[22] Other authors make similar points. Ideals not only stimulate our imagination but also have a practical function in

---

*Empire*; Selznick, *Moral Commonwealth*, and S. Macedo, *Liberal Virtues*, Oxford, Clarendon Press, 1990; for 'aspiration', see Fuller, *Morality of Law*.

[19] This view on ideals is a combination of elements found in Rescher and Selznick. For more elaborate discussions of the concept of ideals see Wibren van der Burg, 'The Importance of Ideals', *Journal of Value Inquiry* 31 (1997) 1, 23-37; Taekema, *Concept of Ideals in Legal Theory*.

[20] Selznick, *Moral Commonwealth*, pp. 55-56.

[21] A field in which the importance of aspirations has been recognized is that of the professional ethics of lawyers. Pleas for renewed attention for ideals of the legal profession are made by Anthony Kronman, *The Lost Lawyer*, Cambridge, Mass., The Belknap Press, 1995, and Mary-Ann Glendon, *A Nation under Lawyers*, Cambridge, Mass., Harvard University Press, 1994. Cf. also David Luban, 'Rediscovering Fuller's Legal Ethics', in Witteveen and Van der Burg, *Rediscovering Fuller*, pp. 93-225; and Wibren van der Burg, 'The Morality of Aspiration', in Witteveen and Van der Burg, *Rediscovering Fuller*, pp. 169-192.

[22] See Nicholas Rescher, *The Validity of Values: A System of Pragmatic Idealism, Volume II*, Princeton, N.J., Princeton University Press, 1993, esp. pp. 129-139. Cf. also Dorothy Emmet, *The Role of the Unrealisable: A Study in Regulative Ideals*, New York, St. Martin's Press, 1994; Gert, *Morality*; Lisa Bellantoni, *Moral Progress: A Process Critique of MacIntyre*, Albany, N.Y., SUNY Press, 2000.

our life – they motivate us to act and even to make sacrifices.[23] Some psychologists go further and hold that the realistic pursuit of ideals may improve the quality of our life; some even regard the commitment to ideals as constitutive of our personal identity and of the meaning of our life. Even if, in our view, the latter claim is too general and too strong, a more moderate version seems to grasp an important dimension of human life. The pursuit of ideals often is part of the identity of persons and may provide them with a purpose in life and, especially if the expectations are realistic and hence frustration for not completely reaching the ideals is limited, may contribute to a happy and good life.[24]

In this respect, however, we should again be careful not to overstate the case for ideal orientation. An exclusive focus on ideals would be as detrimental as an exclusive focus on specific rules. The main thing to worry about is the single-minded pursuit of one ideal; this may cause the neglect of negative effects for other values and a failure to assess the means used to achieve it. Therefore, an ideal-oriented theory should be attuned to a plurality of ideals and be aware of possible conflicts and necessary trade-offs between them.[25] Additionally, the context is important for the appropriateness of advocating ideals. There are many situations in which the main problem is the disregard of basic rules; in such a context ideal orientation may be completely out of place.

Ideals are best regarded as one of the elements in a theory of normative practices, not superior to, but on a par with, other elements. A convincing theory of morality, politics or law needs to pay attention to the normative standards – that is, rules, principles and ideals – in relation to concrete judgments in specific situations and to the relevant facts.[26] Our standpoint is not that ideals should be regarded as the foun-

---

[23] See Gert, *Morality*; Bellantoni, *Moral Progress*; Nathan L. Tierney, *Imagination and Ethical Ideals: Prospects for a Unified Philosophical and Psychological Understanding*, Albany, N.Y., SUNY Press, 1994.

[24] On the basis of his empirical research, the psychologist Mihaly Csikszentmihalyi (*Flow: The Psychology of Optimal Experience*, London, Harper Collins, 1990) argues that happiness and a good life require an attempt to transcend personal restrictions and expand one's own limits (or in words that Csikszentmihalyi does not use, but fit well into his view, to pursue ideals). A similar point is made by Irving Singer, *The Creation of Value*, Baltimore, Md., and London, Johns Hopkins University Press, 1996.

[25] In legal philosophy, one of the most interesting theories of the tension between values (or ideals) is that of Gustav Radbruch, *Rechtsphilosophie*, in A. Kaufmann (ed.), *Gustav Radbruch Gesamtausgabe Band 2*, Heidelberg, Müller Verlag, 1993; see esp. pp. 302-307.

[26] In our view, the best theoretical approach combines pragmatism with a constructivist version of reflective equilibrium. See Wibren van der Burg and Theo van Willigen-

19

dation of normative theory, but that they are elements with a prima facie weight equal to all other elements.[27] As it was indicated in the discussion of ideals and basic rules, each is necessary, and it depends on the problem or field at hand which becomes more prominent.

## 2. Three Additional Theses

These remarks lead us to some additional, more specific theses. Ideals are not always equally relevant. If we want to study social reality, we need an eye for variation. Our general idea is that ideals play some role in social reality, but this is still a very general statement. Their role is not always equally important, and it is certainly not always the same. For the study of some phenomena, we can easily neglect ideals; for others we would miss essential dimensions if we were to do so. A strong orientation towards ideals is not always beneficial either; idealism has had very positive results, but it has also resulted in unproductive projects and social disasters. So we should try to develop more specific insights regarding the relevance of ideals.

We may identify three issues for which ideals are especially important: the phenomena of pluralism (and underlying unity), of controversy and debate, and of development. Our descriptive claim is that if we want to study these phenomena, attention for ideals is usually highly fruitful. And in a more normative approach our claim is that if we want to respond to these phenomena, we must do justice to the role of ideals in order to act effectively and adequately. Below, we will briefly discuss each of them and connect the role of ideals in these three phenomena to the characteristics that were mentioned above. This will provide a general theoretical explanation for the question why ideals are relevant to those phenomena. A more elaborate discussion of these roles of ideals will be given in various articles in this volume, where they will also be illustrated with the help of materials from concrete case studies. We suggest the following more specific theses.

---

burg (eds.), *Reflective Equilibrium: Essays in Honour of Robert Heeger*, Dordrecht, Kluwer Academic Publishers, 1998, and Taekema, *Concept of Ideals in Legal Theory*.

[27] We thus take an anti-foundationalist position with regard to the role of ideals, similarly to that of Lon Fuller, Ronald Dworkin and John Rawls. For a different view, see Rescher, *Validity of Values*, p. 192.

## Thesis 4: *Ideals are key elements in pluralism*

Ideals can be used to explain the existing pluralism of normative practices in two ways: because ideals may give rise to a plurality of interpretations and because a plurality of ideals may exist. First, broad pluralism may exist with regard to ideas and practices connected to the same ideal. Because ideals have a surplus of meaning, going beyond attempts to formulate their meaning and implications, they are open to different and even conflicting interpretations. This scope for pluralism increases when we add that they are not completely realizable. This leaves an even greater variation not only in emphases on different and sometimes conflicting aspects of the same ideal, but also in different and sometimes conflicting ways to try to realize those aspects. Once we acknowledge that people orient their actions and their thoughts at least partly towards ideals, then we become aware that this introduces a major source of ambiguity and controversy – in other words, a source of continuing pluralism – in social interaction.[28]

We may illustrate this with the existing diversity with regard to democratic institutions.[29] Although many states are democracies, they differ in institutional structure and political culture. And different political parties offer different views of what democracy is and how it should be implemented. For example, in the Netherlands some political parties argue that the introduction of a referendum is a democratic requirement, whereas others claim that it would conflict with the basic characteristics of the Dutch democratic institutions. These differences can be regarded as the result of emphasizing different aspects of the democratic ideals. Democratic ideals may even lead to conflicting requirements within one system of belief. On the one hand, democracy requires that every political party is free to propagate its ideas, but if these ideas are anti-democratic, democracy may also require that measures are taken against this party. The problem of tolerance of the intolerant remains such an intangible dilemma precisely because both mutually exclusive alternatives are based on the same ideals of liberal democracy.

Second, pluralism in practice may be connected to a plurality of ideals. Disagreeing social groups or individuals are often committed to different or conflicting ideals, and in this sense ideals may be a source

---

[28] For the suggestion that ideals are a source of pluralism (as well as of dynamics), see Philip Pettit, *Republicanism: A Theory of Freedom and Government*, Oxford, Clarendon Press, 1997, p. 146.

[29] Cf. A. Ross, *Why Democracy?*, Cambridge, Mass., Harvard University Press, 1952, for the related suggestion that democracy can best be understood in connection with an ideal-type.

of pluralism in society. In Western societies, there are widely varying ideals of marriage, such as same-sex marriage, polygamous marriage and traditional heterosexual monogamous marriage. Which ideal of marriage should the political institutions support?

These examples suggest that ideals do not give rise merely to superficial pluralism. In the case of interpretations of one ideal, the pluralism at stake is not (at least not always) that of a common clear core of meaning and only some differences in the penumbra.[30] It is more pervasive. Existing democracies differ on essential characteristics such as whether or not they have a written constitution, a presidential system or a monarchy, proportionate representation or a district system. These are the core elements of democratic systems. Ideals may even give rise to tragic conflicts because of the pluralism within one system of thought, such as in the dilemma of toleration of the intolerant.[31] In the case of different ideals, the pluralism involved can be one of different world views or perspectives of which the ideals concerned are part. In such cases, pluralism is serious or even radical: different ideals are connected to different understandings of normative practices and their meaning. One of the areas in which this is apparent is in the education system: there is a plurality of opinion about the values which are to be taught in public education. Should the display of a crucifix in the classroom be forbidden? Conflicts about such questions demonstrate different ideals of church and state.

Again we should be careful here. Ideals are, in our view, not the main source of pluralism. Social conditions, historical developments, personal psychological characteristics, et cetera, are all part of the explanation of pluralism. Ideals merely offer a part of the explanation.

The other side of the insight that different interpretations of one ideal are a source of pluralism is that such an ideal may also be a source of unity behind pluralism. If we look at the details of the institutions, we find little in common between the British and the Dutch systems of democracy. But when we look at the more general ideals, we find that many of these are shared. Similarly, there are many forms of friendship;

---

[30] As in H.L.A. Hart's idea of the open texture of language, which can explain pluralism and controversy in the penumbra of the meaning of concepts, but which does not explain controversy with regard to the core of concepts; cf. H.L.A. Hart, *The Concept of Law*, Oxford, Clarendon Press, 1961, p. 124.

[31] Bert van den Brink (*The Tragedy of Liberalism*, New York, SUNY Press, 2001) argues that liberalism gives rise to tragic conflicts, because the liberal ideal on the one hand requires the protection of liberal values and on the other hand requires doing justice to the views of non-liberal citizens and thus tolerating their non-liberal practices. See also his contribution to this volume.

but a large part of the diversity disappears when we look at the shared ideals behind this variation. Again it is not the full explanation; it would be naive to suggest that behind every variation there is always one common ideal. But it is often easier to find commonalities at the level of ideals than at the level of concrete problems or specific rules.

These insights about how ideals constitute both plurality and unity can also be used in normative theory. It is not to be avoided that normative theories are, despite aspirations and claims of universality, always contextually and culturally biased. They emphasize elements that in specific historic and economic situations are relevant and neglect others that seem less relevant. Some of the pluralism (and controversy) between different normative views and theories may thus be understood as emphasizing different aspects of common ideals. We can use this insight to deal with new situations. We may enrich our normative theories by going beyond the concrete rules and principles to the underlying ideals and see how they fit into new circumstances and which new rules and principles would be justified in the light of both these ideals and the different circumstances. For example, democracy should mean something different in the context of universities or companies than in the political realm; yet it need not be completely irrelevant in those contexts. Rather than merely transplanting some specific procedures (such as "one man, one vote") in contexts where they do not belong, we should try to develop a plurality of democratic institutions for different contexts. Democracy within the university need not imitate political democracy, but it should be developed in the light of the same fundamental ideals of democracy, and be applied to the specific context of an institution where education and research are the primary values but do not exclude the relevance of democratic ideals either.

In the case of different and conflicting ideals, making use of underlying ideals as a source of unity is often impossible. In some cases, our interpretation of conflicting ideals may be reconstructed to show that they refer back to a more abstract ideal. Often, however, different ideals will be embedded in different systems of thought without a unifying underlying ideal. Then, explicating the relations between different ideals is still useful, but it may be more fruitful to focus on specific issues instead of the underlying ideals. What a focus on ideals can do is lay bare the connections between different ideals and the interdependence of meaning between them, although this may only improve our understanding of what is at stake without pointing towards a solution.[32]

---

[32] Cf. Gustav Radbruch's description of the connections between the three different values of the *Rechtsidee* which both require and contradict each other. According to him, such contradictions are unavoidable even within one system of thought.

## Thesis 5: Ideals are key elements in controversy and debate

The next thesis is closely connected with the role of ideals in pluralism. We can often understand normative debates as debates between different interpretations of the same ideal or as debates in which the parties put the emphasis on different ideals. Understanding the role of underlying ideals in such debates may, moreover, not only provide a better understanding, for example why agreement is so difficult to reach, but also provide a strategy for solving the controversy, or even for stimulating debates where they are desired.

Ideals are often a source both of pluralism and of underlying unity in systems of thought and in practices. It is this double characteristic which accounts for their function in debates. Ideals may sometimes provide a common frame of reference, a common starting point in a discussion or in a pluralist practice, but they may also be strongly divisive, for example, if one party focuses on the ideal of equality and the other on freedom. Their emotive appeal may be essential in situations where, e.g., national unity is required and in cases where political leaders try to rally support for certain political groups and parties. Therefore, appeals to shared ideals are often made in political debates to get a positive emotive response and thus assent from the audience, which may be the political community at large but also a specific subgroup.

That ideals may constitute a common framework and thus enable discussion can be observed in various contexts. Appeals to the fundamental ideals of a legal order, such as legality, due process or human rights are made in court to argue for or against legal claims.[33] In situations where the legal doctrine is unclear or ambiguous, an appeal to the underlying purpose or values is often made by both parties to a legal discussion. Similarly, in public debates in which parties seriously try to convince each other rather than merely affirm their own position in front of the public forum, we sometimes observe that parties refer to certain shared ideals and try to establish that their view does justice to those ideals. The emotive appeal that ideals such as justice and democracy have adds power to the rational argument and makes it less easy for the opponent to simply ignore the argument.

The opposite observation that ideals can sometimes be divisive factors and make controversies more insoluble is also connected with their emotive appeal. People are reluctant to give up or revise their cherished ideals and there is no pressing need for revision because ideals cannot

---

[33] Usually, the term 'ideals' is avoided, probably because it implies the – in our view incorrect – connotation that they are not yet part of positive law and therefore not authoritative.

be directly refuted by empirical reality. The fact that reality does not match the ideals need not be a reason to abandon (the interpretation of) those ideals. This is most clearly visible when initially open doctrines have been transformed into closed ideologies. Ideals are often elaborated in ideological systems of thought; for example, ideals of freedom have been elaborated in a number of liberal and libertarian doctrines. Sometimes these doctrines have become ideologies; they have become immune against criticisms and empirical testing and revisions. The history of Marxism-Leninism provides a good example of such an ideological immunization against any revision in the light of the facts or of different views. This risk of ideological immunization is inherent in a strong commitment to ideals.[34] In those cases, debates often seem futile, because they are merely a repetition of ideological stances, and do not offer any chances that those views are changed or adapted as a result of the debate. The fact that people often strongly identify with their ideals and with their ideologies based on those ideals makes an open debate even more problematic.

Ideals thus may play a number of roles in debates and controversy. Understanding these roles offers various cues for more normative purposes. Sometimes explaining a position in terms of the underlying ideals may help to bridge (part of) the divide between adversaries. Seeing in which ways the adversary position is based on the same ideals as the ones one holds oneself may at least help to appreciate the position of the adversary. In some cases, it may show a way out of the controversy, because if both aim at the same ideal, the discussion may focus on which interpretation of the ideal is the most suited for the concrete situation and which is the best way to approach the ideal.

Even in the case of highly ideological debates, such an approach may be fruitful. Understanding the mechanism of the creation of ideologies may also show the way to reopen debates, namely by showing that there may be other interpretations of the original ideals and other ways to realize them in the light of the changing historical circumstances. Thus even in cases of ideological stalemate, understanding the role of ideals may be a contribution to reopening the debate.

Certainly, such an appeal to shared ideals is not always productive. Analysis of the underlying ideals may show that parties to a debate appeal to conflicting ideals (or to conflicting sides of the same ideal). An appeal to ideals may then prove to be counterproductive, and even reinforce the existing antagonism. This will happen most frequently

---

[34] See Melvyn L. Fein, *The Limits of Idealism: When Good Intentions Go Bad*, New York [etc.], Kluwer Academic/Plenum, 1999.

when the positions are strongly ideological in character. In such situations, it may be helpful to focus on concrete problems and find compromises on those rather than trying to search for consensus at the level of general ideals. However, there is also the possibility of reflecting on the different ideals and trying to construct new ideals that are acceptable to both parties. Such an approach would fit into the idea of frame reflection as suggested by Schön and Rein.[35] A good example is the attempt made by Sophie van Bijsterveld to construct a new ideal of human rights protection in the European Union to bridge two seemingly opposed ideals.[36]

The insights into the role of ideals in debates may also be used in legislative strategies. In societal fields and practices with great variation and change, such as medical practice, detailed regulation is often impossible and ineffective. In such situations, legislators may switch from the level of rules and guidelines to the more abstract level of principles and ideals. They may choose to lay down the more fundamental ideals and principles. This may serve two functions.[37] First, they may express the basic commitments of the political community. And second, they may serve as common points of orientation for a discussion about how to interpret and implement these ideals in varying contexts and for the actual implementation. Such a focus may fit into communicative approaches to legislation as suggested by Bart van Klink and Willem Witteveen.[38]

---

[35] D.A. Schön and M. Rein, *Frame Reflection: Toward the Resolution of Intractable Policy Controversies*, New York, Basic Books, 1994.

[36] Cf. S.C. van Bijsterveld, 'Grundrechte in der Europäischen Union: Über Ideale und Wertvorstellungen', in K.H. Kästner, K.W. Nörr und K. Schlaich (eds.), *Festschrift für Martin Heckel*, Tübingen, Mohr Siebeck, 1999, pp. 707-724. She argues that so far the debate on human rights protection in the European Union has been dominated by two seemingly antagonistic views. One ideal is that of a unifying Europe; the other that of respect for the free citizen. Her suggestion is that we can see the two ideals as connected and mutually supportive if we focus on the ideal of a balanced and integrated society, in which the antagonism between state and citizen is replaced by a more complex network of relations between state, individual and society.

[37] See Wibren van der Burg and Frans W.A. Brom, 'Legislation on Ethical Issues: Towards an Interactive Paradigm', *Ethical Theory and Moral Practice* 3 (2000), 57-75, and Wibren van der Burg, 'The Expressive and the Communicative Functions of Law', *Law and Philosophy* 20 (2000), 31-59.

[38] See Bart van Klink and Willem Witteveen, 'Is Soft Law Really Law?', *RegelMaat* (1999), 126-140.

## *Thesis 6: Ideals are key elements in enabling development*

The third theme which we want to highlight is the role of ideals in change. Ideals are important factors in enabling change.[39] There are various explanatory elements for this role. First, ideals are never completely realized. This means that there is always a gap between our ideals and reality which gives us a reason to improve it. Second, ideals have a surplus of meaning and can never be exhaustively formulated in moral, legal or political doctrines. This means, for example, that even if there is a strong institutional support for a legal doctrine on privacy or environmental law in authoritative legal texts, it can always be criticized and amended with an appeal to those dimensions of the underlying ideals that have not yet been fully recognized. Ideals thus constitute a resource for criticism, they provide for a critical perspective that highlights the respects in which social practices or our normative views and doctrines could be improved.

Second, and in line with this, they provide points of orientation and inspiration for new directions. As they are not yet fully realized, we can use them for guidance in deciding which direction to take in further development. If our current legal system does not protect human rights adequately, we should find ways to do better. If our current rules and principles do not offer guidance for dealing with new technological problems such as biotechnology, the ideals of the legal system, with their surplus of meaning, may suggest (authoritative) directions in which we could search for solutions. Ideals always provide the possibility of breaking open our legal and moral doctrines and offer points of reflection and discussion to find solutions for new problematic situations.[40]

Third, we noted above that ideals may promote debate and open discussion. They stimulate discussion, whether in the legal context, the political institutions or the public at large, both about what is wrong and about how it can be improved. Thus they offer not only cognitive resources for criticism and guidance, but also actually stimulate social mechanisms of discussion that may lead to practical change, in law, in public policies or in everyday life.

---

[39] This connection of ideals with processes of change may be found in Nonet and Selznick, *Law and Society in Transition*, in Rescher, *Ethical Idealism*, in Emmet, *Role of the Unrealisable* and in Bellantoni, *Moral Progress*. See also Wibren van der Burg, 'Ideals and Ideal Theory: The Problem of Methodological Conservatism', in Van der Burg and Van Willigenburg, *Reflective Equilibrium*, pp. 89-99.

[40] See for example Sophie van Bijsterveld, *The Empty Throne: Democracy and the Rule of Law in Transition*, Utrecht, Lemma, 2002.

Fourth, ideals have an emotive appeal. People often are committed to them, engage in the project of realizing them. People may make sacrifices for them; they may even be prepared to die for the cause of democracy or dedicate their lives to the cause of social justice. Rules usually do not have this strong emotive appeal. If people have such a commitment to ideals, this may be an important impetus for social change. Without social movements like the Civil Rights Movement or leaders such as Nelson Mandela, strongly committed to ideals of justice, social developments would certainly have been different.

We should explicitly remark here that this emotional dimension need not always be beneficial. Idealistic movements are often committed to immoral causes or may be prepared to sacrifice too much for the good cause.[41] A commitment to ideals may lead to blindness for the costs and for other values, it may even lead to ruthless axioms such as that the end justifies the means. But even if we abhor the ends or the means of such groups, we cannot deny the force of ideals in bringing about social change.

This analysis may suggest that ideals are unchanging, eternal elements in our changing practices and systems of thought. And indeed, most of our ideals have a long history and have lived through many different cultures and interpretations. They are the more stable and enduring elements of our moralities, of our law or political systems. The ideals of democracy and human rights have proven to be more enduring than the continuously changing ways in which they have been interpreted in constitutional provisions (at least in countries where the constitution may be changed), legal rules and political practices. Nevertheless, in a pragmatist view, ideals may be relatively more stable and enduring but certainly not eternal and unchanging.[42] New ideals such as those of privacy or biological diversity may emerge, old ideals such as that of the full-time housewife as a role model for women may fade or be explicitly abandoned. Even if their role in change is largely due to their relatively

---

[41]   Cf. Isaiah Berlin, 'The Pursuit of the Ideal', in *The Crooked Timber of Humanity*, Princeton, N.J., Princeton University Press, 1990, pp. 1-19. A highly critical analysis of the negative consequences of uncritical idealism may also be found in Fein, *Limits of Idealism*. Fein also emphasizes the combination of a strong emotional attraction and a lack of critical reflection in the light of reality, both inherent risks of idealism, as the main cause for derailment. We are, however, less pessimistic than Fein about the possibilities to cope with these risks.

[42]   The main pragmatist criticism is Dewey's; see his *Reconstruction in Philosophy*, in Jo Ann Boydston (ed.), *The Middle Works, 1899-1924, Volume 12*, Carbondale [etc.], Southern Illinois University Press, 1988. The Platonist idea that ideals are eternal has, of course, been criticized by other philosophical traditions as well. For a Whiteheadian view largely similar to ours, see Bellantoni, *Moral Progress*.

stable and more general character, this does not imply that ideals are completely unchanging.

A good example of how ideals play a role in legal dynamics is offered by the European Convention on Human Rights. The European Court explicitly and repeatedly declared that the Convention is a living instrument which must be interpreted in the light of present-day conditions. In its case law, the European Court has continuously expanded the scope of human rights protected by the Convention. This process of progressive clarification and implementation has been made possible by the fact that the Convention is phrased in very broad and vague terms. These terms, however, are not merely vague – as such they would not provide much guidance. Both the rights and the exception clauses refer to fundamental ideals of human rights and democracy, which are open to continuous reinterpretation in the light of changing circumstances and changing ideas.

Again, these insights into how ideals may play a role in change may also be used for normative and practical purposes. For example, if moral and legal norms are still unclear and evolving, it may be unwise to lay down strict legal rules that would frustrate further development. In such cases, it may be a good suggestion to choose for more interactionist and communicative legislative strategies. Formulating only the basic ideals as a common framework of reference that is open to further normative evolution and stimulates discussion may then be a sound strategy.[43]

These three themes are not meant to be exhaustive. There are many phenomena which can be fruitfully explored with special attention for the role of ideals. Ideals are, for example, central to professional ethics; we cannot understand issues such as the emphasis on professional autonomy if we do not recognize the fact that professions are partly oriented towards professional ideals.[44] Taking the role of ideals in law seriously may lead to fresh perspectives on eternal debates such as that between legal positivism and natural law.[45] It may also shed light on more concrete debates on the role of the judge in political issues, the development of international environmental law,[46] or on controversies

---

[43] Cf. Van der Burg and Brom, 'Legislation on Ethical Issues'.

[44] Cf. Wibren van der Burg *et al.*, 'The Care of a Good Caregiver: Legal and Ethical Reflections on the Good Health Care Professional', *Cambridge Quarterly of Health Care Ethics* 3 (1994), 38-48.

[45] Taekema, *Concept of Ideals in Legal Theory.*

[46] Jonathan Verschuuren, *Principles of Environmental Law: The Ideal of Sustainable Development and the Role of Principles of International, European and National Environmental Law*, Baden-Baden, Nomos, 2003.

regarding the rule of law in semi-autonomous government agencies. We believe that a whole range of interesting issues may still be fruitfully explored with an eye for ideals combined with an eye for variation. The essays in this volume are a first attempt to demonstrate the importance of such an approach.

## 3. The Contributions to This Volume

What these authors have in common is an approach, a perspective, rather than a theory. They all support the general idea that attention for ideals may help us to understand social reality better. The focus on ideals has certainly proven fruitful, not only in the specific themes of this book, but also in our much wider research programme in the past years. However, beyond this common core, the authors have widely varying interests and hold different views regarding the precise role of ideals. Some focus on the role of ideals in dynamics, others on their role in debates. Some are very positive about the advantages of focusing on ideals, others are more sceptical, because with regard to their objects of research the additional value of focusing on ideals is limited. Some authors highlight the negative aspects of the role ideals have, whereas others are more positive about the contributions that ideal-orientation and idealism may have for social problems. And finally, some authors share the editors' pragmatist inclinations, whereas others have different philosophical backgrounds.

This variation is not something we deplore; it is rather what we aspire for. Social reality is highly diverse and it would be a surprise if ideals were to play the same role in every context. We need a pragmatist eye for variation here as well. For philosophical analysis, the most useful conception of ideals may differ from those which prove most helpful for studies in positive law or in empirical sociology. In our view, we have only begun to explore the wide variation with regard to the role of ideals in various sectors of social reality. Therefore, in line with the three themes identified earlier, we could also regard the study of ideals also as an ideal-oriented project. The full understanding of the importance of ideals is our ideal. But we are still far from understanding what this really implies, let alone from realizing it. As a result, there is much room for pluralism, and for a continuous development of our views. But most importantly, there is still much need for open discussion. The authors of this volume greatly enjoyed their internal discussions, and we hope that the publication of this book will stimulate further pluralism, further discussion and further development.

Sanne Taekema discusses the conceptual groundwork of a theory of ideals. If we claim that ideals need to be an integral part of our descriptive theories, what concept of ideals should be defended and in what way does that concept relate to understanding the normative dimension of social reality? According to Taekema, the best theory about ideals and social reality is a pragmatist theory, which sees ideals as complex and dynamic values rooted in social practices. She argues that ideals should not be seen as essentially abstract notions or universal human values, but as guiding standards to everyday problems. They are not purely subjective either, because they are rooted in experience and can be justified by a method of inquiry. The central ideals of important practices are complex values with continuing relevance over time. The way in which such ideals operate is illustrated in many of the other chapters.

Embracing a pragmatist theory of ideals and their role in society implies a broader theory of what social science is and what the right approach to researching law or politics is. That question is dealt with in the chapters by Wouter de Been and Marc Hertogh. De Been traces the theoretical roots of pragmatist social science back to the early pragmatists and shows how important the notions of purpose and ideal orientation are in their views. More specifically, he argues that the contemporary uses made of pragmatism in legal and social science neglect the purposive nature of pragmatist theory to their detriment. Pragmatism is reduced either to a positivistic model in which human relations are viewed deterministically or to a view of knowledge as situated and generated by practice without substantive claims. Such contemporary views forget that pragmatist theorists wanted to use social science to change policy, arguing that inquiry needs to embrace conscious change and experiment in order to progress. Ideals are creatively reimagined by theorists as part of their attempts to shape society by law and policy. This also means that a pragmatist theory, according to De Been, combines descriptive and normative aims, claiming that social science should be purposive and ideal oriented.

It is precisely the combination of descriptive and normative aims that is rejected by Marc Hertogh: he underscores the importance of paying attention to ideals without the normative presuppositions of the social scientist himself. Hertogh criticizes the blurring of the boundary between empirical research and normative claims by the pragmatist sociologist Selznick and sketches an alternative view of empirical research of legal ideals inspired by the sociology of Eugen Ehrlich. In a bottom-up approach, the different views of people about the ideal as they see it in everyday practice are the basis for what Hertogh calls the 'living *Rechtsstaat*'. In a case study, officials working in a residential area are shown to emphasize other values of the *Rechtsstaat* than are usually seen as the core of this ideal by jurists. Hertogh shares the pragmatist view of ideals as constructive, pluralistic and pragmatic: he sees ideals as constructed by people in response to social situations as they try to deal with them. However, in his view, the pluralism of ideals can be more easily detected and charted with a non-normative approach: it is not a question of assessing whether people act according to a preconceived ideal of the *Rechtsstaat*, but of discovering what ideal of the *Rechtsstaat* they hold dear.

An empirical approach to the *Rechtsstaat* is also central to the article by Caroline Raat. She uses the method of narrative analysis to uncover the values implicit in organizational cultures of housing foundations. She argues that the ideal of the *Rechtsstaat* is as relevant to private organizations in a position of power, such as agencies dealing with the allocation of houses, as it is to government. Sociological research regarding such organizations can show whether their culture has the moral commitment to values connected with the *Rechtsstaat* which is necessary for a responsible exercise of power. Raat's analysis of the stories told within a particular housing foundation reveals the sense of responsibility and justice shared by the employees, but also shows the danger of preferential treatment which may threaten the ideal of equality. More than Hertogh, she uses her empirical material to draw normative conclusions: to trust the responsible attitude of street-level workers and focus on the internalization of the ideal of the *Rechtsstaat* instead of using traditional legal norms.

The ideal of the *Rechtsstaat* or the rule of law is a highly complex one, allowing a variety of interpretations. The possibility of new interpretations and the inevitable divergence between ideal and actual practices create a challenge for legal scholars and courts. Willem Witteveen argues that a simple conversion of the ideal into a set of rules and doctrines is attractive but inadequate. He criticizes the Dutch Supreme Court's doctrinal interpretation of the rule of law in the *Pikmeer* cases as unpersuasive, lacking constructive potential and failing to provide normative guidance. A convincing approach to the ideal of the rule of law needs to combine idealism and realism. Each of these perspectives brings its own focus to a problematic case, at the same time calling for the other perspective. Realizing that the ideal of a balance of powers can never be completely attained leads to a realist consideration of actual power relations; the realist notion of prudential self-binding of the government extends easily to an idealist understanding of reciprocity. Thus, the two perspectives are complementary: both are necessary for a convincing interpretation of the rule of law in a democratic polity. Witteveen finds a basis for this attitude of realist idealism in the works of various authors and, perhaps surprisingly, especially of authors labelled as realist, including Machiavelli and Llewellyn.

The theses that ideals are important to understand pluralism and debate are addressed by Bert van den Brink and Roland Pierik in the context of political philosophy. Both authors discuss and systematize plurality of opinion in political debates with the help of ideals, but do so at different levels of abstraction. Van den Brink focuses on the debate about political philosophy which can be analysed as being about different ideals of doing political philosophy. He argues that there are different substantive ideals which focus on certain aspects of philosophy and entail different approaches to philosophy and different answers to the questions political philosophers pose. He highlights two ideals: political philosophy *sub specie aeternitatis*, an impartial perspective aiming to formulate general principles of practical reasoning, and political philosophy as hermeneutical perspectivism, not separating philosophical from political issues and confronting opinions with each other. The ideal of hermeneutical perspectivism embraces plurality because critique consists in the confrontation of different views and theories. This makes it possible to recognize the ability of individuals to engage in criticism and makes room for their creativity; these are substantive ideals that are obscured by the perspective of eternity. In stressing individual creativity and the continuity between philosophy and political practice, Van den Brink extends the pragmatist ideas put forward by Taekema and de Been.

Roland Pierik applies the ideal-oriented approach to a debate in contemporary liberalism. The ideal of equality can be used to clarify the debate between liberal egalitarians and multiculturalists because it shows where they are in agreement and where they differ. Pierik sees the concept of equality as equal respect and concern as an ideal which underlies a range of more specific conceptions of equality. The liberal egalitarian Ronald Dworkin defends a distributive conception of equality: government's distribution of resources should be sensitive to the choices of individuals and insensitive to their endowments. That conception of equality is challenged by multiculturalists who focus on the inequalities resulting from group characteristics. Although the differences between these positions are on some points substantial, an ideal-oriented approach provides a common frame of reference and thus offers a possibility to bridge the differences. Pierik reinterprets multicultural criticism as an argument for recognizing social endowments as a ground for redistribution within liberal theory.

Wibren van der Burg uses the ideal-oriented approach to clarify the debate on the relationship between law and morality. He shows that there are two different models of law, the product and the practice model, which conceptualize law and its connection to morality in a particular way, seeing law as a set of norms and concepts or as a dimension of interaction, respectively. Law is essentially ambiguous in that we can only understand it fully if we use both models. According to Van der Burg, the problem with the debate between natural law and legal positivism is that it largely ignores law as a practice: both positions focus on law as it supposedly really is and overlook the insight that law is constantly being constructed. In order to construct a defensible third, interactionist position, we should take law as a practice seriously as well and recognize ideals as a bridge not only between the two models, but also between legal and moral discourses. Interactionism therefore leads to the idea of a relative autonomy of law, in which part of the legal development may be attributed to ideals. Like Witteveen and Van den Brink, Van der Burg's article is an argument for perspectivism: for the method of switching between two models, which are both necessary but not commensurable.

The thesis that ideals enable development is dealt with in a fairly abstract manner by Van der Burg, but it is also interesting to see whether there is any evidence supporting the thesis when we look at particular fields or problems. The chapters by Blok and Verschuuren and Oudenaarden both address the thesis with regard to legal development, and both come to the conclusion that there is indeed a significant role for ideals in legal development. Their assessment of this influence of ideals is rather different, however. Peter Blok sketches the enormous influence of the ideal of privacy in the development of data protection law. The literature and the legislation and adjudication dealing with the problem of protecting personal data have analysed it in terms of a threat to privacy. According to Blok, this ideal orientation has expanded the legal meaning of privacy from protecting a private sphere to including fair dealing with data, and enabled a discussion on an abstract level showing the connections between different problems, which all turned out to have some relation to privacy. The abstraction involved has had a downside, however, which for Blok is reason to be sceptical about the appropriateness of ideal orientation in law. The invocation of the abstract ideal has not been combined with what Selznick would call an eye for variation. Consequently, it has obscured the diversity of underlying reasons to be concerned about data processing and made it difficult to solve the problems with an appeal to already available legal instruments not directly connected with the ideal of privacy.

Jonathan Verschuuren and Timon Oudenaarden are also cautious in their conclusions about the positive effects of ideals on legal development, but, unlike Blok, they do not see the solution as a matter of choice between abstract ideals and concrete rules. They emphasize the need for a combination of ideal orientation with legal principles and institutional support. In their analysis of international environmental law they focus on two influential ideals: sustainable development and biodiversity. They show how these ideals have stimulated the discussion about new regulation and have enabled international actors to formulate a common purpose in order to start joint action. They argue that it is important to distinguish between enabling legal development and providing guidance. According to Verschuuren and Oudenaarden, ideals facilitate development because their open character stimulates discussion, but the same openness makes that they provide limited, if any, guidance for the choices to be made when new environmental rules need to be adopted. Another advantage of the open character of ideals is that local and regional circumstances can be taken into account when steps towards implementation are taken. Even if ideals do not provide direct guidance, they can influence legal development indirectly. A careful analysis of international environmental law demonstrates how intermediate steps, such as formulating principles of sustainable development and adopting a framework convention on biodiversity, may be useful mechanisms to realize environmental ideals.

# References

Alexy, Robert, 'Rechtsregeln und Rechtsprinzipien', *ARSP Beiheft* 25 (1985), 13-29.

Bellantoni, Lisa, *Moral Progress: A Process Critique of MacIntyre*, Albany, N.Y., SUNY Press, 2000.

Berlin, Isaiah, 'The Pursuit of the Ideal', in Berlin, *The Crooked Timber of Humanity*, Princeton, N.J., Princeton University Press, 1990, pp. 1-19.

Cotterrell, Roger, *Law's Community*, Oxford, Clarendon Press, 1995.

Csikszentmihalyi, Mihaly, *Flow: The Psychology of Optimal Experience*, London, Harper Collins, 1990.

Dewey, John, *The Quest for Certainty*, in Jo Ann Boydston (ed.), *The Later Works, 1925-1953, Vol. 4*, Carbondale [etc.], Southern Illinois University Press, 1984.

———, *Reconstruction in Philosophy*, in Jo Ann Boydston (ed.), *The Middle Works, 1899-1924, Volume 12*, Carbondale [etc.], Southern Illinois University Press, 1988.

Dworkin, Ronald, *Taking Rights Seriously*, Cambridge, Mass., Harvard University Press, 1978.

———, *Law's Empire*, Cambridge, Mass., The Belknap Press, 1986.

Emmet, Dorothy, *The Role of the Unrealisable: A Study in Regulative Ideals*, New York, St. Martin's Press, 1994.

Fein, Melvyn L., *The Limits of Idealism: When Good Intentions Go Bad*, New York [etc.], Kluwer Academic/Plenum, 1999.

Fuller, Lon L., *The Morality of Law*, New Haven, Conn., Yale University Press, 1969.

Galston, W.A., *Liberal Purposes: Goods, Virtues, and Diversity in the Liberal State*, Cambridge, Cambridge University Press, 1991.

Gert, Bernard, *Morality: A New Justification of the Moral Rules*, New York, Oxford University Press, 1988.

Glendon, Mary-Ann, *A Nation under Lawyers*, Cambridge, Mass., Harvard University Press, 1994.

Hart, H.L.A., *The Concept of Law*, Oxford, Clarendon Press, 1961.

Jaeger, Gertrude, and Philip Selznick, 'A Normative Theory of Culture', *American Sociological Review* 29 (1964), 653-669.

Kronman, Anthony, *The Lost Lawyer*, Cambridge, Mass., The Belknap Press, 1995.

Llewellyn, Karl, 'The Normative, the Legal, and the Law-Jobs: The Problem of Juristic Method', *Yale Law Journal* 49 (1940), 1355-1400.

Luban, David, 'Rediscovering Fuller's Legal Ethics', in Willem J. Witteveen and Wibren van der Burg (eds.), *Rediscovering Fuller: Essays on Implicit Law and Institutional Design*, Amsterdam, Amsterdam University Press, 1999, pp. 193-225.

Macedo, S., *Liberal Virtues*, Oxford, Clarendon Press, 1990.

MacIntyre, Alasdair, *After Virtue*, Notre Dame, Ind., University of Notre Dame Press, 1981.

Margalit, Avishai, *The Decent Society*, Cambridge, Mass., Harvard University Press, 1996.

Nonet, Philippe, 'For Jurisprudential Sociology', *Law & Society Review* 10 (1976), 525-545.

Nonet, Ph., and Ph. Selznick, *Law and Society in Transition: Toward Responsive Law*, New York, Harper & Row, 1978.

Peters, Antonie, 'Law as Critical Discussion', in Gunther Teubner (ed.), *Dilemmas of Law in the Welfare State*, Berlin/New York, De Gruyter, 1986, pp. 250-279.

Pettit, Philip, *Republicanism: A Theory of Freedom and Government*, Oxford, Clarendon Press, 1997.

Radbruch, Gustav, *Rechtsphilosophie*, in A. Kaufmann (ed.), *Gustav Radbruch Gesamtausgabe Band 2*, Heidelberg, Müller Verlag, 1993.

Rawls, John, 'Justice as Fairness: Political not Metaphysical', *Philosophy and Public Affairs* 14 (1985), 223-251.

Rescher, Nicholas, *The Validity of Values: A System of Pragmatic Idealism, Volume II*, Princeton, N.J., Princeton University Press, 1993.

Ross, A., *Why Democracy?*, Cambridge, Mass., Harvard University Press, 1952.

Schön, D.A., and M. Rein, *Frame Reflection: Toward the Resolution of Intractable Policy Controversies*, New York, Basic Books, 1994.

Selznick, Philip, 'Sociology and Natural Law', *Natural Law Forum* 6 (1961), 84-108.

———, 'The Sociology of Law', in *International Encyclopedia of the Social Sciences*, 1968.

———, *Law, Society and Industrial Justice*, New York, Russell Sage Foundation, 1969.

———, 'Rejoinder to Donald Black', *American Journal of Sociology* 78 (1973), 1266-1269.

———, *The Moral Commonwealth*, Berkeley, Cal., University of California Press, 1992.

Singer, Irving, *The Creation of Value*, Baltimore, Md., and London, Johns Hopkins University Press, 1996.

Taekema, Sanne, *The Concept of Ideals in Legal Theory*, The Hague, Kluwer Law International, 2003.

Tamanaha, Brian, *Realistic Socio-Legal Theory*, Oxford, Clarendon Press, 1997.

Tierney, Nathan L., *Imagination and Ethical Ideals: Prospects for a Unified Philosophical and Psychological Understanding*, Albany, N.Y., SUNY Press, 1994.

Van Bijsterveld, S.C., 'Grundrechte in der Europäischen Union: Über Ideale und Wertvorstellungen', in K.H. Kästner, K.W. Nörr und K. Schlaich (eds.), *Festschrift für Martin Heckel*, Tübingen, Mohr Siebeck, 1999, pp. 707-724.

———, *The Empty Throne: Democracy and the Rule of Law in Transition*, Utrecht, Lemma, 2002.

Van den Brink, Bert, *The Tragedy of Liberalism*, New York, SUNY Press, 2001.

Van der Burg, Wibren, 'The Importance of Ideals', *Journal of Value Inquiry* 31 (1997) 1, 23-37.

———, 'Ideals and Ideal Theory: The Problem of Methodological Conservatism', in Wibren van der Burg and Theo van Willigenburg (eds.), *Reflective Equilibrium: Essays in Honour of Robert Heeger*, Dordrecht, Kluwer Academic Publishers, 1998, pp. 89-99.

———, 'The Morality of Aspiration', in Willem Witteveen and Wibren van der Burg (eds.), *Rediscovering Fuller: Essays on Implicit Law and Institutional Design*, Amsterdam, Amsterdam University Press, 1999, pp. 169-192.

———, 'The Expressive and the Communicative Functions of Law', *Law and Philosophy* 20 (2000), 31-59.

———, and Frans W.A. Brom, 'Legislation on Ethical Issues: Towards an Interactive Paradigm', *Ethical Theory and Moral Practice* 3 (2000), 57-75.

———, and Theo van Willigenburg (eds.), *Reflective Equilibrium: Essays in Honour of Robert Heeger*, Dordrecht, Kluwer Academic Publishers, 1998.

———, *et al.*, 'The Care of a Good Caregiver: Legal and Ethical Reflections on the Good Health Care Professional', *Cambridge Quarterly of Health Care Ethics* 3 (1994), 38-48.

Van Klink, Bart, and Willem Witteveen, 'Is Soft Law Really Law?', *RegelMaat* (1999), 126-140.

Verschuuren, Jonathan, *Principles of Environmental Law: The Ideal of Sustainable Development and the Role of Principles of International, European and National Environmental Law*, Baden-Baden, Nomos, 2003.

Winston, Ken, (ed.), *The Principles of Social Order, Selected Essays of Lon L. Fuller*, Durham, N.C., Duke University Press, 1981.

———, 'The Ideal Element in a Definition of Law', *Law and Philosophy* 5 (1986), 89-1211.

———, (ed.), *Law and Philosophy* 13 (1994) 3 (special issue).

Witteveen, Willem, and Wibren van der Burg (eds.), *Rediscovering Fuller: Essays on Implicit Law and Institutional Design*, Amsterdam, Amsterdam University Press, 1999.

# What Ideals Are: Ontological and Epistemological Issues

## Sanne TAEKEMA

## 1. A Proposition

When ideals are given a prominent role in a discussion or theory, there will usually be someone who wonders about what is meant by the term. Such a person is not content simply to use the term ideals, to talk about ideals on the basis of a vague understanding of what the term might mean. In this chapter, I will address these philosophical concerns. I will defend a particular conception of ideals against objections from other perspectives. I will go into the ontological status of ideals, the epistemology of ideals, and the implications of these issues for the concept of ideals.

In my opinion, we should regard ideals as follows. Ideals are values,[1] of a complex and dynamic nature, which are embedded in social practices. That is, they are desirable states of affairs which are difficult to realize completely, which provide direction in problematic situations. Ideals have an objective and a subjective component. Their objectivity is found in their roots in social reality, in the constraints provided by the way the world is. Their subjectivity is found in the creativity necessary to imagine the desirable possibilities that can supply guidance to action. Our knowledge of ideals is empirical and experiential, and especially the knowledge of the central ideals of practices is largely implicit and acquired by participating in such practices. However, when used in concrete problem-solving, dimensions of ideals need to be explicated to provide specific guidance.

In the following, I will defend this conception of ideals, which builds on the pragmatist theories of John Dewey and Philip Selznick, against objections from different perspectives. Important traditions in thinking

---

[1] Thus, I do not make a principled distinction between ideals and values. Values have characteristics (such as being difficult to realize completely) which can be seen as ideal aspects and which justify referring to them as ideals. I use the terms as equivalents of each other.

about ideals are the Platonic and the Kantian traditions, which object to the kind of objectivity claimed here, seeking a different basis for the objectivity of ideals. Other objections can be derived from subjectivist and emotivist theories, which deny the objective basis of ideals. I will not present these as rival theories as such, but I will try to formulate their objections to the view proposed here as forcefully as possible, and refute them where I can. In the next section, I will sketch the basic picture of ideals and the arguments against it. In section 3, I will go into the place of ideals in the context of practices, and in section 4, I will discuss the epistemological process of inquiry into ideals.

## 2. The Dynamics of Ideal and Problem

To explain what ideals are, the first and most difficult issue to tackle is in what way ideals can be said to exist. Confronting the issue of their existence leads us to the question of the reality of ideals: Are ideals real, that is, are they part of the fabric of the world?[2] My answer to that question is not a straightforward yes or no. My claim is that ideals *can* be real and that they are always at least rooted in reality, but that they are usually not completely inherent in reality. The easiest way to explain this position is by introducing a twofold, dynamic model of ideals.

The starting point for the model is an ideal situation: a situation that is good in every significant aspect and leaves nothing to be desired. For example, the holiday I spent in Australia last year was an ideal holiday: it was everything a holiday should be. Such a situation has value as it exists, or we could say that the ideal or value is an aspect of the actual situation.[3] When this is the case, the ideal is real because it is part of the existing situation: the desirable state of affairs is the way things are now. I should note that not every pleasant situation is also desirable: in order to know whether it is worthwhile, examination of its bearing upon other things is necessary.[4] However, the important point in regard to the

---

[2] The phrase 'part of the fabric of the world' was introduced by Mackie to discuss realism about values; J.L. Mackie, *Ethics: Inventing Right and Wrong*, London, Penguin, 1990, p. 15.

[3] Cf. what Hilary Putnam says about the interpenetration of fact and value in statements such as 'Caligula was a cruel emperor' (*Pragmatism: An Open Question*, Oxford, Blackwell, 1992, pp. 57-58).

[4] John Dewey, *The Quest for Certainty*, in Jo Ann Boydston (ed.), *The Later Works, 1925-1953, Volume 4*, Carbondale [etc.], Southern Illinois University Press, 1988, pp. 212-213. The key arguments of a pragmatist theory of values are epistemological: we can only say that something has value when it has been critically examined. These arguments are discussed in section 4.

existence of ideals is that here the ideal is part of the existing state of affairs.

Contrasted with the ideal situation is a problematic situation, a situation that is unsatisfactory. In such a situation, the ideal is not an aspect of what exists, but the standard used to judge in what way the situation is unsatisfactory and, at the same time, the standard providing guidance to improve the situation. In a problematic situation the ideal is not real in the sense that it is part of the way things are; the ideal is a desirable state of affairs that has yet to be realized. The dynamics of the model are found in the connection between the two situations: when the right ideal standard is adopted and used as a guide, the problematic situation can become an ideal situation. The ideal is in principle capable of being realized, of becoming real. This does not imply that ideals will usually be realized, only that the obstacles impeding the realization of an ideal are practical, caused by other aspects of the situation or by a conflict with other ideals. Although the ideal situation is the key to understanding in what sense an ideal can be real, the problematic situation is the more interesting. The reason is that in connection with a problem the ideal prompts us to act: it can be used to improve things.[5]

The basics of this conception of ideals leave much to be explained, especially about the way in which the ideal as a standard in a problematic situation is rooted in reality. Most directly, the ideal has roots in the problematic situation itself. The ideal is subject to constraints engendered by the problem itself: the ideal is a possibility for improving the situation, but the character of the situation itself limits what is possible. Not everything is a genuine possibility: the actual sets boundaries on what can appear as a possibility for improvement. When I feel hot on a warm day, I know that a cool drink or moving to a shady spot will help me cool down, while hot tea or a seat in the bright sunshine will not. Similarly, an ideal is a possibility that is prompted by the actual problem; it does not come out of the blue. Apart from these roots in the concrete situation in which the ideal is to be used, the ideal has roots in a broader context of previous experience and social practices. In what way the ideal is embedded in that context is the subject of section 3. First, I want to address objections that can be raised against the first part of my account of ideals.

---

[5]   It is in the practical contribution of ideals that pragmatism is interested. See John Dewey, *Reconstruction in Philosophy*, in Jo Ann Boydston (ed.) *The Middle Works, 1899-1924, Volume 12*, Carbondale [etc.], Southern Illinois University Press, 1988, pp. 77-201, p. 151.

## Objections

The most urgent of these objections calls into question the dynamic nature of ideals and the characterization of ideals as potentially an aspect of an existing situation. This objection is raised from the contrasting view that ideals are abstract values which can never completely inhere in concrete, everyday reality. According to this view, when we talk about the ideal of beauty, we do not speak of an aspect of a concrete thing but of a notion that in itself presents a perfect idea. In the Platonist view, the relation between ideal and reality is such that the perfect idea has a separate, transcendent, origin, which enables us to understand the phenomena in the world around us. There is a realm of ideas, a perfect world formed by the pure ideals of goodness, truth, and beauty, which can explain our having mental images of such notions.[6] How else can we recognize what strikes us as beautiful in a concrete thing if we do not have a prior notion of what beauty is? In short, the objection is that my conception of ideals fails to acknowledge the abstract and perfect character of ideals and the way they guide our grasp of the world by reducing ideals to aspects of everyday reality.

The appeal of this objection draws on an intuitive idea about ideals, namely the feeling that ideals are grand and overarching high values, which stand apart from our everyday life of base wants and needs. With that intuition in mind, regarding a holiday as ideal is a perversion of the term, because it ties the ideal to an everyday, personal satisfaction. Ideals are part of the higher concerns of man such as aesthetics, morality, and pure science. Although I believe there are indeed aesthetic, moral, and scientific ideals, I think it is a mistake to think that only such values deserve the name. This is because such a view creates an unacceptable division between higher and lower values, while there is a whole range of ideals without a clear hierarchy or classification. To be sure, there is a difference in subject matter and range between the aesthetic ideal of beauty and the economic ideal of efficiency, but both have a guiding function, express possibilities of improvement, and are difficult to realize completely. Both, in short, display the features that ideals have (and note that the argument at this point does not depend on a particular conception of the features of ideals: both can also be regarded as perfect and abstract to the same extent, if that is the preferred

---

6 Although the term 'ideal' as a substantive is fairly recent (dating from the eighteenth century), the adjective 'ideal' was already used by the Greeks to refer to ideas, which are comparable to what we now call ideals. According to Plato, ideas can be causes of our physical reality because they are external to it, because they are transcendent (Giovanni Reale, *A History of Ancient Philosophy, Part II: Plato and Aristotle*, Albany, SUNY, 1990, p. 58).

conception). There is no good reason to reserve the term ideal for higher values only.[7]

There is, however, a more fundamental line in the Platonic objection: the argument that only the prior existence of abstract ideals can explain that we recognize the occurrence, and the extent of the occurrence, of the ideal in reality. The strength of this objection lies in the experience of knowing an ideal even if it is not even remotely realized in social reality. A good explanation of this experience is that abstract forms or ideas – to follow Platonic terminology – have a separate existence that causes us to think of them.[8] However, although this explains knowledge of unrealized ideals, it is not the best explanation available, not the least because it is based on an implausible ontology. The separate existence of ideals means an existence in a realm of ideas, a dimension filled with abstract, perfect entities. The existence of such a realm is troublesome: the only indications for it are the intuited notions we have of ideals. That will only do as proof of the separate existence of ideals, if separate existence is necessary to cause us to think of ideals. This is not the case. There are at least two other ways to explain the mental image of an ideal without resorting to a previous occurrence in reality.

First, it can be explained by subjective imagination: people are capable of fantasizing and creativity, of imagining things that are well outside our reality. To the extent that original fantasy is possible, thinking of ideals is possible as well. (Actually, I think originality is limited, but I will come back to this point when I discuss subjectivism.) Secondly, the image of an ideal can be explained by a negative relation to reality.[9] Instead of saying that the ideal is recognized as a positive aspect of experience, we can argue that it arises from a negative experience, that is, as the reverse of the situation encountered. For instance, the experience of serious inequality can give rise to an ideal of equality. It is questionable whether an ideal can be completely grounded in negativity, but in combination with a positive basis in reality a convincing argument can be made. If we say that the experience of inequality can make explicit an inarticulate notion of equality, we can say that the full-fledged ideal arises from the negative experience, while the rudiments of

---

[7] Cf. Dewey, *Reconstruction in Philosophy*, esp. pp. 148-155.

[8] T.K. Seung argues that we intuit abstract and general ideals, which we then use as a starting point to construct more concrete standards. His argument is negative: since there is no other way to develop critical standards, these must have a transcendent source (*Intuition and Construction: The Foundation of Normative Theory*, New Haven, Yale University Press, 1993, pp. 194-196 and 209-210).

[9] See Bert van den Brink, *The Tragedy of Liberalism: An Alternative Defense of a Political Tradition*, Albany, State University of New York Press, 2000, pp. 152-153.

it were present but not apparent in prior unproblematic experiences. I will return to the basis of ideals in prior experience in the next section. Since there are two plausible alternatives to explain the existence of ideals, there is no need to appeal to a pre-existing realm of ideas.

The Platonic objection is that my proposed conception does not give due attention to the perfect and abstract character of ideals. Another line of criticism is pursued from a subjectivist perspective: the proposed conception is wrong in claiming roots of ideals in reality because ideals are no more than subjective thoughts or feelings.[10] A strong point in subjectivist positions, which also served as a counterargument to Platonism, is the central place of individual imagination: it recognizes the individual's own conception of an ideal as developing out of personal creativity. In conjunction with this, a subjectivist position recognizes the importance of individual commitment to ideals, the importance of the emotional ties a person has to his cherished ideals. A person's ideals influence his world view, meaning that ideals in part determine the way a person sees the world.

A subjectivist conception of ideals seems capable of explaining important phenomena related to ideals, such as the continuing controversies in matters of morality and politics and the miscommunications about the meaning of ideals. Different people, each committed to their own idiosyncratic ideals, will have difficulty to agree on, and even to understand, a direction provided by a common ideal. Although I do not want to deny the occurrence of such disagreements, I think it is an overemphasis of one type of phenomenon connected to ideals, neglecting the positive role of ideals and the possibility of sharing ideals. Underlying this refutation is the idea that a subjectivist view claims too much for the individual forming ideals by himself. If we think of social movements that have tried to realize of certain ideals, it does not seem true that the people involved in these movements were all pursuing their own individual values. The first feminist movement marched under the banner of equality for women with a shared sense of equality meaning equal political rights. And, although there was fierce opposition to their views at first, the political equality of women was eventually recognized. This is an example of the more general point that ideals are often shared and capable of exerting influence and gaining broader appeal, eventually overcoming disagreement. Secondly, the first feminists did

---

[10] Some subjectivist positions reduce value or ideal to an emotional state or reaction: the theory of emotivism (e.g. Charles Stevenson, *Facts and Values: Studies in Ethical Analysis*, Westport, Greenwood Press, 1963). Because this seems unduly reductive – ideals are about the world too – I restrict the discussion to the more plausible view that combines emotive and imaginative components.

not *invent* equality: they extended ideas that had been uttered before. There was an imaginative effort involved in thinking through the implications of the earlier ideal for women, but it was not completely original. This is true of practically all ideals: although the individual has a part in extending or rethinking the meaning of an ideal, this is a reworking and combining of what was already in play in social practices. And speaking of social practices, it is time to consider these in more detail.

## 3. The Context: Experience and Practice

Above, I presented ideals as part of problem-solving and I connected the roots of ideals in reality to problematic situations. However, the larger part of the explanation of the roots of ideals lies in the context in which a problem arises. The person confronted with a problem sees it in the light of previous experience and operates within a social environment, which means that the situation is embedded in a context of experience and social practices.[11] Such a context provides opportunities for finding ideal standards and it puts constraints on the applicability of the ideal. Previous experience yields ideals that have been useful in other situations and which are therefore candidates for application to the present problem. To return to the earlier example of my holiday in Australia: if I do not know where and how to spend my next summer holiday, I can use the experience of my ideal holiday in Australia to decide where to go and what to do. Because the wildlife and the beauty and the quiet of the landscape made it ideal, I can use that ideal as a standard to pick out a new holiday destination. Such an ideal is an abstraction from past reality: I have picked out the most important features and generalized them, but as such the ideal has its roots in that reality; the ideal is based on my concrete experiences of seeing kangaroos and Ayer's Rock. It is no longer completely inherent in it, because it is an abstracted standard for the present situation. My holiday this year will be different, for instance, because I do not have the money for an expensive destination such as Australia.

The most significant part of the context in relation to ideals is the social practice: the assessment of a problematic situation takes place against the background of meaning-giving practices. In a collective, social form, practices have a role similar to individual previous experi-

---

[11] According to pragmatism, both our action and our thinking start from a place within a context of previous and future events. From that context we select what is interesting from the present standpoint (which depends on the problem confronting us). See John Dewey, 'Context and Thought', in Richard J. Bernstein (ed.), *On Experience, Nature and Freedom: Representative Selections*, New York, Liberal Arts Press, 1960, pp. 88-110.

ence: they are a source of ideals and of knowledge about the relevance and usefulness of ideals. Practices are therefore another place to locate the roots of the ideal. Practices can be described as complex forms of socially established cooperative human activity that are value-laden.[12] They constitute a medium for people's actions in a social setting, a way of acting that makes smooth cooperation possible. A practice ensures that people have similar expectations because it is a way of sharing knowledge. A participant in a practice learns methods, norms and ideals from the others involved in it.

Some ideals have a special place in practices. There are ideals central to specific practices that provide overall guidance to the actions taking place in those practices. As Selznick says about, for example, democracy: 'A democracy is a normative system in that much complex behavior, as well as many specific norms, is governed by a master ideal. Behavior, feeling, thought, and organization are all bound together by a commitment to the realization of democratic values.'[13] When a problem arises within a particular practice, its occurrence in that context indicates the relevance of the central ideals of that practice for a solution.

Such central ideals are values that have historically grown and continued to exist as ideals relevant to the people involved in a practice. Practices are ways of passing on and extending knowledge and values over generations. The central ideals of a practice, which can be identified by observing the activities that make up the practice, are complex values. One reason is that they consist of different constituting elements, which together determine the meaning of the ideal. Consider the ideal of justice, a central ideal of the practice of law. It can be argued that justice consists of two core notions: the notion of equal treatment – treating like cases alike – and the notion of fairness – giving each person his due.[14] Thus, justice makes different demands that may have prominence in different situations, demands that can even conflict at times. A judge, for instance, has to be fair to the individual about whom he must decide,

---

[12] For theories of practices, see Alasdair MacIntyre (*After Virtue: A Study in Moral Theory*, 2nd ed., Notre Dame, University of Notre Dame Press, 1984, pp. 187-196) and Michael Oakeshott (*On Human Conduct*, Oxford, Clarendon Press, 1975, pp. 54-60). I combine their ideas with Selznick's pragmatism in my account (Philip Selznick, 'Sociology and Natural Law', *Natural Law Forum* 6 (1961), 84-108, at pp. 86-91).

[13] Selznick, 'Sociology and Natural Law', pp. 86-87.

[14] There is a debate over the question whether the two notions form the core meaning of justice. Some theorists argue that equal treatment is the core of justice, while others focus on fairness. The view that they are both central is also held by Neil MacCormick (*Legal Reasoning and Legal Theory*, Oxford, Clarendon Press, 1978, p. 73).

but also needs to beware that he applies the norms equally to similar individual cases. A second reason is that the meaning of any specific core ideal depends on its interrelations with other ideals. Whenever we inquire into the specific demands such an ideal makes, we find that it is necessary to refer to other values to capture its meaning. Consider justice again.[15] If we focus on justice in its meaning of treating like cases alike, it is immediately apparent that we need other values to determine what is to count as being equal: it is a reference to the moral values of equality and desert. On the other hand, the notion of equal treatment also presupposes the stability of a norm: there can be no equal treatment without a norm that is applicable over time to comparable cases. Therefore, justice is also connected to legal certainty.

Although such ideals keep their relevance, their meaning is not fixed. Because they are at the centre of practices, they partake of the changes that occur in these practices. Most importantly, they evolve in the interactions of people with the practice. Because practices are open to whomever learns to use them, and can be modified by their users, participants also have a voice in criticizing and adapting core values. Both practices and their central ideals are subject to change by innovative users. However, such changes are usually gradual and slow: the ideals of a practice most often proved to be highly important in running a practice well. Justice has been a central ideal of law for ages, and although its meaning has shifted in some respects, its focal points are remarkably stable.[16]

## Objections

In my view, the continuing relevance of some ideals is a contingent, historical fact: it is because they turned out to remain useful that central ideals are enduring. Against this one might argue that the enduring character of important ideals has a much stronger basis: namely that the realization of such values is part of the nature of mankind and society. This is advanced by (neo-)Aristotelian theories of ideals: these argue

---

[15] The following analysis is not my own; I borrowed it from Gustav Radbruch, who distinguishes three values – justice, purposiveness (which equals societal, moral values) and legal certainty – as the three constituents of the idea of law. According to Radbruch (and I agree with him on this point), the values governing law presuppose and conflict with each other (*Rechtsphilosophie*, in A. Kaufmann (ed.) *Gustav Radbruch Gesamtausgabe Band 2*, Heidelberg, Müller Verlag, pp. 205-450, pp. 302-309).

[16] E.g., there are still elements of the Aristotelian theory of justice in present-day conceptions. For a more elaborate description of justice, see my *The Concept of Ideals in Legal Theory*, The Hague, Kluwer Law International, 2003, pp. 191-194.

that there are some essential human characteristics that include the need or tendency to realize certain values.[17] Universal features of human life are value-laden: for instance, as social beings it is important for us to love and be loved.[18] Thus, Aristotelians are able to argue for a list of universal ideals as aspects of the proper end of human life. Their objection could then be that ideals in my conception lack a necessary foundation, because they are merely internal to historical practices, and that they thus lack critical force. Universal ideals by being grounded in human nature are justified independently of the practices in which they function and are therefore a more secure source for bringing about social change.[19]

Although the attractiveness of universal standards may be granted, there are a number of reasons why I think the Aristotelian argument need not affect my position.[20] First, because vague universals are not as useful as they might seem; secondly, because internal criticism fares better than one might think; and thirdly, because the connection between ideals and human nature is problematic, which affects the basis of the argument.

A theory of human nature tries to identify the common core of human beings of all cultural backgrounds. The ideals that follow have to be applicable to all, in every context. This makes such ideals necessarily vague: they must have a link with a general feature of human beings and they must be relevant to people in different cultural settings. However,

---

[17]  E.g., Martha Nussbaum, 'Human Functioning and Social Justice: In Defense of Aristotelian Essentialism', *Political Theory* 20 (1992), pp. 202-246. In modern natural law theory, the appeal to human nature is more veiled, but it is there, in the background, as Pauline Westerman argues (*The Disintegration of Natural Law Theory: Aquinas to Finnis*, Leiden, Brill, 1997, pp. 253-258).

[18]  Nussbaum, 'Human Functioning', pp. 216-223; George Santayana, *The Life of Reason, Volume Two: Reason in Society*, New York, Dover Publications, 1980, pp. 9-11.

[19]  Cf. Nussbaum, 'Human Functioning', p. 229, who uses her essentialist theory to criticize public policy in developing countries. See also Larry Arnhart, who argues that slavery and female circumcision are against human nature (*Darwinian Natural Right: The Biological Ethics of Human Nature*, Albany, SUNY, 1998, p. 248).

[20]  Although my ideas are inspired by Philip Selznick, on this point they differ from his. Selznick combines an Aristotelian view of human nature with a pragmatism position, seeing both as varieties of naturalism (*The Moral Commonwealth: Social Theory and the Promise of Community*, Berkeley, University of California Press, 1992, p. 24). In my opinion, there is an important difference between grounding ideals in human nature as the Aristotelians (including Selznick) do and the more fluid and provisional basis of ideals in social practices (see Taekema, *Concept of Ideals*, pp. 123-132).

the vagueness of universal ideals detracts from their functioning as standards in specific situations. That it is valuable for human beings to engage in play and laughter does not tell us much more than that there should be opportunities for playing and laughing, not how or even to what extent. If attention is paid to the specific context in which an ideal functions and its meaning is allowed to be dependent on context, the ideal will have greater relevance.

Secondly, the search for universal standards implies a distrust of internal criticism within a practice which is unwarranted. An argument for universal ideals is often made to counter cultural relativism: to avoid the wholesale acceptance of, or indifference to, all the values of a given culture, universal ideals are put forward as an alternative to enable criticism. Such an argument overlooks the possibility of profound criticism in terms of the ideals of a society or practice itself.[21] If a particular society is committed to equality, it can be criticized internally for not living up to that commitment, for instance, because it does not do as it claims or because it misinterprets the ideal.[22] Because ideals provide direction towards an as yet unrealized situation, they have a critical potential even if their origin lies within the practice itself. The additional advantage of using internal ideals is that criticism is more easily accepted if it is given in terms of commitments of the practice or society itself.

Thirdly, it is questionable whether ideals can be grounded in human nature in a meaningful way. In an Aristotelian theory, striving for universal ideals is seen as part of the natural course of human life: people are said to have the tendency to realize these values. This teleological view is problematic, because the link between human capacities and the positive tendency to realize the corresponding ideals is dubious. It can convincingly be argued that human beings have the capacity for reasoning and for play, and the need to love. But similarly, one can argue that human beings have the capacity to be cruel and to be lazy, and have the need to vent anger. Why should one connect the ideals of reason and love to a human being's positive capacities without connecting the negative counterparts to his capacities for badness? There is no apparent reason to conclude that the tendency to realize positive ideals is any more natural than the tendency towards negative ones. The link between

---

[21] Cf. Michael Walzer, *Interpretation and Social Criticism*, Cambridge, Harvard University Press, 1987, pp. 39-45.

[22] The difficult question remains whether every society *should* be committed to equality. This, however, cannot be solved by appealing to human nature's universals either. See Louise Antony, 'Natures and Norms', *Ethics* 111 (2000), 8-36, at p. 30.

human nature and the realization of ideals is not proven so easily, which provides another reason for not appealing to human nature as a ground.

Another kind of objection can be raised against the claim that practices have central ideals. It can be argued that practices and the values involved in these are not so coherent that central governing ideals can be identified. The existence of central ideals is dependent upon a view of practices as essentially cooperative and oriented towards a unified or unifying goal, and such a view is mistaken. Practices are less coherent than I assume, according to this line of thinking, and the ideals or values that are involved in them are better characterized as the personal ideals of participants than as the central ideals of the practice.[23]

The strength of the objection depends on a particular interpretation of practices and their ideals that I do not embrace.[24] I do not think that practices are essentially coherent activities, but the existence of central ideals does not depend upon such a view of practices. As long as central ideals are not seen as identifying the unity of the practice but as open to interpretation and change by participants in the practice, an overly monolithic view can be avoided. Practices should not be seen as closed circuits: they are activities with their own governing values, but these are connected to other practices through the participants in the practice and through the relations between ideals, which extend to different practices. Governing ideals can be identified by investigating particular practices: it is not a necessary relation but an empirical one. By studying practices and talking to participants central ideals can be discovered. The identification of central ideals does not imply that all participants agree about the meaning of the ideals: discussion about different interpretations is one of the key factors that explain change and development of ideals. Nor does it imply a unified view of practices or a close identity between ideal and practice: the identification of central ideals often also lays bare conflicts between such ideals or between the constituting elements of complex ideals.

---

[23] My account of this line of criticism is an extension of familiar criticism of MacIntyre's view of practices; see Brian Tamanaha, *Realistic Socio-Legal Theory: Pragmatism and a Social Theory of Law*, Oxford, Clarendon Press, 1997, p. 170. Tamanaha, however, does not focus specifically on the values involved in practices.

[24] Such an interpretation can indeed be found in MacIntyre and (to a lesser extent) in Selznick. See for criticism of Selznick's master ideals, Taekema, *Concept of Ideals*, pp. 179-184.

# 4. Knowledge and Justification of Ideals

Seeing in what way ideals are involved in the reality in which they work does not yet yield a clear picture of the way we know and justify the ideals we use. The attractiveness of the pragmatist conception is the application of a general theory of inquiry to the search for ideals. As follows from the previous explications, the first intuitive knowledge of an ideal comes from the context of experience and practice. The person confronted with a problem will use these contexts as a starting point for imagining possible ideals. Such a first impression of an ideal has the status and function of a hypothesis:[25] it is a proposition for a solution, which needs to be tested to see whether it leads in a fruitful direction. Ideally, such a test would be a controlled experiment, which would show the conditions and consequences of the realization of the ideal. However, in many social contexts the room for experimentation is limited[26] and the test will be more of an imaginary test: thinking through the proposed ideal's specifics, the conditions required and the consequences likely to follow. As the result of this process of testing, adopting the ideal is objectively justified. Still, the ideal is only warranted as a provisional ideal: the process of inquiry is not foolproof and it would be a mistake to award an examined ideal absolute status. The pragmatist view of inquiry is fallibilistic, or, in the words of Hilary Putnam: 'Pragmatists hold that there are no metaphysical guarantees to be had that even our most firmly-held beliefs will never need revision.'[27]

Thus, the process of inquiry has subjective and objective components: the person formulating the ideal and carrying out the inquiry brings in subjective elements by using his own creativity to formulate the hypothetical ideal and by structuring the testing of the ideal. Preferably, the process of inquiry will be controlled intersubjectively: the methods of testing and the way of applying these are open to public scrutiny and should be checked by other people who are involved in the practice or are part of the circle of researchers. Unfortunately, especially in fields such as law, morality and politics such a socially shared method is not generally found and the process of inquiry is often dependent on

---

[25] Dewey, *Quest for Certainty*, p. 221.

[26] Although there is more room for experiment in social matters than we sometimes think. Education, local politics, health care are all practices in which small-scale implementation of new ideas can be used to find out the set of values that makes for the best solution. The pragmatist philosopher John Dewey created a laboratory school at the University of Chicago in the 1890s to test his educational theory (see Alan Ryan, *John Dewey and the High Tide of American Liberalism*, New York, Norton, 1995, pp. 135-136).

[27] Putnam, *Pragmatism*, p. 21.

the efforts of an individual researcher.[28] The creativity of the individual subject is something both necessary and positive: imagination is essential for achieving a wider range of desirable possibilities and moving in new directions, which cannot be done without the particularities of individual minds. However, the social aspect of inquiry should not be brushed aside too quickly: even when there is no consensus on the precise method of inquiry, criticism by others is essential to ensure the quality of the inquiry.[29] Conducting the inquiry intelligently is the only guarantee for a satisfactory justification of ideals: epistemological objectivity of ideals is gained by subjecting the ideal to the inquiry into its conditions and consequences.[30] This means serious reflection upon what is necessary to bring the ideal closer and upon the changes likely to come about when the ideal is adopted as a guiding standard.

## Objections

This view of the justification of ideals has an empirical basis: an ideal is justified if the results of an inquiry into the factual consequences of adopting it are satisfactory. It is challenged by a view that sees knowledge of ideals not as an empirical matter, but as a thought construct: ideals can be traced by considering the prerequisites of practical thinking and acting. This (neo-)Kantian train of thought justifies ideals by proving their necessity as a priori ideas that enable us to conduct our moral, political, or legal activities.[31] For instance, even if there is no way of knowing that people are free, an ideal of freedom needs to be presupposed for morality to be possible: only then can a person be held morally accountable. The Kantian objection to my proposition is that I wrongly suppose that an empirical test can give objective knowledge of ideals, because ideals cannot be the subject of such an inquiry. Instead, they can be justified as the necessary presuppositions of our practical thinking.

The strong point of this view is that the justification of ideals takes place by way of a rationally grounded method: every rational being can

---

[28]  The original pragmatists were optimists both about the achievements of science in general and about the probable success of applying scientific method to moral subjects in particular. The optimism seems unwarranted, but that does not disqualify the idea as a normative model. See Putnam, *Pragmatism*, pp. 70-72.

[29]  *Ibid.*, p. 71.

[30]  John Dewey, *Experience and Nature*, La Salle, Open Court, 1989, p. 326.

[31]  See Dorothy Emmet, who discusses Kantian ideals as transcendental – being beyond the conditions of empirical knowledge – and as regulative – assigning direction to a practice (*The Role of the Unrealizable: A Study in Regulative Ideals*, New York, St. Martin's Press, pp. 10-11).

find out that a particular ideal is necessary by thinking through the implications of a field of practical reason. However, the same point also generates difficulties, because it is very demanding, and therefore in the end implausible. The demanding nature of the view is found in the necessity claimed for ideals: ideals are justified if they can be shown to be presuppositions of a field of reasoning, but that is not easy to do. It requires arguments that are in principle acceptable to every rational being, establishing that a certain field cannot function, or even be thought, without that ideal. But such arguments depend on choices of perspective that are not evident to everyone by virtue of their rationality. For instance, consider the neo-Kantian argument that the field of law is necessarily oriented towards justice.[32] Radbruch argues that law can only be understood as the part of reality that means to serve the value of justice. This argument depends on a controversial thesis about law being a value-oriented reality, and if that is accepted on the further controversial thesis that justice is the supreme value of law. Although I find no fault with the conclusions – I happen to believe in justice as one of the supreme values of law myself – it cannot be taken for granted that there is a necessary relationship between law and such a value, so it must be demonstrated that law and justice are related. It is much more plausible to do this by pointing out the prevalence of the ideal of justice in existing legal systems than by seeking an a priori justification. An empirical method also allows for the recognition of variety of meaning and can move beyond the formal values to which an a priori argument can be applied. Because of the demanding method, the view is overly restrictive: only a limited number of ideals is fully justified by this model, namely, the formal and abstract ideals that can be rationally justified in this way.

## Fact and Value: A Return to Ontology

A more general critique, but one that can also be voiced from a Kantian perspective, concerns the fundamental, and recurring, issue of fact and value. In my view, as the reader will have noticed, fact and value cannot be separated. Ideals have roots in reality, and the inquiry into ideals has the same basic structure and method as an inquiry into facts. In this, my view is exactly that of classical pragmatism.[33] Therefore, it is subject to the same objection: neglecting the distinction between fact

---

[32] See Radbruch, *Rechtsphilosophie*, pp. 255-256. Radbruch is an exponent of early twentieth-century German neo-Kantianism. See further Taekema, *Concept of Ideals*, pp. 71-77.

[33] See Selznick, *Moral Commonwealth*, pp. 20-23; Putnam, *Pragmatism*, p. 7; Tamanaha, *Realistic Socio-Legal Theory*, pp. 50-51.

and value.[34] There are different applications of the distinction: in science, it is the distinction between observable facts and the values that the scientist brings to his inquiry; in ethics or law, it is the distinction between factual beliefs and value judgments, between the belief about the facts of the case and the judgment on what ought to be done or what is good. In my, pragmatist, view these are aspects of the same reality which can be distinguished, though not separated. The disagreement is with any position saying that fact and value are different things, e.g. that fact refers to observable objects and value to human feeling or desire. The objection against pragmatism can be more precisely formulated as saying that the fact/value distinction made by a pragmatist is not clear enough, because it is not grounded in an account of the differences between fact and value.

This objection aims at the root of my account of ideals, which rests on a holistic view of the world, in which everything is connected and in which separations cannot be sustained. It means that what is seen as reality is that in which we find ourselves: what is real is not what can be verified, but what we can experience. Starting there, we can make a distinction between observable hard facts and soft value judgments, though both start from experiences: the sensation of a hard object when you bump your head against the kitchen cupboard, or the feeling that the yelp of a dog when you pull its tail signifies pain. We need to distinguish the way things are from the way they ought to be, or we want to them to be, in order to cope with the world. The fact/value distinction is made from our situated place in the world, or as Tamanaha puts it: '*Given* that we cannot perceive the world except from within a perspective, the fact/value distinction must be understood as arising out of our acting in the world, where both values (preferences, ideals, *oughts*) and facts (*is*) are naturalistically conceived as functionally distinct aspects of our experience.'[35] It is true that my view depends on this holistic world view, and that a critic may reply that what I call reality does not refer to what is real but to what I experience as real. Against my broad view of reality that critic may counterpose a narrower view of reality as that which can be observed or proven. Such a critic takes the fact/value distinction too far. For instance, where does that leave the unobservable social structures such as legal institutions, which are there nonetheless? Or consider the moral judgment that killing foetuses is wrong: Can one

---

[34] *Locus classicus* of the distinction is Hume: the argument that we cannot derive ought from is. It is also defended by Kant. On both, see Stuart Hampshire, 'Fallacies in Moral Philosophy', in Steven M. Cahn and Joram G. Haber (eds.), *Twentieth Century Ethical Theory*, Englewood Cliffs, Prentice-Hall, 1995, pp. 162-173.

[35] Tamanaha, *Realistic Socio-Legal Theory*, p. 51, commenting on Dewey.

really separate a subjective feeling of it being wrong from the factual belief about what a foetus is? If I believe that a foetus is as much a human being as a newborn baby, the judgment that killing a foetus is wrong is easier to make than if I believe that there is a clear distinction between the life of a foetus and that of a baby. The distinction can be made, but the interaction between the two is too significant to claim that they are separate things altogether. Such phenomena can best be accommodated in a theory that connects fact and value in an encompassing world view.

## 5. Conclusion

I have made a case for a particular conception of ideals and defended it against rival conceptions. Doing so, I discarded a number of features traditionally associated with ideals. In my view, ideals do not have a transcendent origin; ideals are not grounded in human nature; they are not essentially abstract values nor are they necessary aspects of our thought. Thus, I have stripped ideals of much of their character of grand and important notions. This does not mean, however, that they have been reduced to irrelevant or whimsical personal preferences. I have tried to defend a view that avoids both extremes, a view that claims neither too much nor too little. I have indicated how a subjective interpretation of ideals is bound by the social practices in which that interpretation occurs. Additionally, the dangers of subjectivity are limited by the method of inquiry of ideals, by justifying them in terms of their conditions and consequences. Thus, I have shown how ideals can be objectively justified without having to turn to problematic theories of transcendence or human nature.

The important contribution of a pragmatist theory of ideals is that it points out the strong connections between ideals and everyday reality. This is done, first, by showing that ideals arise out of, and are guiding standards to, concrete problems and, secondly, by explaining how they are rooted in experience and social practices. The continuing focus is on the use made of ideals in social activities: in coping with problems in the context of social practices. To do this well, the activities must include inquiry to ensure that the ideals adopted for guidance do not have pernicious effects and do not interact negatively with other values. The complexity of practices and of ideals themselves may make this difficult, but as long as we realize that all attempts at formulating and justifying ideals are provisional, we can and should keep trying.

# References

Antony, Louise, 'Natures and Norms', *Ethics* 111 (2000), 8-36.

Arnhart, Larry, *Darwinian Natural Right: The Biological Ethics of Human Nature*, Albany, SUNY, 1998.

Dewey, John, 'Context and Thought', in Richard J. Bernstein (ed.), *On Experience, Nature and Freedom: Representative Selections*, New York, Liberal Arts Press, 1960, pp. 88-110.

————, *The Quest for Certainty*, in Jo Ann Boydston (ed.), *The Later Works, 1925-1953, Volume 4*, Carbondale [etc.], Southern Illinois University Press, 1984.

————, *Reconstruction in Philosophy*, in Jo Ann Boydston (ed.), *The Middle Works, 1899-1924, Volume 12*, Carbondale [etc.], Southern Illinois University Press, 1988, pp. 77-201.

————, *Experience and Nature*, La Salle, Open Court, 1989.

Emmet, Dorothy, *The Role of the Unrealizable: A Study in Regulative Ideals*, New York, St. Martin's Press, 1994.

Hampshire, Stuart, 'Fallacies in Moral Philosophy', in Steven M. Cahn and Joram G. Haber (eds.), *Twentieth Century Ethical Theory*, Englewood Cliffs, Prentice-Hall, 1995, pp. 162-173.

MacCormick, Neil, *Legal Reasoning and Legal Theory*, Oxford, Clarendon Press, 1978.

MacIntyre, Alasdair, *After Virtue: A Study in Moral Theory*, 2nd ed., Notre Dame, University of Notre Dame Press, 1984.

Mackie, J.L., *Ethics: Inventing Right and Wrong*, London, Penguin, 1990.

Nussbaum, Martha, 'Human Functioning and Social Justice: In Defense of Aristotelian Essentialism', *Political Theory* 20 (1992), 202-246.

Oakeshott, Michael, *On Human Conduct*, Oxford, Clarendon Press, 1975.

Putnam, Hilary, *Pragmatism: An Open Question*, Oxford, Blackwell, 1992.

Radbruch, Gustav, *Rechtsphilosophie*, in A. Kaufmann (ed.), *Gustav Radbruch Gesamtausgabe Band 2*, Heidelberg, Müller Verlag, 1993, pp. 205-450.

Reale, Giovanni, *A History of Ancient Philosophy, Part II: Plato and Aristotle*, tr. John R. Catan, Albany, State University of New York Press, 1990.

Ryan, Alan, *John Dewey and the High Tide of American Liberalism*, New York, Norton, 1995.

Santayana, George, *The Life of Reason, Volume Two: Reason in Society*, New York, Dover Publications, 1980.

Selznick, Philip, 'Sociology and Natural Law', *Natural Law Forum* 6 (1961), 84-108.

————, *The Moral Commonwealth: Social Theory and the Promise of Community*, Berkeley, University of California Press, 1992.

Seung, T. K., *Intuition and Construction: The Foundation of Normative Theory*, New Haven, Yale University Press, 1993.

Stevenson, Charles L., *Facts and Values: Studies in Ethical Analysis*, Westport, Greenwood Press, 1963.

Taekema, Sanne, *The Concept of Ideals in Legal Theory*, The Hague, Kluwer Law International, 2003.

Tamanaha, Brian Z., *Realistic Socio-Legal Theory: Pragmatism and a Social Theory of Law*, Oxford, Clarendon Press, 1997.

Van den Brink, Bert, *The Tragedy of Liberalism: An Alternative Defense of a Political Tradition*, Albany, State University of New York Press, 2000.

Walzer, Michael, *Interpretation and Social Criticism*, Cambridge, Harvard University Press, 1987.

Westerman, Pauline, *The Disintegration of Natural Law Theory: Aquinas to Finnis*, Leiden, Brill, 1997.

# Pragmatism and Ideal-Oriented Socio-Legal Study

Wouter DE BEEN

## 1. Introduction

Wibren van der Burg and Sanne Taekema note in the introduction to this volume that an important inspiration for the ideal-oriented approach discussed in this book is American pragmatism. The pragmatists, they claim, believed that any adequate understanding of a social practice like law involved taking into account the ends or ideals that were implicit in it. In this contribution I will take their claim a step further and defend the view that from a pragmatic perspective the task of the legal scholar and the social scientist is not only to analyse and describe these implicit ideals, but also to work towards their creative re-imagination and adaptation. Moreover, I will argue that this imaginative and creative aspect is crucial for a pragmatic approach, even though it is an aspect that is all but absent from the contemporary revival of pragmatism in legal scholarship.

In a recent, authoritative statement of pragmatic philosophy, the American philosopher Hilary Putnam recounted four core principles of pragmatism that he was taught as an undergraduate:

1) Knowledge of facts presupposes knowledge of theories.

2) Knowledge of theories presupposes knowledge of facts.

3) Knowledge of facts presupposes knowledge of values.

4) Knowledge of values presupposes knowledge of facts.

Of these four principles, according to Putnam, number (1) was once highly controversial, but is now widely accepted. Today, few academics would doubt that fact and theory interpenetrate one another, that all facts are necessarily theory-laden, and that before you can observe anything empirically you first need to define, according to the criteria of some theory, what you are looking for. However, principle (3), Putnam notes, is still as controversial today as it was when William James and John

Dewey first defended it.[1] The idea that facts, and especially facts about the social world, are shaped and coloured by the standards of evaluation on which their classification depends is not widely accepted. Indeed, the fact/value distinction still holds such a strong grip over the imagination that even neo-pragmatist legal scholars, who adopt many of James's and Dewey's basic insights, are loath to give it up. Thus, Brian Tamanaha, a self-styled neo-pragmatist legal scholar, asserts that pragmatism for him means a 'descriptive, non-normative approach', and Richard Posner, another convert to pragmatism, asserts that a pragmatic, empirically oriented legal scholar should always avoid substantive issues.[2]

Such claims fit very well in with a positivist understanding of science, but are quite problematic when you adopt a pragmatic stance. For the positivist, the social scientist was more or less an outside observer, somebody standing apart from the social setting who could explain in a rational, impartial and disinterested fashion, on the basis of objective empirical data, what was going on. From such a perspective it makes eminent sense to call for a strict separation of the "Is" and the "Ought," and to propose a social science that largely steers clear of the substantive concerns of the people studied. Yet, the pragmatists always rejected this positivist model. For them the social scientist could never be somebody standing apart from the social setting, but was always somebody firmly rooted in that setting and necessarily working with the assumptions, prejudices, standards, concerns, and concepts current in it. For the pragmatists, in other words, the social scientist was just as situated in a certain time and a certain place, with all the biases that entailed, as the social actors she was studying. As a result, the pragmatic conception of the social scientist was not that of the disinterested, outside observer, but that of the active participant engaging with the concerns of her society and doing so intelligently with the use of the time-tested methodology of science.

What is curious about such neo-pragmatist legal scholars as Tamanaha and Posner is that they reject the epistemology of positivist social science, but still cling to its image of the social scientist as an impartial and disinterested observer; and that they embrace a pragmatic epistemology, but reject its image of the social scientist as an active participant involved in the projects of her society. In effect, Tamanaha and Posner claim *both* that the notion of neutral and impartial research is a naive illusion from a bygone era, *and* that research which is not neu-

---

[1]  Hilary Putnam, *Pragmatism: An Open Question*, Oxford, Blackwell, 1995, p. 14.

[2]  Brian Z. Tamanaha, *Realistic Socio-Legal Theory: Pragmatism and a Social Theory of Law*, Oxford, Clarendon Press, 1997, p. 253; Richard Posner, *The Problematics of Moral and Legal Theory*, Cambridge, Mass., Harvard University Press, 1999, p. 46.

tral and impartial is seriously flawed and morally reprehensible. The basic thesis defended in this contribution is that such a mixed signal is incoherent. If you want to adopt something like a pragmatic epistemology – and both Posner and Tamanaha have good reasons for wanting to do so – then you are also committed to a substantively informed social science. A pragmatic theory of truth wedded to positivist notions of social science, in short, is not a match made in heaven, but little more than a marriage of convenience that will not last.

## 2. The Pragmatic Conception of Ideals and Human Volition

To understand the pragmatic conception of social science as 'ideal-oriented' more fully, a small excursion into the early days of pragmatism will be helpful. Hans Joas, a chronicler of pragmatism, has argued that a central feature of classical pragmatism was the realization that only if the naive nineteenth-century belief in mechanistic and teleological scientific progress was given up '… can we move forward to understanding the openness of the historical future, the risk- and responsibility-laden nature of present action'.[3] The pragmatists, in other words, did not conceive of scientific method as a routine that would automatically deliver social improvement, but as a 'tool which, provided that it could be comprehensively institutionalized and applied to the problems of social reform under democratic conditions, would render further progress possible'.[4] For the pragmatists there was no predetermined ideal state of society that science would automatically move humanity towards. People made their own future, and scientific method was only there to help them make it sensibly and deliberately. The point was that the method of science could not substitute for human creativity and imagination in dealing with social questions, but could only help to test, improve, and discipline creative intuition. Science was not a self-executing programme, but a helpful tool to be used in shaping a desirable future. Hence, for the pragmatists science did not efface human intentionality, but only improved and extended the potential of human beings to remake their world.

---

[3] Hans Joas, *The Creativity of Action*, Chicago, University of Chicago Press, 1996, p. 250.

[4] *Ibid.*, p. 249.

This pragmatic notion of science was basically a reaction against the type of stark Social Darwinism that dominated American intellectual life at the end of the nineteenth century.[5]

One of the hallmarks of this Social Darwinist thought was the fatalistic notion that humanity was inexorably evolving towards a state of optimal adjustment to its living environment which was believed to be beyond human control. For the classic Social Darwinists, evolution was a mindless process, in which humanity moved slowly but surely towards perfect adaptation to the fixed circumstances of life. As Herbert Spencer himself put it: 'The social state is a necessity. The conditions to greatest happiness under that state are fixed. Our characters are the only things not fixed. They then must be moulded into fitness for the conditions. And all our moral teaching and discipline must have for its object to hasten this process.'[6] The way to hasten this process of moral improvement involved doing very little. The best way to serve human progress was non-interference and letting nature run its course. Interference with the harsh struggle for life would only impede the natural processes through which human nature was perfected. Left to their own devices people would slowly but surely adapt to existing conditions and finally develop to reach moral perfection, understood as the perfect adaptation to the static circumstances of life.

Pragmatism should be understood, in part, as an effort to show that the theory of evolution had an alternative application in the social realm. As the intellectual historian Edward Purcell has argued, in the beginning of the twentieth century the Darwinist vogue started to develop into what he calls 'scientific naturalism'. Pragmatic philosophers like William James and John Dewey, Purcell notes, began to define evolutionism as 'broadly humanitarian and democratic'.[7] They contended that

---

[5]     Charles Darwin's theory of evolution and Herbert Spencer's Social Darwinism had an enormous influence in the United States. Indeed, the late nineteenth-century obsession with evolutionism is hard to exaggerate. As Stephen Jay Gould has noted: 'The concept of evolution transformed human thought during the nineteenth century. Nearly every question in the life sciences was reformulated in its light. No idea was ever more widely used or misused' (Stephen Jay Gould, *The Mismeasure of Man*, London, Penguin, 1996, p. 142). Likewise, the English intellectual historian J.W. Burrow describes Darwin's theory of evolution as an 'all-embracing intellectual fashion' in the nineteenth century, which 'in a human context could be all things to all men' (J.W. Burrow, 'Editor's Introduction', in Charles Darwin, *The Origin of Species*, London, Penguin, 1968, pp. 11-48, at pp. 45-46).

[6]     Herbert Spencer, *Social Statistics, Abridged and Revised – Together with The Man Versus the State*, Osnabrück, Zeller, (1892) 1966, p. 34.

[7]     Edward A. Purcell, Jr., *The Crisis of Democratic Theory: Scientific Naturalism and the Problem of Value*, Lexington, University Press of Kentucky, 1973, p. 10.

in its collective struggle with the environment, humanity was cooperative and sympathetic, rather than competitive and mutually hostile. Most
significantly, however, the pragmatists began to stress the importance of
human intelligence in the process of evolution. For Spencer, evolution
had been an impersonal, cosmic process slowly moving humanity
towards the predetermined end of blissful adjustment to the fixed circumstances of life. The pragmatists, however, did not believe that
humanity evolved by this slow and mindless process of natural selection.
In the struggle for life, humanity had developed intelligence and this had
radically changed the evolutionary process. Thus, William James observed that human beings were not merely passive witnesses of the
world around them:

> The knower is an actor, and coefficient of the truth on one side, whilst on
> the other he registers the truth which he helps create. Mental interests, hy-
> potheses, postulates, so far as they are bases for human action – action
> which to a great extent transforms the world – help to make the truth which
> they declare. In other words, there belongs to mind, from its birth upward, a
> spontaneity, a vote. It is in the game, and not a mere looker-on; and its
> judgments of the *should-be*, its ideals, cannot be peeled off from the body of
> the cogitandum as if they were excrescences, or meant, at most, survival.[8]

Not mindless adaptation to, but conscious and willed change of, their
living conditions was the salient aspect of human development.

Similarly, John Dewey criticized theories like Spencer's for locating
reason and purpose in the natural process itself, rather than in the actions of humanity. '[I]ntelligence is not an outside power presiding
supremely but statically over the desires and efforts of man, but is a
method of adjustment of capacities and conditions within specific
situations.'[9] Consequently, he derided Spencer's 'philosophy of the
fixed environment and the static goal' as an 'animistic survival'.[10]

As a result, pragmatism developed the concept of evolution into directions, radically different from Spencerian Social Darwinism. If in the
nineteenth century, as Purcell puts it, 'many intellectuals still placed
Darwinian terms in an essentially static conceptual framework, one that
assumed a comprehensive religious or rationalistic ordering principle',
then in the beginning of the twentieth century they began to understand
Darwinism in a fully naturalistic perspective, which '... saw change as

---

[8]  Cited in Richard Hofstadter, *Social Darwinism in American Thought 1860-1915*,
    Philadelphia, University of Pennsylvania Press, 1945, p. 111.

[9]  John Dewey, *The Influence of Darwin on Philosophy and Other Essays*, Amherst/
    New York, Prometheus, (1910) 1997, p. 68.

[10]  *Ibid.*, p. 72.

given, order as accidental, process as nonteleological, behavior as adaptive, values as experiental, and absolutes of any kind as superstitions'.[11] Darwin had presented a picture of a world in constant flux; a world in which nothing was fixed and everything in a permanent process of change and adaptation. Not even the natural species themselves possessed timeless form. The pragmatists translated this view in an antifoundationalist epistemology. If nothing was fixed, if certainties and absolutes were not to be had, then there no longer was any reason to believe that a firm foundation could be provided for scientific knowledge and social institutions either. The only thing that human beings could do was pull themselves up by their bootstraps and work with the partial concepts and contingent scientific procedures inherited from earlier generations to frame the best possible solutions for the problems thrown up by an ever-changing world.

Hence, even though the pragmatists believed that certainty was unattainable, they did not discard science as an illusion. According to Putnam, this amounts to, '*the* basic insight of American pragmatism', namely that 'one can be both fallibilistic *and* antisceptical', that one can both believe that no independent and objective proof can ever be provided for even our most firmly held beliefs *and* that total doubt about all our knowledge of the world is misplaced. For the pragmatists objectivity and truth in any absolute sense were not in the cards because scientific knowledge could never rise above the biases of the socio-cultural setting in which it was produced. However, that there could be no access to a preconceptual world of facts untainted by a conceptual framework did not invalidate scientific inquiry for the pragmatists. What the pragmatists understood, according to Putnam, was '… that access to a common reality does not require access to something *preconceptual*. It requires, rather, that we be able to form *shared* concepts.'[12] All that was needed for scientific inquiry, from the pragmatic viewpoint, was a community of scholars with shared concepts, a shared conception of the world, engaged in a collaborative effort of debating, testing and criticizing each other's work and trying to arrive at some measure of intersubjective agreement on what theory fitted best in with, and worked best in, the external world that was still believed to be out there and not simply to conform to our conception of it. Hence, for the pragmatists the possibility of testing theories on a preconceptual realm of uncontaminated facts simply was not a precondition of science. Science only required a democratic community of scholars working within a shared conceptual framework, freely and openly testing and criticizing each other's work

---

[11] Purcell, *Crisis of Democratic Theory*, p. 9.

[12] Putnam, *Pragmatism*, p. 21.

according to shared scientific standards, standards that themselves were open for discussion and change, and, thus, trying to achieve an unforced consensus on what theory was preferable. That these scientific truths, in the end, remained relative to a certain conceptual framework did not worry them. Theories could still be tested on the consequences they predicted and evaluated on whether their consequences were desirable.

## 3. The Rejection of Pragmatic Social Science as Determinism

If the classic pragmatists went to great lengths to distance themselves from the view that social science would deliver progress towards a fixed ideal, then these efforts have largely been lost on the postmodern critics of pragmatic social science within the legal academy. The way the postmodern wing of American legal theory – Critical Legal Studies (CLS) – received the work of their pragmatic forebear – American Legal Realism – makes this abundantly clear. In their reception of Realism, Critical Legal scholars did not treat the use of scientific method as a form of creative action, but as a dissolution of creativity. Social science to them signals determinism. Creativity is a term they attach to the capacity of human beings to conceptually and symbolically re-imagine the world they inhabit, not to what they see as the routine application of scientific procedure geared towards the explanation of the legal status quo as a near-perfect functional optimum. This misunderstanding of pragmatism with regard to creativity lies at the heart of CLS hostility to social science in general and its embrace by pragmatists and Legal Realists in particular.

The Legal Realists of the 1920s and 1930s were heavily influenced by pragmatism, of course. From the pragmatists they adopted, among other things, a social-engineering outlook on law, a commitment to the empirical methodology of the social sciences, and a contextualist conception of law as an institution organically interwoven with the social, cultural, and historical setting of a particular society in a particular period. Critical Legal Studies has revived this Realist theory and today is often called the contemporary heir to Legal Realism. Yet, CLS has not been enthusiastic about everything the Realists had to offer. CLS has built on the contextualist aspect of legal realism, but has dropped most of its programme for the social scientific study of law. Critical legal scholars tend to view the Realist embrace of social science as a misguided effort to ground legal theory in empirical fact, whereas they tend to see their contextualism as an early and visionary attempt to come to terms with the cultural and historical contingency of law. In their rejection of Legal Realist social science Critical Legal scholars have written

65

a great deal about the shortcomings of the pragmatic, social-engineering stance that the Realists favoured. This social-engineering view, Critical Legal scholars claim, has debilitated the Realist movement. According to them, it led Legal Realism to embrace a kind of reductive functionalist analysis; a determinist functionalism which sought to present law and legal change as something that does not follow from substantive choices, but from the push of the facts, from the functional requisites inherent in the social and economic circumstances. This blunted the critical edge of Realism, CLS adherents argue, and turned it into a movement that acquiesced in the status quo.

Thus, the Critical Legal scholar Robert Gordon claims that there 'are apologetic aspects' in the Realist view of law 'that the Critics feel compelled to resist'. The problem with the Realist view on law and legal history is 'that by taking the world as we know it as largely determined by impersonal social forces, evolutionary-functionalists obscure the ways in which these seemingly inevitable processes are actually manufactured by people who claim (and believe themselves) to be only passively adapting to such processes'.[13] Gordon, in contrast, believes that there is no independent social reality that shapes the legal system, because our understanding of social reality is constructed out of the – very often legal – concepts and categories we use. Such a thing as '[t]he economy is no more "real" than "legal ideas,"' he maintains, 'it's an assemblage of conventions of which "legal ideas" such as property, contract, promissory and fiduciary obligation, not to mention money itself, are indispensable elements and propagators.'[14] Hence, Gordon argues the power of the legal system mainly resides in its capacity to narrow people's imaginations with its categories and concepts, and thus to predetermine how existing social and economic arrangements will be conceived. And Critical Legal analysis, building on the contextualist themes in Legal Realism, tries to show how contingent these structures of categories and concepts are and to what extent they predetermine our understanding of social reality.

Thus, CLS can be understood as an approach that wants to unfreeze the world, that wants to see the political and legal set-up as unnecessary rather than predetermined, plastic rather than inflexible. Roberto Unger, arguably the foremost visionary of the CLS movement, claims that this can be achieved by taking 'the last and most surprising step in the itinerary of modern historicism', and to recognize 'that the quality of our

---

[13]  Robert W. Gordon, 'Critical Legal Histories', *Stanford Law Review* 36 (1984), 57-125, at p. 70.

[14]  Gordon, 'Critical Legal Histories', p. 117.

relation, as context-revising agents, to the institutional and imaginative contexts we establish and inhabit is itself up for grabs in history. We can construct not just new and different social worlds but social worlds that more fully embody and respect the creative power whose suppression or containment all societies and cultures seem to require.'[15] The vision Unger puts forward is one of extensive autonomy. The development of legal and social arrangements should not be understood as necessitated by existing empirical conditions, Unger claims, but purely as the product of the contingent political choices embodied in our conceptualizations of reality.

The CLS critique with its stress on the importance of creative transformation points to an important aspect of ideals – the imagination of unrealized possibility. But it would be wrong to accept the CLS verdict that this imaginative dimension necessarily gets lost in a pragmatic approach such as Legal Realism, which sought legal change based on empirical knowledge. Indeed, pragmatism was in large part a reaction against exactly this type of functional determinism in nineteenth-century Social Darwinist theory. Realist views were very much in line with the pragmatist faith that human beings could shape their own destiny. Like the pragmatists, the Realists saw people as efficacious agents shaping their own life conditions. Indeed, the whole point of Legal Realism seems to be that intelligent human effort can make a difference in this world. Thus, it seems odd to charge Realism with a deterministic view of social development. To the Realists, functionalism *did* mean that there were social and economic constraints on what could be done with law; that it paid to research those constraints; even that knowledge of those constraints could help decide between policy alternatives; but not that those restraints should preclude all choice. The whole point of their turn to social science, after all, was not to acquiesce in existing conditions, but to change and reform them to fit in with human ends.

## 4. The Revival of Pragmatism in Legal Scholarship

If Critical Legal scholars overstate the scope of pragmatic social science when they criticize it as an all-encompassing, technocratic social vision, then some present-day converts to pragmatism underestimate it as only a theory of truth which steers clear of all substantive issues. In fact, much of the present appeal of pragmatism among empirical legal scholars appears to derive from its epistemology, which seems resistant

---

[15] Roberto Mangabeira Unger, *False Necessity: Anti-Necessitarian Social Theory in the Service of Radical Democracy,* Cambridge, Cambridge University Press, 1987, p. 1.

to postmodern critiques of science, such as the one provided by CLS. Since the heyday of pragmatism, positivist notions of science have been so fiercely criticized, that little credibility remains for the idea that the procedures of science can provide us with a true, impartial, and objective account of social world. Yet, because pragmatism shares many of the insights that have been marshalled against positivism, it still seems to provide a plausible account of what social science can be without the discredited positivist notions of objectivity and truth.

This observation certainly holds true for Tamanaha. The notion that all perception and understanding is mediated by our contingent and biased conceptual paradigms and, therefore, not true in any absolute sense, from Tamanaha's point of view, does not make much of a difference for the practice of science. We simply cannot perceive the world except from within a perspective, Tamanaha argues. Hence, the practice of science is necessarily informed by the conceptual distinctions arising out of our socio-cultural setting. To deny the validity of scientific knowledge on this ground, is to be a disappointed absolutist, he claims, 'lashing out in disappointment at our inability to rise above the conditions of our existence'.[16] Pragmatists, instead, simply accept that absolutes are not attainable and proceed with the concepts, standards, and values that are part of their given existential setting. If these are partial and limited, they still suffice to produce scientific knowledge which is both reliable and valid for the circumstances at hand (and the only kind of knowledge situated and finite human beings can hope to generate, anyway). As a result, according to Tamanaha, pragmatism mainly leaves things as it finds them. By and large, it reassures scientists that even without firm foundations they can keep on doing what they have always done, only now without the illusion that they are uncovering any ultimate truths about the world around them.

This leads Tamanaha to claim that pragmatism is a substantively thin philosophy. Although pragmatism is useful to brace empirical socio-legal research per se, it is markedly less useful for the advancement of any particular substantive theory of law. This is so, according to Tamanaha, because pragmatism principally involves a methodology of inquiry and a theory of truth, and does not itself 'say what the good is, how to live, what economic or political system to develop, or anything else of that nature'.[17] Other than a rejection of legal formalism and a renunciation of absolutist notions of truth, pragmatism provides the legal

---

[16] Tamanaha, *Realistic Socio-Legal Theory*, p. 30.
[17] *Ibid.*, p. 34.

scholar with very few recommendations about what would be desirable in law.

As a result, Tamanaha argues that substantive questions are best left out of a pragmatic conception of legal study altogether. Pragmatism, to him, suggests a 'descriptive, non-normative approach'.[18] In plain, common sense terms this means, according to Tamanaha: '... carefully watching what people do, figuring out why they are doing it, and trying to grasp how it all comes together.'[19] A pragmatically inspired approach to legal study would at most provide a testing ground for normative legal theories provided by others, he asserts, but would itself be careful to stay out of the politically contentious world of substantive theory. In other words, a pragmatic approach means going back to the 'scientific basics', to 'impartial and disinterested investigation', and giving up 'the impotent politics and the debunking anti-law attitude', characteristic, especially, of much CLS scholarship. It means a renewed focus on the 'accumulation of knowledge', Tamanaha believes, which is 'a valuable project that stands on its own merit'.[20]

By and large Tamanaha is right to suggest that pragmatism does not entail any full-fledged, substantive theory. Yet, from the observation that pragmatism does not 'say what the good is' it does not logically follow that pragmatism understood as a methodology of inquiry must therefore not be interested in the good. Even if pragmatism itself does not provide a particular view of the good, it can nonetheless demand that research be directed at *a* view of the good. And, indeed, as we saw that is exactly what pragmatism does seem to demand. Pragmatism entails what could be called a *commitment to commitment*; a dedication to scientific research that is not aloof, neutral, and descriptive but aimed at the achievement of a substantive end. This makes Tamanaha's insistence that his pragmatic socio-legal theory should be 'a descriptive, nonnormative approach' problematical.

Fundamental to the pragmatic conception of social science is the idea that inquiry is furthered by acting on the world, by consciously trying to bring about a socially desired state of affairs. Only by actively trying to achieve a certain result do we learn anything about how it can be achieved. Hence, the pragmatic stance is not to collect a great deal of information on social phenomena in the hope that this will decide for us what we should want to achieve. (In that case, the equation of social science with determinism would be entirely valid.) Rather the pragmatic

---

[18]   *Ibid.*, p. 253.

[19]   *Ibid.*, p. 57.

[20]   *Ibid.*, pp. 254-255.

approach is first to decide what we want to achieve and then to learn from the efforts to bring it about. Put differently, pragmatist epistemology revolves around the idea of social science as an experimental and purposive practice, as a practice aimed at making a difference. Dewey, indeed, fiercely rejected the notion that pure description of social phenomena would amount to a social science:

> Observing, collecting, recording and filing tomes of social phenomena without deliberately trying to do something to bring a desired state of society into existence only encourages a conflict of opinion and dogma in their interpretation. If the social situation is itself confused and chaotic because it expresses socially unregulated purpose and haphazard private intent, the facts themselves will be confused, and we shall add only intellectual confusion to practical disorder. When we deliberately employ whatever skill we possess in order to serve the ends which we desire, we shall begin to attain a measure of at least intellectual order and understanding.[21]

This should not be taken to suggest that pragmatism leaves social scientists free to embrace any possible grand design of society they like as a basis for social experimentation. Ideals, goals and desired ends in pragmatism are always understood as imaginative extensions of the values and purposes already inherent in existing social practices.[22] Hence, pragmatism demands that social science is informed by substantive goals; and that these substantive goals, in turn, are continuous with the values already inherent in the social practice in question.

This purposive aspect of the pragmatic notion of social science is not some optional accessory that can simply be discarded and replaced with something like non-normative description. The pragmatic conception of social science as a purposive practice seems intimately connected to its epistemology. Why should social scientists acquiesce in the given, historically contingent, conceptual framework of their cultural group, after all, unless they saw themselves as sharing in its project and trying to edge it on to a new stage of development? Tamanaha's promotion of descriptive and non-normative social research, in contrast, seems more in keeping with positivist or critical rationalist notions of social science, aimed at making contributions to the body of knowledge that are independent of the biases of time and place. These positivist or critical

---

[21]    John Dewey, 'Social Science and Social Control', in Larry A. Hickman and Thomas M. Alexander (eds.), *The Essential Dewey: Volume I: Pragmatism, Education, Democracy*, Bloomington, Ind.: Indiana University Press, (1931) 1998, pp. 369-371, p. 371.

[22]    For the pragmatic conception of ideals, see Sanne Taekema, *The Concept of Ideals in Legal Theory*, The Hague, Kluwer Law International, 2003, pp. 32-35.

rationalist approaches, however, presuppose notions of transhistorical and transcultural objectivity, that are open to exactly the kind of anti-foundationalist critique that led Tamanaha to embrace pragmatism in the first place.

Like Tamanaha, Richard Posner adopts many of the central tenets of pragmatism into his own Law-and-Economics approach to law:

> Pragmatism in the sense that I find congenial means looking at problems concretely, experimentally, without illusions, with full awareness of the limitations of human reason, with a sense of the 'localness' of human knowledge, the difficulty of translations between cultures, the unattainability of 'truth,' the consequent importance of keeping diverse paths of inquiry open, the dependence of inquiry on culture and social institutions, and above all the insistence that social thought and action be evaluated as instruments to valued human goals rather than as ends in themselves. These dispositions, which are more characteristic of scientists than of lawyers (and in an important sense pragmatism is the ethics of scientific inquiry), have no political valence.[23]

Posner's 'pragmatist manifesto' lists many of the elements that have been associated with classical pragmatism in this contribution: It accepts the unattainability of 'truth', and openly recognizes the myriad influences of time and place on the construction of knowledge; but, nevertheless, keeps faith with science as the single best method for determining what is most warranted to believe; and it proposes an instrumentalist perspective which focuses primarily on the practical consequences of legal rules, rather than on their doctrinal logic and propriety. Yet, again like Tamanaha, the idea of a substantively informed social science, or even of substantive legal theory, is something from which Posner clearly wants to distance himself. Social scientists, Posner argues, '... can criticize moral codes by showing lack of functionality, of instrumental efficiency or rationality', but such types of criticism are more properly styled 'value clarification' than 'value argument'.[24] Social scientists, in other words, can show that certain ends are ill-conceived because they do not fit in very well with existing social and economic circumstances, or do not have a realistic chance of succeeding. Yet, they cannot tell society which ends it should prefer:

> The point is that the expert, the scholar, does not choose the goal, but is confined to studying the paths to the goal and so avoids moral issues. If, as is sometimes the case, the goals of society are contested – some people want

---

23 Richard Posner, *The Problems of Jurisprudence*, Cambridge, Mass., Harvard University Press, 1990, p. 465.

24 Posner, *Problematics of Moral and Legal Theory*, p. 45.

prosperity while others would sacrifice prosperity to equality – then all the expert can do is show how particular policies advance or retard each goal. He cannot arbitrate between the goals unless they are intermediate goals – way stations to a goal that commands a consensus.[25]

If this is taken to suggest that ultimately moral and political theory are crucial for law, then that would be misconception. Moral and political philosophy, according to Posner, are incapable of resolving contentious issues. Hence, he strongly opposes their use in law.

This avoidance of substantive issues is strange, because Posner's own approach is so clearly geared towards a substantive vision. In his work, Posner leaves little doubt about his preference for a neo-conservative, free-market order. This is not meant as criticism. There might be something wrong with the content of Posner's substantive view, but from a pragmatic perspective there is little wrong with his commitment to *a* vision. It lends coherence and purpose to his law-and-economics approach. There is a *point* to Posner's varied research projects. In this, Posner resembles the Realists, who also had a substantive view of the direction in which law should be moving, although one diametrically opposed to Posner's – i.e. towards the development of the very administrative welfare state that Posner seeks to scale down. Thus, Cardozo's famous maxim for adjudication, that 'there can be no wisdom in the choice of a path unless we know where it will lead', seems to be applied by the Realists and Posner not just to law, but also to their own research projects.

## 5. Conclusion

Pragmatic ideal-oriented socio-legal study itself, in conclusion, still remains very much a misunderstood ideal. Its critics, mainly from the CLS movement, have confused pragmatic social science with its discredited bigger brother, positivist social science. Yet, even though pragmatism sometimes seems to walk and talk like positivism, it should not be confused with positivism. Hence, however effective the CLS critique might be with regard to positivist notions of social science, it is mostly beside the point when it comes to pragmatism.

Oddly, a similar confusion can be observed in some of today's proponents of pragmatic social science. Even though they are very keen to persuade people that pragmatic social science does not suffer from the same ills as its positivist sibling and claim that it is wholly resistant to the onslaught of its postmodern critics, they seem to find it very hard to

---

[25] *Ibid.*, p. 46.

dissociate the two. Thus, some of the characteristic traits of positivist social science – most notably its purported value-free objectivity – seem to blur into the image of the pragmatic alternative. Such half-hearted pragmatism, as I hope to have shown, leads to a confused and inconsistent approach to socio-legal study and should be avoided.

A pragmatic approach to socio-legal study should give up the pretence of value-free objectivity and return to an ideal-oriented, experimentalist approach. To paraphrase James, it should seek to make, rather than find, the truth which it declares. This advice has largely been forgotten, even by self-declared neo-pragmatist social scientists. Hence, social science has principally become synonymous with what Dewey derisively described as 'observing, collecting, recording and filing tomes of social phenomena without deliberately trying to do something'. This has mainly encouraged confusion about social phenomena and has led to the present-day platitude that society has proven to be far too complex to be consciously shaped through law or policy. As a result, social science has become the handmaiden of the acquiescent who maintain that empirical research only shows society to be far too perplexing to allow for any deliberate tinkering, however well meaning. Although this vexing-complexity-of-the-social-world view is often presented as some profound new insight, Dewey, as we saw, already warned that a social science which simply focused on describing the given state of society would in all likelihood bog down in the confusion of social phenomena and only add 'intellectual confusion to practical disorder'. Dewey, consequently, opted for a purposive social science because we *can* learn from an orderly effort to achieve a socially desired state of affairs. This presupposes a committed, ideal-oriented, rather than an aloof, value-free social science. Without a purpose, there can be no purposive social science.

## References

Burrow, J.W., 'Editor's Introduction', in Charles Darwin, *The Origin of Species*, London, Penguin, 1968, pp. 11-48.

Dewey, John, *The Influence of Darwin on Philosophy and Other Essays*, Amherst/New York, Prometheus, (1910) 1997.

———, *Experience and Nature*, 2nd ed., Chicago, Open Court, (1929) 1997.

———, 'Social Science and Social Control', in Larry A. Hickman and Thomas M. Alexander (eds.), *The Essential Dewey: Volume I: Pragmatism, Education, Democracy*, Bloomington, Ind.: Indiana University Press, (1931) 1998, pp. 369-371.

Gordon, Robert W., 'Critical Legal Histories', *Stanford Law Review* 36 (1984), 57-125.

Gould, Stephen Jay, *The Mismeasure of Man*, London, Penguin, 1996.

Hofstadter, Richard, *Social Darwinism in American Thought 1860-1915*, Philadelphia, University of Pennsylvania Press, 1945.

Joas, Hans, *The Creativity of Action*, Chicago, University of Chicago Press, 1996.

Posner, Richard, *The Problems of Jurisprudence*, Cambridge, Mass., Harvard University Press, 1990.

————, *The Problematics of Moral and Legal Theory*, Cambridge, Mass., Harvard University Press, 1999.

Purcell, Edward A., Jr., *The Crisis of Democratic Theory: Scientific Naturalism and the Problem of Value*, Lexington, University Press of Kentucky, 1973.

Putnam, Hilary, *Pragmatism: An Open Question*, Oxford, Blackwell, 1995.

Spencer, Herbert, *Social Statistics, Abridged and Revised – Together with The Man Versus the State*, Osnabrück, Zeller, (1892) 1966.

Taekema, Sanne, *The Concept of Ideals in Legal Theory*, The Hague, Kluwer Law International, 2003.

Tamanaha, Brian Z., *Realistic Socio-Legal Theory: Pragmatism and a Social Theory of Law*, Oxford, Clarendon Press, 1997.

Unger, Roberto Mangabeira, *False Necessity: Anti-Necessitarian Social Theory in the Service of Radical Democracy*, Cambridge, Cambridge University Press, 1987.

# The Living *Rechtsstaat*:
# A Bottom-Up Approach
# to Legal Ideals and Social Reality

Marc HERTOGH

> When legal reality is compared to an ideal
> with no identifiable empirical referent, such as
> the 'rule of law'..., the investigator may inad-
> vertently implant his personal as the society's
> legal ideals. At this point social science ceases
> and advocacy begins. ... [I]t involves, perhaps
> unwittingly, moral judgment at the very point
> where it promises scientific analysis.[1]

## 1. Legal Ideals and Social Science[2]

Crime fighting and the protection of human rights, the development
of modern governance, and the future of the multicultural society: many
contemporary debates on these and other issues circle around the legal
ideal of the *Rechtsstaat*. These are predominantly normative debates that
focus on what legislators, judges, or administrators should or should not
do in the light of this ideal. But how do administrators and others experience these debates? Which elements of the *Rechtsstaat* do they
value most? And what is the impact of this ideal in administrative
decision-making? To tackle these and similar empirical questions, we
need to supplement the conventional – normative – approach with an
alternative – empirical – way of looking at the *Rechtsstaat*. The aim of
this chapter is to develop a way in which we can include the *Rechtsstaat*
and other legal ideals in an empirical study and to demonstrate how this

---

[1] Donald Black, 'The Boundaries of Legal Sociology', in Donald Black and Maureen
Mileski (eds.), *The Social Organization of Law*, New York, Seminar Press, 1973,
pp. 41-56, at p. 45.

[2] The main argument of this paper is developed further in Marc Hertogh, *De levende
rechtsstaat: Een ander perspectief op recht en openbaar bestuur* [The Living
*Rechtsstaat*: An Alternative Perspective on Law and Public Administration], Utrecht,
Uitgeverij Lemma, 2002.

may contribute to a better understanding of the role of ideals in social reality.

Empirical analysis of legal ideals evokes important methodological questions, with regard to both the relation between law and social science and the role of social science in general.[3] One of the most interesting debates on this subject – the controversy between the American sociologists Philip Selznick and Donald Black – dates back to the early 1970s, and has lost little of its relevance since. They differ considerably on what they consider meaningful social science.[4] According to Selznick, law is dominated by the 'master ideal' of legality.[5] 'A legal order faithful to itself seeks progressively to reduce the degree of arbitrariness in positive law and its administration.'[6] In *Law, Society, and Industrial Justice,* Selznick identifies a 'strain toward legality' that is 'natural' to bureaucracy.[7] Considering this 'receptive institutional setting', he argues that – as a tendency of 'moral evolution' – legal ideals previously monitoring the exercise of public authority can now be extended to the regulation of private authority, particularly to that lodged in the industrial employment relationship. Black objects to this conclusion. He considers the empirical arguments in Selznick's study biased because they are based on a mix of normative and descriptive analysis. 'His conclusion has no empirical grounding and is saturated with ideology and evaluation and interest.'[8] According to Black, 'he interprets the law... this is where Selznick leaves sociology and enters jurisprudence.'[9] This critique is also expressed in the citation at the top of this chapter. Selznick rejects these objections. 'I admit that a spirit of advocacy carries the risk of loss of objectivity. But should we be fearful of addressing issues of social policy on that account? Social science has

---

[3]   See the chapter by Wouter de Been in this volume: 'Pragmatism and Ideal-Oriented Socio-Legal Study'.

[4]   See, e.g., C.J.M. Schuyt, 'Normen en feiten in de rechtssociologie', in C.J.M. Schuyt, *Tussen macht en moraal: Over de plaats van het recht in verzorgingsstaat en democratie,* Alphen aan den Rijn, Samsom, 1983, pp. 84-115.

[5]   Philip Selznick, 'Sociology and Natural Law', *Natural Law Forum* 6 (1961), 84-108, at p. 94.

[6]   Philip Selznick, *Law, Society, and Industrial Justice,* New York, Russell Sage Foundation, 1969, p. 12.

[7]   Selznick, *Law, Society, and Industrial Justice,* p. 93.

[8]   Donald J. Black, 'Book Review of *Law, Society and Industrial Justice* by Ph. Selznick', *American Journal of Sociology* 78 (1972), 709-714, at p. 712.

[9]   Black, 'Book Review', p. 712.

much to gain from an intimate association with genuine problems as they are experienced by acting persons or groups.'[10]

Among other things, this debate draws our attention to two different strategies of empirical inquiry: a *top-down* and a *bottom-up* perspective. In the first perspective, the investigator applies a normative (legal) definition of the *Rechtsstaat* and analyses the effectiveness of these values in influencing social behaviour. In this chapter, it will be argued that this strategy of problem formulation is similar to Roscoe Pound's contrast between the 'law in the books' and the 'law in action', and his focus on the 'gap problem' in law. It will also be demonstrated that this type of analysis is bound to produce empirical findings with a normative bias. Yet, unlike Selznick argued, this bias is neither unavoidable nor desirable. Unlike Black argued, however, this does not mean that we should abandon the empirical study of legal ideals either. Here it will be argued that it is possible – and desirable – to develop an alternative model of empirical research based on a bottom-up perspective on law and society. In this model, based on the idea of 'living law' that was first developed by Eugen Ehrlich, the investigator seeks to apply a non-normative concept of the *Rechtsstaat* and focuses on the social definition of this ideal.

This argument will be illustrated by a case study of the Indonesian quarter, a neighbourhood in the Dutch town of Zwolle. This study is not meant to give an exhaustive account of everyday life in this town, but serves as an illustration of how empirical research can add to our conventional understanding of the *Rechtsstaat*. Section 2 first offers a brief introduction to the Indonesian quarter. Section 3 looks at the significance of the *Rechtsstaat* in this neighbourhood, in particular with regard to the legal values of legality and equality. Section 4 introduces two empirical models of the *Rechtsstaat*. The first model has already been applied in our analysis in section 3; the second model is used in an alternative empirical analysis of the Indonesian quarter in section 5. Finally, section 6 discusses the conclusions of this paper.

## 2. The Indonesian Quarter in Zwolle

The Indonesian quarter is a small and predominantly blue-collar neighbourhood in Zwolle, a provincial town in the eastern part of the Netherlands and the birthplace of Jan Rudolf Thorbecke (1798-1872),

---

[10] Philip Selznick, 'Rejoinder to Donald J. Black'', *American Journal of* Sociology 5 (1972), 1266-1269, at p. 1268.

one of the founding fathers of the Dutch Constitution.[11] Many consider this area, which is wedged between a busy motorway and a small industrial area, the seedy part of town. There are about 350 houses in this area, most of which are part of social housing projects that provide accommodation for some 1,000 inhabitants. Unemployment figures in this area are extremely high. Many people depend on social security for their income and many of them have serious financial problems. Most children leave school early and social life in this community is very limited. The crime rate is the highest in Zwolle. When the Dutch Minister for City Development visited the Indonesian quarter, part of the programme was a bicycle tour of the area. However, when he and his party returned after a brief walk in the neighbourhood, one of the bicycles turned out to be stolen.[12]

In the Spring of 1994, after a series of smaller incidents, the Indonesian quarter was the scene of severe street violence. After a fight, a black family that had only just moved to Javastraat were forced to leave their home by other people in the neighbourhood. A curfew and police in riot gear were necessary to restore public order. In the aftermath of these events, many people left their houses and moved to other parts of town. In response to these events, Joop (a social worker concerned primarily with homeless young people), Wessel (a local policeman), and Freddie (an official from the local housing association) decided it was time for a change. Together they started the so-called Neighbourhood Intervention Team Zwolle (NITZ) to help restore the sense of community and security in the Indonesian quarter. Their work has recently been evaluated.[13] The overall conclusion is that their approach is controversial but successful. The Indonesian quarter is no longer considered a 'no-go area', more people are involved in voluntary community work, less damage is done to the local houses, and the crime rate has dropped considerably.

---

[11] The name of the Indonesian quarter (*de Indische buurt*) refers to the former Dutch colony of Indonesia (Dutch East Indies). The streets in this neighbourhood carry names such as 'Javastraat', 'Sumatrastraat' and 'Bankastraat'.

[12] 'Fiets gestolen: Minister geeft wethouder een lift', *Zwolse Courant*, 28 October 1999.

[13] Joyce Hes (and Jasper Veldhuis), *Recht doen aan de buurt*, Dordrecht, Stichting Maatschappij, Veiligheid en Politie, 2001.

# 3. A Top-Down Perspective

The ideal[14] of the *Rechtsstaat* is usually understood to include the legal values of legality, equality, fundamental human rights, the separation of powers, and the right to an independent court.[15] To assess the significance of the *Rechtsstaat* in the Indonesian quarter, we will apply the results of the evaluation study of the NITZ. This study was conducted in the Summer of 1999 and took six months. It was based on informal interviews with the inhabitants of this neighbourhood, members of the intervention team themselves, social workers, town officials and local politicians as well as on observations during relevant local meetings.

A complete picture of the Indonesian quarter includes both the opinions of town officials and the views of the inhabitants of this neighbourhood. Most of the empirical material available, however, emphasizes the views of the officials. Moreover, public officials are the primary subjects of the *Rechtsstaat*; the ideal of the *Rechtsstaat* is aimed at controlling *their* actions. This makes it especially relevant how officials themselves relate to this ideal. In the light of these arguments, we will focus on the actions and opinions of the members of the NITZ team and other public officials only. To be sure, later studies should also include the views of the people of this neighbourhood.

## 3.1 Legality

According to Dutch constitutional and administrative law, the principle of legality requires that every administrative act that affects the rights and freedoms of an individual has a statutory basis.[16] All official action should be based on official law. For the members of the NITZ team and some of their colleagues, however, the principle of legality does not seem to play a very significant role in their day-to-day decision making. Most decisions concerning the internal organization of the NITZ team are, for instance, largely informal and are in no way based

---

[14] With the editors of this volume, the conceptual category of ideals is interpreted as follows: 'Ideals are best understood as values that are usually not completely realizable. They are usually implicit in legal, moral and political practices and are often difficult to formulate exactly. They function as points of orientation for these practices and thus play a role in motivating action and in justifying decisions and opinions.' See Wibren van der Burg, 'The Importance of Ideals', *Journal of Value Inquiry* 31 (1997), 23-37.

[15] See, e.g., M. Scheltema, 'De rechtsstaat', in J.W.M. Engels *et al.* (eds.), *De rechtsstaat herdacht*, Zwolle, W.E.J. Tjeenk Willink, 1989, pp. 11-25.

[16] See, e.g., A.J.C. de Moor-van Vugt and B.W.N. de Waard, 'Administrative Law', in J. Chorus *et al.* (eds.), *Introduction to Dutch Law*, 3rd rev. ed., The Hague, Kluwer Law International, 1999, pp. 331-354, at p. 331.

on official rules and regulations. As a result, those who are not closely connected to the team often have a hard time figuring out the responsibilities of each individual team member.[17] The way in which public officials in the Indonesian quarter play down the importance of legality is also illustrated by the attitude of the local police towards privacy. During her fieldwork for the NITZ evaluation, the researcher had noticed that the police discussed and exchanged private information about tenants without much restraint. When she confronted them with some of the provisions of Dutch privacy law, their typical reaction was as follows:

> Privacy? That's something I infringe on every day... Privacy cannot be handled by legislation, but should be considered in each individual case instead.[18]

Perhaps the most telling example of the way in which the members of the NITZ team think about legality is reflected in their most controversial scheme in the Indonesian quarter: the allocation of low-rent houses. Their approach (which will be explained below) consisted of neglecting the general rules and regulations of official housing policy and replacing them by their own 'rules'. About these and other examples in the Indonesian quarter, the evaluation study concludes: 'To defend the good cause, official rules are often put aside.'[19] And: 'The fact that something "works" is considered far more important than whether it is legally permissible'.[20] Although the way in which the NITZ team decides on the allocation of local houses goes against official rules and regulations (see below), the then mayor of Zwolle, Mr J. Fransen, openly defended this approach. In an interview with a national newspaper he claims:

> Sometimes it is better to put the rules aside, provided that you have a clear concept and your policy is supported by the town council.[21]

In their efforts to restore public order and security in the Indonesian quarter, the NITZ team is sponsored by an organization called the 'Stichting Maatschappij, Veiligheid en Politie' (the Dutch Foundation

---

[17]  Hes, *Recht doen aan de buurt*, p. 41.

[18]  *Ibid.*, p. 40 (my translation).

[19]  *Ibid.*, p. 119 (my translation).

[20]  *Ibid.*, p. 107 (my translation).

[21]  J. Groen, 'Zet soms regels opzij in achterstandswijk: Politici pleiten voor onorthodoxe aanpak gemeentebesturen na succes in voormalige Zwolse crisiswijk', *de Volkskrant*, 26 January 2001, p. 1 (my translation).

for Police, Security and Society). With regard to the role of the police, the managing director of this organization argues as follows:

> Murder, theft and violence – these are all things the police can never tolerate; in these cases strong police action is called for. In other cases, however, it might be beneficial to bend the rules somewhat or to be flexible in the implementation of the rules.[22]

Some national politicians endorse this 'creative' policy. According to one Member of Parliament: 'In some circumstances you should be able to bend the rules somewhat.'[23] Whereas the legal ideal of the *Rechtsstaat* puts great emphasis on the 'rule of law, not of men', the members of the NITZ team and other public officials seem to have changed this principle into a 'rule of men, not of law'.

## 3.2 Equality

The principle of equality – all equal cases should be treated equally – is anchored both in the Dutch Constitution and in statutory law. Article 1 of the Constitution guarantees equal treatment of all persons in the Netherlands in equal circumstances. In addition, the Equal Treatment Act seeks to ban discrimination on the grounds of religion, belief, political opinion, race, sex, hetero- or homosexual orientation, or marital status.

In 1994, police in riot gear were sent to the Indonesian quarter after local citizens had forced a black family to leave their newly rented house in Javastraat. To prevent similar incidents in future, the NITZ team decided to develop a completely new, and highly controversial, policy. Before 1994, the distribution of low-rent houses in Zwolle (and in most other Dutch towns) was subject to a detailed housing policy. This policy gave all citizens in Zwolle in equal circumstances equal opportunities to rent a house. All future tenants were awarded a number of 'housing credits' for the number of family members and the time they had been listed on a waiting list. On the basis of these credits, town officials decided who was eligible for a house in Zwolle (including the Indonesian quarter). After the events in 1994, however, the NITZ team chose to put the official system aside, and decided to control the allocation of low-rent houses in the Indonesian quarter themselves. Town officials no longer decided on who was eligible for which house on the basis of someone's housing credits, but from now on the members of the

---

[22]  J. Groen, 'Beetje soepel met de regels', *de Volkskrant*, 26 January 2001, p. 9 (my translation).

[23]  Groen, 'Zet soms regels opzij', p. 1 (my translation).

NITZ team themselves decided who they thought would be the most suitable for a particular house. Team member Freddie explains:

We [the members of the NITZ team] conducted several interviews, and we considered whether a newcomer would fit into the neighbourhood and the neigborhood would fit in with him.[24]

In effect, this meant that tenants from ethnic minorities were excluded from social housing in the Indonesian quarter, because people in this neighbourhood felt that they did not fit in. This raised great controversy among many people in other parts of Zwolle, who not only objected to the discrimination against foreigners but also complained that those who happened to live in the Indonesian quarter did not have to comply with the general housing policy and were thus given preferential treatment.

## 3.3 Assessment

From a *legal* point of view, this case study offers a rather grim picture of life in the Indonesian quarter. Two major elements of the legal ideal of the *Rechtsstaat* – legality and equality – do not seem to play a significant role in the day-to-day decision making of the NITZ team and other public officials. Rules and regulations are put aside in favour of more informal solutions and the allocation of houses favours some tenants in the Indonesian quarter rather than others.

From a *sociological* point of view, it is obvious that this image of the Indonesian quarter is coloured by a normative interpretation of the *Rechtsstaat*. The evaluation study was used to measure the social impact of the legal values of legality and equality. The definition of these values was derived from the Constitution, statutory law and from writings in constitutional and administrative law. This is a clear example of what Black refers to as a study in *legal effectiveness*: '... a comparison of legal reality to a legal ideal of some kind.'[25] Apparently, the normative definition of the *Rechtsstaat* itself – as it is agreed upon among most lawyers – is taken for granted and its social value is considered self-evident. But how do people in the Indonesian quarter feel about this ideal? What do they consider important? What is *their* ideal of the *Rechtsstaat*? Thus far, these questions have been left unanswered. A normative definition of the *Rechtsstaat* is applied to analyse life in the Indonesian quarter from a *top-down* perspective.

---

[24] Groen, 'Beetje soepel met de regels', p. 9 (my translation).
[25] Black, 'Boundaries of Legal Sociology', p. 42.

*Law, Society, and Industrial Justice* takes a similar approach. Although this study claims to work with a 'weak definition' of law and legal ideals,[26] much of the empirical analysis applies a different method.[27] According to Selznick, someone's sense of justice is variable. Yet, 'despite variation in detail' these different interpretations do share several 'universal attributes'. *'Equal treatment, respect for personal dignity*, and *getting what one deserves* may be basic ingredients of a sense of justice, but the mode and the measure of their achievement hinge upon the realities of group life.'[28] No evidence is provided to substantiate this claim. This (hardly spacious and inclusive[29]) 'definition' is applied in a survey of employee attitudes in a way that leaves little room for alternative interpretations. This is first reflected in the fact that Selznick chose to study employee attitudes by means of a survey with pre-structured questions to which the respondents could only reply with a simple 'yes' or 'no'. A more inclusive research design would have opted for open-ended interviews and observation. Secondly, the questionnaire that was used in the survey is a direct translation of Selznick's own normative ideas about justice and fairness (based on three 'universal attributes'). Employees were asked to check which of the following phrases describes the primary meaning of their fair treatment best: (1) getting the same treatment that other employees get – no favouritism; (2) having one's abilities recognized by management; (3) having management live up to its promises; or (4) some other meaning. Finally, although some forty employees indicated that, to them, justice and fairness represented 'some other meaning', their beliefs and attitudes were not analysed.[30] The survey offered no possibility for these respondents to express their interpretation of justice and no follow-up interviews were conducted either.

According to Black, 'the value of legal-effectiveness research of this kind is bound to be precarious, for it involves, perhaps unwittingly,

---

[26] '[W]e have no wish to argue for a special and restrictive definition; a weak definition is inclusive [and] its conditions are easily met'; Selznick, *Law, Society, and Industrial Justice*, p. 4.

[27] Selznick (*Law, Society, and Industrial Justice*, p. 103) interviewed forty-four personnel directors to study their reactions to seven hypothetical cases. However, since these were all based on actual cases in grievance arbitration – and they were specifically designed to assess the correspondence between legal doctrine and the orientation of these managers – this analysis was not completely open and inclusive either.

[28] Selznick, *Law, Society, and Industrial Justice*, p. 184 (emphasis added).

[29] *Ibid.*, p. 9.

[30] *Ibid.*, p. 186.

moral judgment at the very point where it promises scientific analysis'.[31] Unlike Black argues, however, this does not imply that *all* types of empirical research on the legal ideal of the *Rechtsstaat* should be abandoned completely. To analyse some of the foundations of much legaleffectiveness research and to explore possible alternatives, we need to go back to the beginning in sociology of law.

## 4. Two Empirical Models of the *Rechtsstaat*

Roscoe Pound (1870-1964) and Eugen Ehrlich (1862-1922) are considered two major contributors to modern sociology of law. Pound had a long and distinguished career in American law schools, including a deanship at Harvard, and his ideas are still very influential today. Ehrlich was a professor of law in the former Austrian empire and his ideas are far less known to the modern reader. Whereas 'Pound's concerns have become today's orthodoxies',[32] Ehrlich – a 'prophet without honor'[33] – left no similar inheritance. Many commentators take the view that their ideas on law and society are very similar and that Pound's 'law in action' in fact builds on Ehrlich's 'living law'.[34] Yet, despite the fact that they were near contemporaries and both had a special interest in legal reality, their approaches are in fact very different and produce two different empirical models of the *Rechtsstaat*.

### 4.1 Pound and Ehrlich

The richness of both Pound's and Ehrlich's ideas warrants an extended analysis that goes well beyond the limited scope of this chapter. Some of their main arguments, however, can be summarized as follows. Central to Pound's view on law and society is the way he distinguishes the 'law in books' from the 'law in action': 'the rules that purport to govern the relations of men' and 'those that actually govern them.'[35] According to Pound, courts should not make their decisions on the basis of the common law system of fundamental rules and principles, but they should accommodate for those principles and values in society that are

---

[31] Black, 'Boundaries of Legal Sociology', p. 45.

[32] David Nelken, 'Law in Action or Living Law? Back to the Beginning in Sociology of Law', *Legal Studies* 4 (1984), 157-174, at p. 158.

[33] James F. O'Day, 'Ehrlich's Living Law Revisited: Further Vindication for a Prophet without Honor', *Western Reserve Law Review* 18 (1966), 210-231.

[34] Klaus A. Ziegert, 'The Sociology behind Eugen Ehrlich's Sociology of Law', *International Journal of the Sociology of Law* 7 (1979), 225-273.

[35] Roscoe Pound, 'Law in Books and Law in Action', *American Law Review* 44 (1910), 12-36, at p. 15.

otherwise overlooked. To Pound, the law is not an autonomous system of formal rules, but an important tool for social change. Judges and other lawyers should act as 'social engineers' and apply the law to prevent or to address social conflict. To be the most effective, the official law needs to be constantly updated and amended to legal reality to bridge the gap between the law in books and the law in action. 'In a conflict between the law in books and the national will there can be but one result. Let us not become legal monks... For the word remains, but man changes.'[36]

To Ehrlich, court rulings and state legislation are 'norms for decision'. These norms tell judges and government officials how to perform their tasks. Society as a whole is considered a collection of social associations; 'a plurality of human beings who, in relations with one another, recognize certain rules of conduct as binding, and generally at least, regulate their conduct according to them.'[37] Ehrlich calls these rules the 'living law'. 'The living law is the law which dominates life itself even though it has not been posited in legal propositions.'[38] To Ehrlich, the need for 'norms for decision' arises only in cases of dispute and conflict, whereas 'living law' prevails under normal circumstances.

The most significant difference between the two views on law and society is their central focus on two completely different objects. Whereas Pound focused on the behaviour of legislators, judges, jurists, and other legal officials, Ehrlich was oriented towards the behaviour of people in social associations (inside *and* outside legal institutions).[39] The 'law in books' refers solely to (official) rules and norms. In this way, it can be distinguished from the 'law in action'; the application of these rules and norms in legal practice. 'Norms for decision', on the other hand, include not only rules and norms but also the actual patterns of decision by legislative and judicial bodies. Conversely, 'living law' is not identical to 'law in action' because it refers essentially to obligatory norms rather than action. Ehrlich's 'norms for decision' therefore encompass most of what Pound meant by both the 'law in books' *and* the

---

[36] Pound, 'Law in Books and Law in Action', p. 36.

[37] Eugen Ehrlich, *The Fundamental Principles of the Sociology of Law*, Cambridge, Mass., Harvard University Press, 1936, p. 39.

[38] Ehrlich, *Fundamental Principles*, p. 493.

[39] Brian Z. Tamanaha, 'An Analytical Map of Social Scientific Approaches to the Concept of Law', *Oxford Journal of Legal Studies* 4 (1995), 501-535, at p. 517, identifies two distinct categories in socio-legal research. 'The first category [including Ehrlich] was oriented towards the behavior of people in social groups or society, the second category [including Pound] towards the behavior of legal actors within legal institutions.'

'law in action'. But Ehrlich's notion of 'living law' has no parallel in Pound's distinction.[40]

## 4.2 Two Models

Both views on law and society can be used as an inspiration for two empirical models of the *Rechtsstaat* (Figure 1). Each model represents a different approach to the empirical analysis of the *Rechtsstaat*.

Pound's central distinction between the 'law in books' and the 'law in action' can be applied to the ideal of the *Rechtsstaat*. The '*Rechtsstaat* in books' then refers to the legal definition of the *Rechtsstaat* that is, for instance, referred to in legal doctrine. The model of the '*Rechtsstaat* in action' looks at the degree to which these legal principles are implemented in legal practice. Whereas the '*Rechtsstaat* in books' can be studied by reading law books and studying court decisions, the '*Rechtsstaat* in action' requires empirical research. Similar to Pound's general theory of law and society, this type of empirical study focuses on the gap between the '*Rechtsstaat* in books' and the '*Rechtsstaat* in action' and on possible ways to bridge this gap.[41]

Ehrlich's central concept of the 'living law' can also be translated into a model for empirical research: the model of the '*living Rechtsstaat*'. This refers to all social norms and values that dominate life itself, even though they have not been posited in law (or in the legal definition of the *Rechtsstaat*). Unlike the previous model, this model is not in any way connected to the official definition of the *Rechtsstaat*. Empirical research based on this second model is not interested in measuring the effectiveness of the legal version of the *Rechtsstaat* in legal practice; instead, it focuses on the values of society itself. In reality, there is probably not just one, but a collection of many different understandings of the *Rechtsstaat*.

---

[40]   Nelken, 'Law in Action or Living Law?', p. 165.
[41]   David Nelken, 'The "Gap Problem" in the Sociology of Law: A Theoretical Review', *Windsor Yearbook of Access to Justice* 1 (1981), 35-61.

## Two empirical models of the *Rechtsstaat*[42]

|  | *Rechtsstaat* in action | living *Rechtsstaat* |
|---|---|---|
| *inspiration* | law in action (Pound) | living law (Ehrlich) |
| *perspective* | top-down | bottom-up |
| *definition* | official | non-official |
| *focus* | action | norms/values |
| *quality* | static | dynamic |

The first model takes the official definition of the *Rechtsstaat* – as it is discussed and agreed upon among most lawyers – as its central reference point to study legal reality (top-down). The second model, on the other hand, focuses on everyday legal practice (bottom-up). The first model is primarily interested in measuring the impact of the *Rechtsstaat* in the actions of government officials and others, the second model looks at what they themselves (and others) consider important social norms and values. Whereas the first model assumes that the official definition of the *Rechtsstaat* is more or less a given fact, the second model stresses the dynamics and constant development of what society thinks should be included in their own definition of the *Rechtsstaat*.

## 4.3 Beyond Legal Effectiveness

Our analysis of life in the Indonesian quarter in the previous section, which demonstrated the limited impact of legality and equality, is a clear example of empirical research based on the '*Rechtsstaat* in action' model. Its central focus on 'legal effectiveness' is closely related to the emphasis on 'the gap problem' in this model and the difference perceived between the 'law in books' and the 'law in action'.[43] This model essentially rests on a *normative* interpretation of what the 'right' ideal of the *Rechtsstaat* should be. This makes the '*Rechtsstaat* in action' model less suitable to study the *Rechtsstaat* empirically. As our case study of the Indonesian quarter demonstrates, an empirical research strategy based on this model unduly limits our observation to those facts that are relevant for a normative interpretation of the *Rechtsstaat*, but neglects those facts that are not.

---

[42] Hertogh, *De levende rechtsstaat*, p. 45.

[43] 'The survey findings reported here suggest that there may be a significant gap between the subjective preferences of many employees and the rules by which they are governed' (Selznick, *Law, Society, and Industrial Justice*, p. 210).

Unlike the first model, the model of the 'living *Rechtsstaat*' is not based on the concept of 'law in action' but on the idea of 'living law'. Consequently, it does not focus on possible gaps between the official law and legal reality. By contrast, the central focus in the model of the 'living *Rechtsstaat*' is not the level of *social support* for legal propositions but the *social definition* of the *Rechtsstaat*. What do members of a given community themselves consider important, regardless of what the law has to say about this (and regardless of any other normative definition)? To see how we can apply this alternative empirical model of the *Rechtsstaat*, we will now venture a second trip to the Indonesian quarter.

## 5. A Bottom-Up Perspective

Unlike many normative studies that evaluate legal practice on the basis of a closed *definition* of the *Rechtsstaat*, a bottom-up empirical study should be based on an open working *model* of the *Rechtsstaat*. This is what separates a legal from a sociological analysis:

> The lawyer needs a test to specify what material can be relied upon in legal argument before a court or in devising legal strategies which may one day be tested in litigation. A social science of law, however, while taking full account of these lawyers' tests of 'the legal' must seek *not to close off inquiry, before it begins, by conclusively specifying the nature of the object of study in a definition.* Sociology of law relies on 'working models' or open conceptions of law which are adequate to guide inquiry and are constructed solely for that purpose.[44]

We need, in other words, a non-normative conception of the *Rechtsstaat*. In our empirical analysis of the Indonesian quarter, we will ask: What do the members of the NITZ team and other public officials working in this neighbourhood consider important social values with regard to the most desirable relation between the law (*Recht*) and the state (*Staat*)?[45] Here, these values are considered important fragments of their ideal of the *Rechtsstaat*.

The evaluation study of the NITZ team attributes much of the team's success to, what is referred to as, the 'personalistic value orientation' of its members.[46] This orientation is characterized by a strong emphasis on the social context of clients and the special circumstances of each

---

[44] Roger Cotterrell, *The Sociology of Law: An Introduction*, 2nd ed., London, Butterworths, 1992, p. 38 (emphasis added).

[45] Of course, other non-normative conceptions of the *Rechtsstaat* are possible. See, e.g., James L. Gibson and Gregory A. Caldeira, 'The Legal Cultures of Europe', *Law & Society Review* 1 (1996), 55-85.

[46] Hes, *Recht doen aan de buurt*, p. 96.

individual citizen. This is reflected in two values that will be referred to as responsiveness and material equality.

## 5.1 Responsiveness

Whereas in the legal definition of the *Rechtsstaat*, the legitimacy of administrative action is its statutory basis (legality), public officials in the Indonesian quarter themselves feel that their legitimacy should be based on their close cooperation with the neighbourhood and its citizens instead (regardless of the legal status thereof). The NITZ team is not oriented towards fitting their individual decisions into a system of general rules, but towards individual citizens and their unique circumstances.[47]

Prior to the start of the NITZ team, people in the Indonesian quarter felt a deep sense of mistrust towards the town authorities.[48] They felt abandoned by the authorities, which, according to them, refused to listen to their complaints and even did not bother to send a police car to their neighbourhood when they reported break-ins. After the 1994 incident, this was one of the first things that Joop, Wessel and Freddie were keen to change. From that moment on, most of their actions were inspired by the central value of responsiveness. Or, as Freddie put it:

> Not a single stone from the pavement should be removed without consulting the local people first.[49]

Public officials in Zwolle consider this one of the 'cultural pillars' of their organization. In a brochure for future employees, the town council summarizes what they see as typical for the 'Zwolle perspective':

> Town government should be at the heart of society, outward-looking and cooperative. Policy is not made from behind a desk; public officials know what's going on in Zwolle and their work is directed at the needs of the client. There is a very close cooperation with all partners in the city.

Town officials and politicians pay regular visits to all quarters of Zwolle. During such visits, either on foot or by bicycle, officials take note of problems in the Indonesian quarter that require further attention, and all members of the community are encouraged to walk or cycle with them. One official summarizes their attitude as follows:

> Our golden rule is: listen to what the residents say. Our second rule: do not shy away from creative solutions.[50]

---

[47] *Ibid.*, p. 95.

[48] *Ibid.*, p. 25.

[49] Groen, 'Beetje soepel met de regels', p. 9 (my translation).

This is also reflected in the interviews with local police officers. According to one policeman:

> Rules are made by the residents themselves; it is our job to help them enforce these rules.[51]

His position is illustrated by the following events. For a long time, many people in the Indonesian quarter have complained about heavy traffic from the nearby motorway that uses the small streets in their neighbourhood to avoid traffic jams. At one point, several inhabitants of the Sumatrastraat decided to block their street with a concrete pole and a wire fence. Only two days after this incident, members of the community met with officials from the neighbourhood intervention team. As a result of this meeting, the Sumatrastraat was formally closed by way of a removable fence, which allows only a limited number of cars to pass. Moreover, local inhabitants have been made responsible for this fence. This solution goes against official traffic rules, and people in other parts of Zwolle have objected to what they consider a 'bonus for anti-social behaviour'.

## 5.2 Material Equality

The 'personalistic value orientation' of the NITZ team is also reflected in their attitude towards equality. In the Indonesian quarter, public officials feel less inspired by the idea of 'general justice' that focuses on official rules and general norms (*Normgerechtigkeit*) and they adhere more to the idea of 'individual justice' that emphasizes individual solutions for specific problems (*Einzelfallgerechtigkeit*). In their opinion, one should not focus on treating all people equally, but consider various ways that may help restore the equal position of individuals instead. It is, in other words, not the *intent* but the *result* of their actions that should promote equality. This does not mean ignoring, but emphasizing individual differences. In some cases, this may require favouring some citizens more than others.

This attitude is most clearly expressed in the way the NITZ team – and the local housing association 'Openbaar Belang' (Public Interest) in particular – used so-called 'special contracts' for the allocation of houses.[52] In these contracts, each tenant is treated differently and each has to fulfill different requirements to be eligible for a house. In one of these contracts, Mrs A., who had been refused a house before, was

---

[50] Groen, 'Beetje soepel met de regels', p. 9 (my translation).

[51] Hes, *Recht doen aan de buurt*, p. 43 (my translation).

[52] *Ibid.*, p. 61.

offered a house under the specific condition that she would *not* allow her two sons to move in with her. Moreover, she was obliged to arrange for other members of her family to take care of her. Both sons of Mrs A., who locally held a somewhat notorious reputation, were offered a house as well. Before the 1994 incident they used to live in a caravan. In their contracts, the men were explicitly prohibited to drink more than one litre of beer a day. In his defence of these and other remarkable contracts, the managing director of the local housing association claimed:

> You may argue, equal cases should be treated equally. But that simply doesn't hold for the Indonesian quarter. Here, there are no equal cases...[53]

With regard to these and other examples, the evaluation study concludes: 'Justice is done by recognizing the importance of individual differences and by treating the neighbourhood favourably.'[54] Whereas the legal definition of the *Rechtsstaat* adheres to a concept of 'formal equality', the members of the NITZ team and others acted upon the value of 'material equality'.[55]

## 5.3 Assessment

The 'living *Rechtsstaat*' model does not approach social reality with a normative definition of the *Rechtsstaat*, but analyses life in the Indonesian quarter from a *bottom-up* perspective. This provides us with a completely different image of the neighbourhood. Unlike the previous grim picture (section 3), this alternative perspective shows how town officials and local politicians are motivated by two central values: responsiveness and material equality. Both values are directly related to the (most desirable) role of their own public institutions and the role of the law (*Recht*) and the state (*Staat*) in general. Accordingly, to most officials involved in the re-development of the Indonesian quarter, these values represent two important fragments of their own ideal of the *Rechtsstaat*. This analysis is based on an open – non-normative – conception of the *Rechtsstaat*. It does not require the investigator to base his research on a normative interpretation of this ideal, but allows observable life in the Indonesian quarter to speak for itself. The emphasis on responsiveness and material equality does not constitute some degree of more or less *Rechtsstaat*, but a different type of *Rechtsstaat* altogether.

Critics may argue that the 'living *Rechtsstaat*' model is not a completely neutral model either. Since all observation is theory laden, the

---

[53] *Ibid.*, p. 61 (my translation).

[54] *Ibid.*, p. 117 (my translation).

[55] *Ibid.*, p. 106.

definition of the *Rechtsstaat* used in this model has some normative characteristics as well. This *normative* element, however, differs from the normative character of the '*Rechtsstaat* in action' model in at least three important respects. Firstly, a truly normative concept of the *Rechtsstaat* turns attention 'from necessity to fulfilment'; '… instead of concentrating on the minimum conditions that signify its emergence, the emphasis shifts to [its] civilizing potential.'[56] Yet, the 'living *Rechtsstaat*' model focuses on 'all values with regard to the most desirable relation between the law (*Recht*) and the state (*Staat*)', but it does not specify what these values are or should be. As a result, this definition can be little more than a 'minimalist view' of the *Rechtsstaat*.[57] It excludes those potential interpretations that are not directly related to the law and the state, but this exclusion is considerably smaller than an approach that limits the observation of relevant values to those related to, for instance, equal treatment, legality, and the separation of powers. Secondly, the definition used in the 'living *Rechtsstaat*' model is strictly functional and provisional. It is subject to a process of trial and error and to empirical falsification. Regardless of any personal, legal, political, or other normative reservations, it will be applied only for as long as other definitions will not produce better (more inclusive) results. Finally, the normative character of any research project is never fully determined by its definitions only. It is also important to consider how these definitions are applied in the overall research design. Whereas the exclusive use of a survey with pre-formulated questions *maximizes* the closed and normative character of the concepts used, semi-structured interviews and observation promote the open and inclusive character of the findings and may thus *minimize* the effects of any normatively coloured concepts. Here, the 'living *Rechtsstaat*' model was used in open-ended interviews and observation only.

## 6. Conclusion

The world of legal ideals and social reality is a world of extremes. The 'sociological jurisprudence' of Selznick and others has made many of us aware of the importance of values and ideals in law. Yet, in developing their argument, descriptive empirical analysis has become too much interwoven with normative interpretation. At the other extreme, Black's 'pure positivism' has drawn our attention to some of the real risks associated with including values and ideals in an empirical study; it may well end up in normative judgement where it promises scientific

---

[56]  Selznick, *Law, Society, and Industrial Justice*, p. 9.

[57]  *Ibid.*, p. 8.

analysis. However, in making this valuable point Black took the wrong decision to abandon the empirical study of ideals altogether. Here it was argued that the concept of 'living law', that was first developed by Ehrlich, offers an attractive middle position on the continuum between these two ends. The model of the 'living *Rechtsstaat*' allows us to include the ideal of the *Rechtsstaat* in an empirical study, while avoiding a normative bias.

The case study of the Indonesian quarter is by no means a thorough empirical analysis. Most observations are solely based on the evaluation study of the NITZ team and other secondary research. Yet, despite these obvious limitations this case study contains several interesting features of the role of legal ideals in social reality. Supported by more interviews with officials and citizens and other empirical material, these could serve as hypotheses for future research. Based on our analysis of the Indonesian quarter, an empirical study of the *Rechtsstaat* reveals the constructivist, pluralistic and pragmatic character of this legal ideal. Firstly, the ideal of the *Rechtsstaat* is a *constructivist* concept. The case study demonstrates that this ideal is not a given fact, but is something that is constantly shaped in everyday practice. Seen from this perspective, ideals are the answers people formulate among themselves in response to situations they hope to retain or aspire to change. A world without communication is a world without ideals. Secondly, in our case study the *Rechtsstaat* is also presented as a *pluralist* concept. Different people have different ideas about the 'true' values of the *Rechtsstaat*. Some may well be in accordance with the accepted legal definition, others may not.[58] Whereas legislators, judges, and other jurists emphasize the significance of legality and (formal) equality, the members of the NITZ team stress the importance of responsiveness and material equality instead. The inhabitants of the Indonesian quarter and of other parts of Zwolle have, no doubt, their own ideas about the *Rechtsstaat* as well. Finally, the ideal of the *Rechtsstaat* has a *pragmatic* character. Although ideals may be vague and implicit, they can influence the decision-making of public officials. In addition, in an empirical study the only values or ideals of the *Rechtsstaat* that are of any significance are the ones that can be recognized in the actions and opinions of the members of the NITZ team and others. '[S]cience can know only phenomena and never essences. Accordingly, insofar as such ideals as

---

[58] For a similar discussion, see S. Wai Man and C. Yiu Wai, 'Whose Rule of Law? Rethinking (Post-) Colonial Legal Culture in Hong Kong', *Social & Legal Studies* 2 (1998), 147-169.

justice, the rule of law, and due process are without a grounding in experience, they have no place in the sociology of law.'[59]

Taking a top-down perspective, life in the Indonesian quarter has very little to do with the legal ideal of the *Rechtsstaat*. Public officials working in this neighbourhood pay very little attention to the key values of legality and equality. Yet the empirical model of the 'living *Rechtsstaat*' – that views legal reality from a bottom-up perspective – has provided us with a remarkably different image. Although town officials may not always work in accordance with the legally accepted elements of the *Rechtsstaat*, they do adhere to at least two different values instead: responsiveness and material equality. To them, these values represent fragments of their own definition of the *Rechtsstaat*. This leaves, of course, an important normative question unanswered. Do we accept that these alternative values are indeed fragments of the legal ideal of the *Rechtsstaat*? The answer to this question, however, is beyond the scope of this paper. At this point social science ceases and advocacy begins.

# References

Black, Donald J., 'Book Review of *Law, Society and Industrial Justice* by Ph. Selznick', *American Journal of Sociology* 78 (1972), 709-714.

––––––, 'The Boundaries of Legal Sociology', in Donald Black and Maureen Mileski (eds.), *The Social Organization of Law*, New York, Seminar Press, 1973, pp. 41-56.

Cotterrell, Roger, *The Sociology of Law: An Introduction*, 2nd ed., London, Butterworths, 1992.

De Moor-van Vugt, A.J.C., and B.W.N. de Waard, 'Administrative Law', in J. Chorus *et al.* (eds.), *Introduction to Dutch Law*, 3rd rev. ed., The Hague, Kluwer Law International, 1999, pp. 331-354.

Ehrlich, Eugen, *The Fundamental Principles of the Sociology of Law*, Cambridge, Mass., Harvard University Press, 1936.

'Fiets gestolen: Minister geeft wethouder een lift', *Zwolse Courant*, 28 October 1999.

Gibson, James L., and Gregory A. Caldeira, 'The Legal Cultures of Europe', *Law & Society Review* 1 (1996), 55-85.

Groen, J., 'Zet soms regels opzij in achterstandswijk: Politici pleiten voor onorthodoxe aanpak gemeentebesturen na succes in voormalige Zwolse crisiswijk', *de Volkskrant*, 26 January 2001, p. 1.

Groen, J., 'Beetje soepel met de regels', *de Volkskrant*, 26 January 2001, p. 9.

---

[59] Black, 'Boundaries of Legal Sociology', p. 47.

Hertogh, Marc, *De levende rechtsstaat: Een ander perspectief op recht en openbaar bestuur* [The Living *Rechtsstaat*: An Alternative Perspective on Law and Public Administration], Utrecht, Uitgeverij Lemma, 2002.

Hes, Joyce (and Jasper Veldhuis), *Recht doen aan de buurt*, Dordrecht, Stichting Maatschappij, Veiligheid en Politie, 2001.

Nelken, David, 'The "Gap Problem" in the Sociology of Law: A Theoretical Review', *Windsor Yearbook of Access to Justice* 1 (1981), 35-61.

―――, 'Law in Action or Living Law? Back to the Beginning in Sociology of Law', *Legal Studies* 4 (1984), 157-174.

O'Day, James F., 'Ehrlich's Living Law Revisited: Further Vindication for a Prophet without Honor', *Western Reserve Law Review* 18 (1966), 210-231.

Pound, Roscoe, 'Law in Books and Law in Action', *American Law Review* 44 (1910), 12-36.

Scheltema, M., 'De rechtsstaat', in J.W.M. Engels *et al.* (eds.), *De rechtsstaat herdacht*, Zwolle, W.E.J. Tjeenk Willink, 1989, pp. 11-25.

Schuyt, C.J.M., 'Normen en feiten in de rechtssociologie', in C.J.M. Schuyt, *Tussen macht en moraal: Over de plaats van het recht in verzorgingsstaat en democratie,* Alphen aan den Rijn, Samsom, 1983, pp. 84-115.

Selznick, Philip, 'Sociology and Natural Law', *Natural Law Forum* 6 (1961), 84-108.

―――, *Law, Society, and Industrial Justice*, New York, Russell Sage Foundation, 1969.

―――, 'Rejoinder to Donald J. Black', *American Journal of Sociology* 5 (1972), 1266-1269.

Tamanaha, Brian Z., 'An Analytical Map of Social Scientific Approaches to the Concept of Law', *Oxford Journal of Legal Studies* 4 (1995), 501-535.

Van der Burg, Wibren, 'The Importance of Ideals', *Journal of Value Inquiry* 31 (1997), 23-37.

Wai Man, Sin, and Chu Yiu Wai, 'Whose Rule of Law? Rethinking (Post-) Colonial Legal Culture in Hong Kong', *Social & Legal Studies* 2 (1998), 147-169.

Ziegert, Klaus A., 'The Sociology behind Eugen Ehrlich's Sociology of Law', *International Journal of the Sociology of Law* 7 (1979), 225-273.

# Stories and Ideals

## Caroline RAAT

## 1. Introduction

In the Netherlands, there have always been many private organisations with public functions, like public housing, education, welfare, health care, and so on, and their number is still growing. From a legal point of view, these organisations are considered private and are therefore governed by private law. If we look at them through sociological or ethical eyes, what we see is a locus of power. And power can be used and abused. Thus, the fact that they have power urges these organisations to act properly toward their clients, even though positive law sets no such rules.

In Western law, the doctrine of the *Rechtsstaat* has been developed to limit the abuse of state power. But there are more situations of power where abuse may occur. In this chapter, I will argue that the *Rechtsstaat* is an ideal, something worthwhile achieving. The *Rechtsstaat* in this respect is not so much a set of positivised rules; it is based on human values and inner commitment.[1] One of the advantages of such an ideal-based conception is that it can also be used in situations of private power.

An example of private power can be found in private social housing foundations, which allocate most of the houses in the Netherlands. By means of empirical research I tried to get an idea of the institutional setting of such organisations and whether the *Rechtsstaat* as an ideal is of any use in these organisations. I used a method called storytelling, which will be dealt with in this chapter. Stories can be used to reveal attitudes and thoughts that are normally left unspoken. They are a good way to trace down the ideals in an organisational culture. The 'Story of the Decent Vagabond' may illustrate this.

---

[1] 'Ideals are values that are implicit or latent in the law, or the public and moral culture of a society or group that usually cannot be fully realized, and that partly transcend contingent historical formulations and implementations in terms of rules and principles'; W. van der Burg, 'The Importance of Ideals', *The Journal of Value Inquiry* 31 (1997), 23-37, p. 25.

At the end of this chapter, I will make the same point in a more general way: we can speak of *rechtsstaatliche* ideals in organisations, but I will also show that there is the risk of particularism when dealing with clients in hard cases. I believe there are solutions for dealing with this risk. Unlike most jurists, I will not focus on legislation, adjudication, or self-regulation, but I will use insights from organisational ethics and the social sciences to point to the motivational aspect of the *Rechtsstaat*.

## 2. How the Law Limits Power

### 2.1 *The Rule of Law and the* Rechtsstaat: *Answers to Power*

In this contribution, I will use the word *Rechtsstaat* mainly for the reason that my research was done in the Netherlands.[2] Important work in the field of expanding the doctrine to private spheres was done by Philip Selznick in 1969, in his book *Law, Society, and Industrial Justice*. His sociological approach to institutions and the law made him argue that private organisations too should be subjected to the Rule of Law. 'Clearly [a "law of governance"] should apply wherever the social function of governing is performed, wherever some men rule and others are ruled.'[3] The problem is that strictly legally speaking this makes no sense because the Rule of Law only holds for the state and its institutions.[4] In my opinion, the *Rechtsstaat* should be regarded not only as a legal but also as a social, historical, *and* ethical concept. The main reason why the doctrine of the *Rechtsstaat* was created was the wish that those in power would no longer act toward the objects of this power in an arbitrary manner. The clearest way to follow the route from this wish to *Rechtsstaatlichkeit* as an ideal is to divide this route into four steps:

Step one: The organisation is in a position of power.

Step two: The client is an individual with inseparable rights.

Step three: The organisation bears responsibility for this individual.

Step four: The organisation can and should commit itself to the ideal of the *Rechtsstaat*.

---

[2] There is also a more fundamental reason to do this. Many jurists treat the German terms *Rechtsstaat* and *Rechtsstaatlichkeit* and the English term Rule of Law as synonyms because they refer to the same phenomenon, but there are essential differences that made me choose the German concepts. I will mention only one aspect: the Rule of Law seems to have a stronger connotation with positive law than the *Rechtsstaat* does.

[3] Ph. Selznick, *Law, Society and Industrial Justice*, New York, Russell Sage Foundation, 1969, p. 259.

[4] This is an important statement that I will elaborate on below.

Considering all four steps together, we may conclude that what we are actually dealing with is a morality of organisational power. The more power an organisation has over its clients, the more urgent the need for such a morality becomes. The social housing foundations I will discuss below have, indeed, specific features that make control of their exercise of power necessary:

1. It concerns the relation between an organisation and an individual.

2. The organisation has a (semi-)monopoly position, which means that there is no alternative organisation for the client to turn to.

3. The organisation supplies a product or service that constitutes a basic need for the client, such as the right to health, housing, or education.

4. There is no mutual dependency and, therefore, no equality of position.

The special features of the organisation, its product, and its clients are largely the same for many commercial enterprises. Many business ethics theorists these days believe that privately owned companies have social responsibilities.[5] These social responsibilities are even more important for private organisations that have public tasks. Though the Constitution and administrative laws do not apply directly to them, the power of this type of organisations over their clients is enormous. An orientation toward *rechtsstaatliche* ideals can be a way to develop the organisational morality that is required for such a powerful organisation. In the next section, I will try to explain that the legal way people usually look at law and the *Rechtsstaat* is a limited one. In contrast, I would like to suggest that the *Rechtsstaat* can also be seen as an ideal, with a much broader impact than positive law.

## 2.2 A Static-Institutional Approach

Lawyers are taught to think in a positivist way about law, not only in their education but also in their day-to-day practice. Law is generally seen as a body of rules that is outside the persons or organisation(s) it applies to. In legal writings, aspects of law, like coercion and controllability, are emphasised. In Dutch handbooks on constitutional and administrative law, the *Rechtsstaat* is 'positivised': The Netherlands *has* a Constitution, etc., therefore, the Netherlands *is* a *Rechtsstaat*.[6] Oosting calls this traditional view on the *Rechtsstaat static institutional*.[7] By this

---

[5]  See the writings on business ethics, e.g. W.M. Hoffman and R.E. Frederick, *Business Ethics: Readings and Cases in Corporate Morality*, New York, McGraw-Hill, 1995.

[6]  E.g. W.J. Witteveen, *De geordende wereld van het recht*, Amsterdam, Amsterdam University Press, 1996.

[7]  E.g. M. Oosting, 'De last van het recht: Recht als opdracht en als obstakel', in J.W.M. Engels *et al.* (eds.), *De rechtsstaat herdacht*, Zwolle, W.E.J. Tjeenk Willink,

he refers to a traditional lawyer's view on the law and the state. He sees a great risk in this view: if an organisation and its employees only regard the *Rechtsstaat* as something externally imposed on them, they may develop a legalistic manner of rule-following. Webb describes legalism as 'an ethical attitude which encourages individuals to treat moral conduct as rule-following and to use rules manipulatively through forms of creative compliance'.[8] This means that the rule is followed only because it is a rule without taking notice of its content and moral background. Abuse of power easily occurs here.

## 2.3 A Dynamic-Cultural Approach

During the past few centuries, jurists and political philosophers have been working on this concept, not simply as a set of rules that is part of positive law, but as a historical and socially developed concept, based on this very urge to demand responsibility from those who are in power. This makes the *Rechtsstaat* an ideal: something worthwhile achieving. Organisations can and should bind themselves to this ideal, not so much in a legal way, but in a moral way.[9]

For the state and public organisations, the doctrine of the *Rechtsstaat* has been 'positivised' in externally imposed legal rules. For private agencies, the same doctrine has not, or only in part, been codified. This does not mean that the doctrine has no appeal to private organisations. Speaking of the *Rechtsstaat* as an ideal, something worthwhile achieving, every powerful organisation should feel bound to the rules of the *Rechtsstaat*. This is also the case for private powerful organisations, even though legally speaking these rules do not apply to them. Ideally, such an organisation has an internal commitment to abide by these rules, so to speak, because of the moral character of the organisation. If this is the case, it has internalised the norms of the *Rechtsstaat*. This has an enormous advantage: the organisation will act according to the rules even if there is no threat of external sanctioning,[10] just because it *wants* to act according to the rules. Where there are no rules or when rules are

---

1989, pp. 171-183, p. 172 (my translation). Oosting has been the Dutch National Ombudsman for many years, which means that he monitored the *behavior* of the administration towards its clients.

[8] Julian Webb, 'Ethics for Lawyers or Ethics for Citizens? New Directions for Legal Education', *Journal of Law and Society* 25 (1998) 1, 134-150, p. 137.

[9] Both *Rechtsstaatlichkeit* and responsibility can be regarded as organisational virtues, a concept that I will not deal with in this article, but that will be a central issue in my doctoral thesis.

[10] Because there is no legal procedure open or because it is known from experience that the client will not use it (because it lacks bureaucratic competence).

100

unclear, the principles of the *Rechtsstaat* will lead to a better decision. Oosting calls this the dynamic-cultural approach of the *Rechtsstaat*.[11] By this he means that law is more than the law in the books; the moral and sociological background of the law is also taken into account by those who are in power.

A central concept in this dynamic-cultural approach is responsibility.[12] According to Witteveen, power and responsibility are 'mirror images: if you look for the former you will also see the latter. Whoever looks power in the face, demands responsibility.'[13] But is not this the main problem? Those who have no power are not in a position to demand anything.

On the other hand, the urge of responsible execution of power is clear. Most people seem to favour responsible action, but what does this mean in concrete cases? In the day-to-day functioning of organisations, this question is not all that easy to answer. The proof of this can be seen every day: How often do we not talk about organisations acting 'wrongly'? I think that an important contribution can be made by regarding the *Rechtsstaat* as a concept with a broad meaning.

## 2.4 The Ideal of the Rechtsstaat

So far I have explained the difference between two ways of looking at the law and the ideal of the *Rechtsstaat*. I will proceed by explaining what this *Rechtsstaat* means in a more detailed sense. I will confine myself to two major features: governance by rules and principles, and responsiveness.[14] The first one is a more classic way to describe the *Rechtsstaat*, the latter is an addition made by Nonet and Selznick to

---

[11]  E.g. Oosting, 'De last van het recht', p. 172.

[12]  M.A.P. Bovens, 'De veelvormigheid van verantwoordelijkheid', in M.A.P. Bovens, C.J.M. Schuyt and W.J. Witteveen (eds.), *Verantwoordelijkheid: Retoriek en realiteit, Verantwoording in publiek recht, politiek en maatschappij*, Zwolle, W.E.J. Tjeenk Willink, 1989, pp. 17-41, p. 30.

[13]  W.J. Witteveen, 'Retorische constructie', in M.A.P. Bovens, C.J.M. Schuyt and W.J. Witteveen (eds.), *Verantwoordelijkheid: Retoriek en realiteit, Verantwoording in publiek recht, politiek en maatschappij*, Zwolle, W.E.J. Tjeenk Willink, 1989, pp. 81-99, p. 83 (my translation).

[14]  The concept of *responsive law* was developed by Philippe Nonet and Philip Selznick; see Ph. Nonet, and Ph. Selznick, *Law and Society in Transition: Toward Responsive Law*, New York, Harper & Row, 1978. It means that '[a] responsive institution maintains its integrity while acknowledging the legitimacy of an appropriate range of claims and interests'; Ph. Selznick, *The Moral Commonwealth, Social Theory and the Promise of Community*, Berkeley, Cal., University of California Press, 1992, p. 463.

emphasise that law has to be open to the needs of society. Both function as counterweights in a balance. Only if an organisation has both features can we speak of full *Rechtsstaatlichkeit* in this organisation. This concerns the difference discussed above: it will not do for an organisation to display rule-following behaviour only; it also needs a sense of justice and a sense of who its client is. Responsiveness can be defined as having an open mind to the needs of the client. This open mind may prevent the organisation from legalistic ways of applying the law, so that the client has a bigger chance of getting what he is entitled to. In fact, responsiveness is meant to compensate for too much bureaucratic rule-following.

In addition to the previous section, where the *Rechtsstaat* was introduced as an ideal, it may be enlightening to look again at why this doctrine was developed in the first place. One of the features that the *Rechtsstaat* and the Rule of Law have in common is that both have been developed to prevent arbitrariness, because this was and still is experienced as a flagrant violation of most people's sense of right and wrong. It is important to find out why this is so: and this leads us to the question about the values behind the *Rechtsstaat*. There is no consensus about these values. Most authors come up with notions like: autonomy, freedom, security, equality, human dignity, the value of the individual, and so on. In this chapter, I choose to use human dignity,[15] because it is the broadest notion that includes the most important of the others that have been suggested: freedom, equality, and justice.

Each of these three values is connected with elements of the *Rechtsstaat*. Freedom has a negative and a positive meaning, as equality has a formal and a material side. Negative freedom means that every person has the right to be protected from arbitrary intervention by the state.[16] This is protected by legality, the principles of due administration (both addressing obligations to the state and its institutions) and by the individual's constitutional rights, such as the freedom of religion. This type of freedom refers to formal equality: before the law, people are equal, regardless of their personal differences. The state and its institutions of justice must give both parties in a legal procedure equal tools in order to eliminate inequality of power. The image of Justitia with her blindfold is typical for this way of thinking. Positive freedom is closely connected

---

[15]    This does not mean that authors agree on what human dignity means or implies. Bobbio, for instance, regards three values as the moral essence of the Rule of Law: (procedural) equality, individual autonomy, and security. R. Cotterrell, 'The Rule of Law in Transition: Revisiting Franz Neumann's Sociology of Legality', *Social & Legal Studies* 5 (1996) 4, 451-470, p. 459.

[16]    I. Berlin, *Four Essays on Liberty*, Oxford, Oxford University Press, 1969, p. 122.

with material equality: the institutions of justice must not be blind to the material inequalities that exist in reality.[17] The idea of equality of arms developed in the nineteenth-century liberal state might not be enough to truly eliminate inequality, both in legal procedures and in the design of society. Positive freedom is necessary to fully achieve negative freedom. Social constitutional or human rights try to guarantee at least a minimum standard of welfare, health, housing, etc. But these rights do more than that; they are not only a means to achieve positive freedom, they also represent an end in themselves. By introducing social rights and material equality, we enter the domain of justice. Justice, used here as a material notion, means more than freedom and equality. It means that the state fully acknowledges the intrinsic dignity of every individual human being as a value that must be achieved and protected.

## 3. Empirical Research of Ideals

In the previous section, I introduced the *Rechtsstaat* as a moral notion. If we want to find out whether this notion is of any use in reality, we need a sociological framework. The concept of internal morality can be a starting point for such a framework, as it refers to the central normative idea of the *Rechtsstaat* and connects this to law and public administration in such a way that it can be studied empirically.[18] This concept means, according to Selznick, that organisations can get a characteristic that is not based on external enforcement, but on self-limitation. He calls this morality, which can easily be recognised as *rechtsstaatlich*, 'corporate responsibility', a notion often mentioned in business ethics.

> For institutions, as for persons, self-regulation does not mean freedom to do as one pleases. Rather it implies the exercise of options that will... enhance its integrity. ... The great task of institutional design is to build moral competence into the structure of the enterprise. This is the key to corporate responsibility – private as well as public. ... [A] responsible enterprise, like a responsible person, must have an *inner* commitment to moral restraint and aspiration.[19]

Selznick writes about the development of organisations in terms of institutionalisation and culture. 'Internally, as the organisation takes on a distinctive identity the source of integration shifts from goals to values, from specific objectives to ways of thinking and deciding. In short: a

---

[17]   *Ibid.*, p. 131.

[18]   This concept was developed by Lon Fuller in *The Morality of Law* (rev. ed., New Haven, Conn., Yale University Press, 1969).

[19]   Selznick, *Moral Commonwealth*, pp. 344-345.

corporate culture is created.'[20] Organisational culture in this sense can be used as an equivalent for the internal morality of an organisation.

## 3.1 Organisational Culture and Attitudes

Organisational culture has to do with the living norms and values of an organisation. It is strongly connected with opinions and mentalities that are characteristic for the organisation. 'Culture is the basic assumptions and beliefs shared by members of the organisation that operate unconsciously and that defines in a basic, taken for granted fashion an organization's view of itself and its environment.'[21] Values are the core of organisational culture. These values play a vital role in the way people in the organisation treat each other, and, more importantly, their clients. Values, when used in this sociological sense, are not intrinsically good or bad. If we want to connect the concept with ideals that are intrinsically good, we have to add positive terms to our definition, referring to responsibility or *Rechtsstaatlichkeit*. A *rechtsstaatliche* organisational culture will be defined as: a set of opinions of an organisation that is based on and expresses the values the *Rechtsstaat* is meant to protect. This set is also determinative for the way the organisation acts.

What culture is for organisations, is attitude for individuals. This phenomenon can be defined as follows: 'An attitude is a rather stable mental position held toward some idea, or object, or person. ... Every attitude is a combination of beliefs, feelings, and evaluations, and some predisposition to act accordingly.'[22] Just as culture does for (parts of) an organisation, attitude not only refers to opinions, but also to action. Just like culture, attitudes can be good or bad. A *rechtsstaatliche* attitude can be described as a set of opinions of a person that is based on and expresses the values the *Rechtsstaat* is meant to protect. This set is also determinative for the way the person acts.

Culture and attitude do not refer to the same actor; one refers to an organisation or a group, the other to a single person. This does not mean that there is no relation between the two concepts. A major aspect of this relation is socialisation: the process by which an organisation transmits its culture, instilling in new members the values and norms of the organisation, transforming an outsider into an insider.[23] If this process

---

[20] *Ibid.*, p. 237. He calls the development of organisations from goal-driven to value-driven (thick) institutionalisation.

[21] F. Heffron, *Organization Theory and Public Organizations: The Political Connection*, Englewood Cliffs, N.J., [etc.], Prentice Hall, 1989, p. 212.

[22] H. Gleitman, *Psychology*, New York, W.W. Norton & Company, 1991, p. 459.

[23] Heffron, *Organization Theory*, p. 221.

succeeds, we can see 'deep commitment' to the organisation and its goals by its members: the norms have been internalised. This deep commitment is often referred to as loyalty.[24] The link that exists between organisational culture on the one hand and attitude of employees on the other may be called the institutional setting.

If we describe the same phenomena in ethical terms rather than in sociological ones, we can use the term virtues. I regard organisational virtue as the positive *ethical equivalent* of the sociological concept of *organisational culture*. Personal virtues find their equivalent in the social-psychological concept of *attitudes*. Both are important if we want to find out what the ideals of a specific organisation are. The culture of an organisation cannot exist without the moral contribution of its members, and the attitude of the members is influenced by the culture of the organisation. An institutional setting can be called virtuous when it meets the ideal of the *Rechtsstaat*.

## 3.2  Stories: A Key to Ideals

One of the most complicated things to study in practice is organisational culture and attitudes, precisely because the members of the organisation hardly ever write them down. Everyone who works in an organisation can tell you that culture is there and that it is very important. Though this culture is often felt in an unreflected or even half-conscious way, it still influences the way employees think and act, sometimes even more than overt rules do. Studies of this phenomenon have in common that they try to find out what a culture is in an indirect way, precisely because it is not directly visible. If you ask an employee what the local culture is, he will often only be able to describe it in very general notions. How it affects his own functioning is a different matter. This was not different in my empirical study. In order to find a way to get to this unreflected and more detailed level, I used a technique called narrative analysis, which is also referred to as *storytelling*.[25]

The basic thought behind the method of storytelling is that stories told in organisations can teach us a lot about the organisation's charac-

---

[24] Loyalty, however, is a problematic concept with not only a positive, but also a very negative meaning. In my doctoral thesis, I will argue that loyalty to the organisation or to its management is not always good, and that therefore a shift should take place to loyalty to values, such as the values of the *Rechtsstaat*.

[25] I prefer the word 'storytelling' because it indicates what it is. Apart from that the word 'analysis' holds a claim of objectivity and exactness that storytelling does not. See also S. Maynard Moody, and M. Musheno, 'Morality over Legality: Invoking Norms from the Front-Lines of Government', paper presented at the annual meeting of the Law and Society Association, Chicago, May 1999.

ter, its members, what they stand for, and what moral norms and values exist. I use the so-called naturalistic variant, which is a pragmatic, empirical method.[26] The main focus in this variant is on the moral dimension of a practice: values play a central role when it comes to how people experience reality.[27] Stories are reflections of this experienced reality. Storytelling is valuable, not because it gives us an idea about the objective reality, but about the experiences of people and the values involved.[28] Stories are symbolic representations of human action in practical, concrete situations. There they function as an explanation, as a justification, and as a guideline for future action.[29]

Stories do not say so much about objective reality or events, but about meaning and experience. A story is interesting because it says something about the storyteller. Stories can help reveal the norms and values that this person has. When we want to study the ideals of an organisation, storytelling is a good method to make ideals explicit that usually remain implicit in the practice. Stories can show us that they play a role in daily functioning. Ideals can be seen as those goals an organisation or a person regards as worthwhile achieving, such as the ideal of the *Rechtsstaat*. Also, stories can show us how different values, or how values and rules, can be intrinsically conflicting.[30] The ideal situation can function as a critical counterpoint in these cases.[31] Stories often deal with events that show us how ideals and reality can conflict, or how the storyteller can be in conflict with the rest of the world.[32]

---

[26] H. Wagenaar, 'Beleid als fictie: Over de rol van verhalen in de bestuurlijke praktijk', *Beleid & Maatschappij* 1 (1997), 6-20, p. 3.

[27] The word 'practice' was introduced into recent debate by MacIntyre. For an elaborate description of the various ways it is used, see B.Z. Tamanaha, *Realistic Socio-Legal Theory, Pragmatism and a Social Theory of Law*, Oxford, Clarendon Press, 1997, pp. 168-172. I use it here in the way Wagenaar does. He says that a practice is concrete, situated in an institutional setting, intrinsically conflicting, action oriented, and morally loaded.

[28] C. Kohler Riessman, *Narrative Analysis*, Newbury Park, Cal., Sage Publications, 1993, p. 5.

[29] Wagenaar, 'Beleid als fictie', p. 12.

[30] *Ibid.*, p. 10.

[31] In this case, the 'ideal situation' is a situation where the organisation has *Rechtsstaatlichkeit* as a virtue. This ideal situation functions as a kind of *ideal type*, as it was developed by Weber. This means that we can describe a phenomenon in abstracto by certain features and see to what extent a concrete example of this phenomenon meets the description.

[32] Kohler Riessman, *Narrative Analysis*, p. 5.

## 3.3 How to Analyse a Story

There are different ways in which to use stories and to analyse them. Here I will confine myself to a brief description of how I analyse the content of a story. The first way to grasp how people actually tell stories and how they insert their own views of reality into a story is *backward mapping*. By starting at the end, the orientation to the situation and the characters will give a completely different view of a story. Reading from end to beginning, all sorts of useless details and descriptions of characters have to lead to a certain conclusion. This is because the storyteller has a stake in his own version of reality; in order to justify his own behaviour and the fact that he wants to tell you the story at all.[33] One could say that backward mapping reveals the ideal in a strong manner: it forces itself upon you. A second way to show that a storyteller gives you his version of a story, which is not necessarily the only one, is *alternative reading*.[34] A storyteller wants to take you with him in his convictions, experiences, his sympathies, and so on, by presenting events and characters in a certain way. He wants to make you think that the conclusion, the way the story ends, is inevitable and right.

# 4. Ideals in Action

## 4.1 Background of the Story

In this section, I will give an example of a story told to me during an interview. The story is illustrative in many ways, not only because it shows how a conflict of values occurs in practice, but also because it represents many other aspects regarding my research. It tells us something about ideals in reality, about the public-private dichotomy, about the value of pluralism versus the value of the *Rechtsstaat*, about the question whether a private housing foundation is part of the private domain or not, about power and responsibility, and so on. Before telling the story I will briefly introduce the backgrounds of the organisation and the storyteller.

The story takes place in the WSE, a private social housing foundation in E., a middle-sized town. In every Dutch town and city, there are some such foundations, and they usually have a long history. Since the 1980s, the subsidies have stopped and the housing foundations had to become financially independent. They can be financially independent by developing commercial activities, such as selling houses. On the other

---

[33] *Ibid.*, p. 20. She calls these justifying clauses 'the soul of the narrative'.

[34] Wagenaar, 'Beleid als fictie', p. 16.

hand, they are legally still obliged to house 'those who are not able to find housing on the free market'.[35]

The foundation concerned is a large one. It is, like most of them, very modern. The allocation of houses (for which in this town the local government issued rules) is completely computerised. This means that the influence of the employees on allocation is minimised. Here, the chance of arbitrariness is very small. However, there are other tasks that are still 'risky', because the influence of the employees is big. One of these tasks is assigning so-called *priority*. This means that the client gets preferential treatment for social (divorce, etc.), financial, or medical reasons. Though there are rules, of course, and though an independent committee takes the final decision, the employees make a first selection. They do this by 'calculating' the chance that the client will eventually be assigned this priority. The employee concerned said during the interview that she regards 'compassion' both as her own ideal in work and as the most important value of the organisation. Her colleagues also value this highly, so it can be regarded as part of the organisational culture. For the employee, it means she has to empathise with the clients' situation and, if necessary, to put the rules aside to help them.

## 4.2  The Decent Vagabond

This man, who worked in E., came to the office. He had been divorced six months and since then he had stayed in someone else's house. At some point, this other person had said: 'You will have to leave my house within two months, otherwise I'll kick you out.' Then the man tried to get other accommodation; I believe it was a shed or an attic room in a farmer's house somewhere. When he wanted to move in, the farmer told him: 'I'm sorry, but I've changed my mind about the whole thing', and then the man literally was on the street. He would sleep on a bench in the local park, and every time I saw him he looked worse and worse. Officially, he could not get priority because he was not registered as a resident of E. However, he could get a house, because he works in this town. At that time I was working on several furnished apartments with his employer. So I called the employer and asked whether this man couldn't get one of those apartments. After all, the man was his employee. But the employer said he had other plans with the apartments. Of course, I was a bit angry and wanted to give up but then – here I am with my compassion again – of course I'm not sensitive to everything people tell me. But I think it is unacceptable that someone who has a regular income in 1999 should live in the street. Of course you can say: 'Why don't you go to the Salvation Army', or something, but I don't think that is appropriate in a case like this. Then I talked to my colleagues about

---

[35]  This is a rough translation of an Article of the Dutch Housing Act.

this case and asked them: 'Isn't there something we can do for this poor man?' Then we looked again and we found a house that was right for him. It didn't look all that smart, so we had to repair some things. You can't believe how happy the man was. Well, of course you can say: rules are rules are rules, but if someone has to sleep in the street without the possibility of having a shower or changing his clothes... I think this was the right decision.

The argument that a person should not sleep in the street can be regarded as an appeal to human dignity, a motive directly related to the *Rechtsstaat*. The storyteller makes this appeal in a particularistic way: in her opinion someone with a 'regular income', someone she can identify with and whom she regards as a decent person, should not live in the street these days. This is her motive for action. We should note here that she goes much further in her efforts to help the man than normally is to be expected. After all, if she were to help everyone who appeals to her in this way, she would not be able to help many clients because it would take too much time.[36] Besides, the man did not live in E. and had, according to the rules, no right to preferential treatment.

### Backward mapping

The end of the story is that, thanks to the special efforts of the employee, the man gets a house. Not only the fact that he gets a house needs to be justified, but also the special efforts. The first is done by making clear it is not the man's 'own fault' that he lives in the street: he is the victim of a chain of unhappy events. He has a job, an average income, and does not belong to the category of people that should live in the street or should go the Salvation Army. In this case, humanity is a higher good than legal rules. This is the ideal that guides the employee's action.

### Alternative reading

We may retell the story in the following way: There was a man who worked in E. He had been divorced and was obviously stupid enough not to make the right arrangements before leaving his wife. First, the friend he stayed with got tired of him, and then the farmer he was going to rent a room from clearly changed his mind about the whole thing. The result of all this was that he had no accommodation. As the weeks passed, he looked dirtier and dirtier. Officially, he had no right to get priority status. Then I thought to myself: Yeah, of course, you have to be

---

[36] This is called the street-level dilemma. See M. Lipsky, *Street-Level Bureaucracy: Dilemmas of the Individual in Public Service*, New York, Russell Sage Foundation, 1980, p. 99.

human in this business, but I'm not sensitive to everything people tell me. If you have a regular income in 1999, it must be your own fault if you live in the street. And, of course, the Salvation Army is not willing to help him because they are there to help genuinely poor people. Well, I'm not going to do anything extra for this guy and I'm certainly not going to break the rules. He will have to wait his turn like everyone else. After all, he has no right to priority status. And why should someone with a regular income have more rights than someone who has no income? Well, of course you may say that compassion should go before anything else but if you sleep in the street because of your own negligence, then I think it's okay to simply apply the rules.

## 4.3  Conclusions on the WSE

The story told above can be said to reflect the organisational culture and the attitudes of the employees quite well.[37] What I have learned from the interviews is that there is a risk of what I call particularism. By this I mean that the employee's own opinion of people, what they do, and how they live their lives, plays a role in decisions where there is discretion, like the decision to grant someone priority status. More concretely: people who are polite, who are sympathetic, and easy to empathise with seem to have a greater chance of getting what they are entitled to, or even to what they are not entitled to, than people who are not. If it is in any way 'your own fault' to be in a difficult situation, the employees are less willing to help you out. People who are different, for instance from other cultures or from other social backgrounds, are not always understood as easily as 'own' people. There also seems to be a rule that you 'have to do your best' to get a house before asking for priority. All these informal norms are not laid down in the official rules, and can largely be regarded as being opposed to these rules. There seems to be a guiding value behind these informal rules that is in accordance with the norms and values in society at large.[38]

Generally, we can say that the legal, bureaucratic rules that apply to the WSE are followed, partly because of the computer system[39] and partly because of the fact that generally the rationale behind these rules (a fair distribution of houses) is well understood. The following of rules, one major aspect of the *Rechtsstaat*, is met here, and so is respon-

---

[37]  Of course, this short story is merely one example of this organisational culture but it is consistent with my other findings of the interviews. In my doctoral thesis, I will give a detailed description and analysis of these interviews.

[38]  Lipsky, *Street-Level Bureaucracy*, p. 109.

[39]  This system applies the official, external rules.

siveness. The story shows that the WSE is responsive, but in a limited way. The limitation originates from the fact that it is particularistic responsiveness. This is due to the private, and even semi-commercial identity of the organisation that makes the employees think it is justified to distinguish between people, though according to the *Rechtsstaat* idea people should be treated equally.

## 5. General Conclusions on the Ideal of the *Rechtsstaat*

### 5.1 Generalising the Empirical Material

*Rechtsstaatlichkeit* can be seen as an ideal for organisations. This means that it is not, or not only important what external, legal rules apply to the organisation, but that it is the internalised norm that really matters. This internalised norm is based on the main thought behind the *Rechtsstaat* which is that the arbitrary use of power as regards the organisation's clients is not right. Instead, the organisation should develop a sense of responsibility. In sociological terms, we can say that the organisation should have a responsible institutional setting. This means it must have a *rechtsstaatliche* organisational culture and that the employees should have a responsible attitude. In my research on the WSE, I found a certain internal morality that to some extent agrees with that of the *Rechtsstaat*. Customer-friendliness is one of the key words it uses to emphasise that the client is highly valued. The employees are generally responsible people, motivated to do their job as well as they can. They have a sense of justice, which makes them make the right decisions in most of the cases. In hard cases, particularism plays an important role. I believe that in this respect the WSE is not much different from other private housing foundations or from public administration bodies.

Thus, a more or less *rechtsstaatliche* institutional setting may be found in private organisations.[40] This may be called remarkable, regarding the fact that, traditionally, the *Rechtsstaat* only applies to public organisations. Many things may be deduced from this statement. For instance, understanding that the conditions under which an organisational culture will be more or less *rechtsstaatlich*, may shed light on the issue whether the privatisation of public tasks is wise. If we privatise, we abolish the other (legal) safeguard of the *Rechtsstaat*, the control by constitutional and administrative positive law. We could say that even though this setting may exist, it would not be wise to privatise all sorts of public tasks because, legally speaking, they do not have to act accord-

---

[40]  A similar conclusion was drawn by Philip Selznick in his empirical work.

ing to the rules of the *Rechtsstaat*, such as the Constitution and administrative law.

Another conclusion may be that legal scholars, legislators, and policy-makers should not only look to positive law for understanding how certain organisations function, but should also take the sociological aspects into account. One step further, we may say that maybe the organisational culture and the attitude of its employees are of greater importance if we want their clients to get what they are entitled to than when the formal rules are applied to them, and that, therefore, a private organisation may sometimes be even more *rechtsstaatlich* than a public one. These conclusions are spectacular, but still quite speculative as well. What I would like to focus on here is an often-underestimated connection between law, ethics, and social science.

## 5.2 The Motivational Aspect of the Rechtsstaat

As mentioned above, all employees interviewed emphasised their own motivation. This was the contacts with the clients, the variety of people, and the willingness to help people. This motivation does not automatically lead to the 'right' outcome. My question is: How 'bad' is this? The traditional jurist would answer that it is bad, and that we should make more rules to diminish discretion in order to prevent the arbitrary use of power by employees of administrative organisations. In his frame of thinking he may be right. After all, every 'wrong' outcome violates someone's dignity, something the *Rechtsstaat* wants to prevent.[41] However, instead of only focusing on what goes wrong, we might also look at all the good things that happen in this type of organisations, because we can learn a lot if we want to prevent wrong outcomes. And is the motivation to do the right thing not an important key to that? I believe this motivation shows that there is such a thing as a responsible attitude among street-level employees, something that is not very surprising. The fact that some things go wrong only points out that there may be and should be ways to let this attitude grow. We may wonder whether the traditional legal solution is the only option at hand and whether an opposite solution might bring us closer to the *ideal* of the *Rechtsstaat*.

At the beginning of this chapter, I briefly pointed out that following rules simply because they are rules may lead to legalism. This implies that making more rules may have the effect that the employees will regard the rules only as impeding limitations to their freedom and not as

---

[41] In the case of housing agencies: someone entitled to a house does not get this house, which will largely affect his life and well-being.

good guidelines for action. One reason for this is that they might feel distrusted, which is, of course, not very good for motivation. In order to enhance motivation, making people feel trusted and valued for their skills is a better solution. Making more laws is not the way to do this. What then do we need? There is a great variety of ways to improve organisational culture and attitudes. Some of them are based on ethical works on institutional citizenship, loyalty, whistle-blowing, integrity education, and ethical auditing. Others come from legal writings that base their ideas on sociological insights, and deal with self-regulation and internal democracy, and symbolic legislation. Still others are based on literature about organisations, such as a plea for organisational change and persuasive communication.[42]

## 6. Conclusions

This chapter discussed the question: How do we deal with the power that organisations have over individuals? Starting with the traditional legal way of solving this problem by making legislation, I took a step further by looking at the ethical and sociological issues that underlie this problem. These made me develop my thesis that *Rechtsstaatlichkeit* is an ideal that should exist in every powerful organisation. Also, through empirical research I have shown that something like a responsible institutional setting may exist in the type of organisations I am concerned with here, private social housing foundations. An important feature of this setting may be that street-level bureaucrats have a strong motivation to help people, something that may enhance *rechtsstaatliche* behaviour.

It seems that it is not far from this step to the next step, the insight that motivation is a, so far, underestimated aspect of the *Rechtsstaat*. My idea is that if we really want this important doctrine to progress, we must also think about power and responsibility, about what law is and what it has to do with ethics and sociology. If we really want to limit the arbitrary use of power more and more, arguing for organisational change may be more fruitful than writing about new legislation. Of course, there will always be a discrepancy between ideal and real life. This does not mean that it is not and remains not important to strive for this ideal.

---

[42] In this chapter, I can only prelude on my own suggestions for improvement. Value-driven leadership and openness are the main issues I focus on. C. Raat, 'Macht en rechtsstaat: Verantwoordelijkheid als organisatiedeugd in de praktijk', in R.J.M. Jeurissen and A.W. Musschenga (eds.), *Integriteit in bedrijf, organisatie en openbaar bestuur*, Assen, Van Gorcum, 2002, pp. 100-122, esp. pp. 113-120.

# References

Berlin, I., *Four Essays on Liberty*, Oxford, Oxford University Press, 1969.

Bovens, M.A.P., 'De veelvormigheid van verantwoordelijkheid', in M.A.P. Bovens, C.J.M. Schuyt and W.J. Witteveen (eds.), *Verantwoordelijkheid: Retoriek en realiteit, Verantwoording in publiek recht, politiek en maatschappij*, Zwolle, W.E.J. Tjeenk Willink, 1989, pp. 17-41.

Cotterrell, R., 'The Rule of Law in Transition: Revisiting Franz Neumann's Sociology of Legality', *Social & Legal Studies* 5 (1996) 4, 451-470.

Fuller, L., *The Morality of Law*, rev. ed., New Haven, Conn., Yale University Press, 1969.

Gleitman, H., *Psychology*, New York, W.W. Norton & Company, 1991.

Heffron, F., *Organization Theory and Public Organizations: The Political Connection*, Englewood Cliffs, N.J., [etc.], Prentice Hall, 1989.

Hoffman, W.M., and R.E. Frederick, *Business Ethics: Readings and Cases in Corporate Morality*, New York, McGraw-Hill, 1995.

Kohler Riessman, C., *Narrative Analysis*, Newbury Park, Cal., Sage Publications, 1993.

Lipsky, M., *Street-Level Bureaucracy: Dilemmas of the Individual in Public Service*, New York, Russell Sage Foundation, 1980.

Maynard Moody, S., and M. Musheno, 'Morality over Legality: Invoking Norms from the Front-Lines of Government', paper presented at the annual meeting of the Law and Society Association, Chicago, May 1999.

Nonet, Ph., and Ph. Selznick, *Law and Society in Transition: Toward Responsive Law*, New York, Harper & Row, 1978.

Oosting, M., 'De last van het recht: Recht als opdracht en als obstakel', in J.W.M. Engels *et al.* (eds.), *De rechtsstaat herdacht*, Zwolle, W.E.J. Tjeenk Willink, 1989, pp. 171-183.

Raat, C., 'Macht en rechtsstaat: Verantwoordelijkheid als organisatiedeugd in de praktijk', in R.J.M. Jeurissen and A.W. Musschenga (eds.), *Integriteit in bedrijf, organisatie en openbaar bestuur*, Assen, Van Gorcum, 2002, pp. 100-122.

Selznick, Ph., *Law, Society and Industrial Justice*, New York, Russell Sage Foundation, 1969.

————, *The Moral Commonwealth: Social Theory and the Promise of Community*, Berkeley, Cal., University of California Press, 1992.

Tamanaha, B.Z., *Realistic Socio-Legal Theory: Pragmatism and a Social Theory of Law*, Oxford, Clarendon Press, 1997.

Van der Burg, W., 'The Importance of Ideals', *The Journal of Value Inquiry* 31 (1997), 23-37.

Wagenaar, H., 'Beleid als fictie: Over de rol van verhalen in de bestuurlijke praktijk', *Beleid & Maatschappij* 1 (1997), 6-20.

Webb, Julian, 'Ethics for Lawyers or Ethics for Citizens? New Directions for Legal Education', *Journal of Law and Society* 25 (1998) 1, 134-150.

Witteveen, W.J., 'Retorische constructie', in M.A.P. Bovens, C.J.M. Schuyt and W.J. Witteveen (eds.), *Verantwoordelijkheid: Retoriek en realiteit, Verantwoording in publiek recht, politiek en maatschappij*, Zwolle, W.E.J. Tjeenk Willink, 1989, pp. 81-99.

————, *De geordende wereld van het recht*, Amsterdam, Amsterdam University Press, 1996.

# Realist Idealism and the Rule of Law

## Willem J. WITTEVEEN

> It is the case of trouble which makes, breaks,
> twists, or flatly establishes a rule, an institu-
> tion, an authority. If there be a portion of a so-
> ciety's life in which tensions of the culture
> come to expression... that portion of the life
> will concentrate in the case of trouble or dis-
> turbance. (Llewellyn and Hoebel)

## 1. A Democratic Polity under the Rule of Law

Democratic states are characterized by their commitment to the rule of law. The forms and the content of democratic politics can be highly varied, but the effect of democratic governance must always be that the citizens are governed by a 'rule of measures, not of men', as a famous dictum expresses it. So, a democratic polity, functioning under the rule of law, will allow for effective controls on government power, even when the exercise of this power is mandated by a majority of the voters. Under the rule of law, not only the citizens but also the government is subjected to rules and principles that have been accepted in the polity in conformity with valid rules of constitutional law. The rule of law has two faces: the government is entitled to govern through law, but the citizens are entitled to be ruled by laws that also bind the government itself and to which it, in all its sometimes awesome power, is subjected.

The ideal of a democratic polity under the rule of law is a very de-manding one. Like all ideals, it can never be completely realized and it is doubtful whether there will ever be a fundamental agreement as to what it means for practical issues. Ongoing debate about the meaning of the ideal is a sign of vitality of the democratic polity since, if the word democracy means anything at all, it stands for free and open deliberation about public issues. It is also significant as a measure of the quality of the rule of law actually attained: one of the first things that is imperilled when democracy and the rule of law are in jeopardy, is the freedom of expression. The crucial question is always to what extent actual prac-tices of governance are in conformity with the ideal of the rule of law.

Between practices and ideals there is a tension, sometimes a constructive one, sometimes a deadly one. When practices take institutional form in arrangements of procedures, rules, agencies and officially recognized action possibilities, it is thus necessary to keep in mind the imperfection of the institutionalization in light of the ideal which can now be said to 'underlie' the institution and to be 'embedded' in the practice; metaphorical expressions which capture an important fact: that in actual practice the meaning of the rule of law often recedes into the background, as part of normality, of the current concerns, and that it soon becomes invisible.

The picture sketched here is in many ways too simple. An important complication arises from the nature of the rule of law as an ideal, or rather, as a family of related ideals. People invoking the ideal of the rule of law mean different things. They may focus on legality, on transparency, on accountability, on liberty and human rights, on equality and solidarity, on the separation of powers, on standards of good governance. All of these notions are ideals in themselves, and all of these ideals are in some way interpretations of the rule of law. They are not, however, identical; they are interrelated, though not in a uniform manner. The ideals of the rule of law show at most a family resemblance. As in a human family, the members of the family of rule of law ideals are not always in harmony with each other; there are conflicts and inherent tensions. Radbruch's idea of 'antinomies' within the idea of justice captures a truth about the ideals of the rule of law: they can be in accord, indeed, they presuppose each other; but at the same time they are always in tension.[1] Isaiah Berlin's celebrated idea of 'value pluralism' is still more to the point when it comes to the ideals making up the rule of law: there is no deep underlying harmony and the inherent tensions cannot always be resolved; indeed, in some situations tragic choices between different ideals belonging to the family of rule of law ideals must be made.[2] As a consequence of this state of affairs, practices of governance can and must be compared with a number of, sometimes non-compatible, ideals.

And then it is, historically and comparatively speaking, not true either that at all times and places the ideal of the rule of law was invariant. Under this 'master ideal' we find instead a variety of conceptions, competing to be the best interpretation of the rule of law and, in revolution-

---

[1]  Gustav Radbruch, *Rechtsphilosophie*, Stuttgart, Koehler Verlag, 1973, I.9.

[2]  Isaiah Berlin, 'The Originality of Machiavelli', in Isaiah Berlin, *Against the Current*, London, Hogarth Press, 1980, pp. 25-79. In many other essays, Berlin wrote about this idea of value pluralism, but he derived it from the tradition of Machiavellian realism in politics.

ary times, even fighting each other, sometimes remaining implicit as a stable normative background for a prevalent conception of the rule of law in a given culture and period. The rule of law means different things to people in the United States and in the European Union; and in the latter it even differs between the Netherlands and Belgium, let alone between Italy and Sweden. The differences in meaning still further increase when we leave this 'family' of Western and modern states and consider democracy and the rule of law as ideals in South America, Africa or Asia. Also in the history of different political systems, we find large differences in local understandings of the rule of law.

Regardless of this complexity of the ideal and its manifestations, there are clear cases of states that clearly manage to be democratic polities functioning under the rule of law. The Netherlands is one of these. Constitutional scholars commenting on the state of the *rechtsstaat Nederland* are as a rule critical though constructive. In 1958, with an international debate about Hayek's *The Road to Serfdom* sketching great dangers to liberty ensuing from emerging welfare state arrangements, the leading Dutch commentator, F.R. Böhtlingk, was moderately optimistic about the chances that the welfare state would be compatible with individual freedom. He noted the danger of an overly expanding government policy, that would lead to a bureaucracy threatening individual freedom (and this is, in his interpretation, the essence of the rule of law). Nonetheless, Böhtlingk was confident that this tendency could be counterbalanced by way of better and stricter legislation governing administrative measures and through an expanse of administrative law allowing citizens to seek redress through the courts.[3] The first part of this admonition did not materialize – bureaucracy has in fact increased tremendously and it has not been kept in check by better legislation – but the second part did: it is now possible to go to court in almost all instances in which a citizen has a complaint about governmental actions. Not only in administrative law, as Böhtlingk envisaged, but also in private law and in criminal law, the courts are now much more responsive to the need for protection of the values relating to the rule of law than half a century ago; often courts have developed new standards that make the ideal of the rule of law operative in a more concrete way.[4] The protection of human rights through the courts has expanded so much in the Netherlands that it has transformed the law in all fields relating to

---

[3]  F.R. Böhtlingk, *De rechtsstaat Nederland*, Alphen aan den Rijn, Samsom, 1958.

[4]  It is no exaggeration to say that court cases on the basis of Art. 6 ECHR (about due process values) have transformed criminal and civil procedural law in the Netherlands.

citizens and authorities, especially on the basis of the European Convention on Human Rights.

Modern observers, correcting some of Böhtlingk's predictions, usually come to quite similar conclusions about the prospects for the rule of law in the Netherlands at the beginning of the twenty-first century: they see new challenges (such as the emergence of the information society and globalization) and sometimes perceive these as threatening developments, but they are on the whole confident that the rule of law can and will adapt to changing circumstances; there are no arguments suggesting we should give up on the master ideal altogether.[5]

If, as we have said, the crucial problem relating to the ideal of a democratic polity under the rule of law is the divergence (or the degree of conformity) between the ideal and actual practices, this problem is compounded by the dynamics of the ideal itself. It is not a static given of a culture but a normative complex adapting to changing circumstances. The relationship between ideal and practice is confounded by the changes that occur both at the practical and the normative level of the equation. There is thus no conceptual clarity about the meaning of the rule of law, not even among constitutional law scholars who are supposed to be the guardians of the temple. How to deal with this inevitable predicament? It is very tempting to take a legalistic way out: converting the fluidity and openness of the ideal into a set of rules and doctrines that are precise and uniformly applicable. Courts and legislatures, having to settle conflicts involving different conceptions of the rule of law, are attracted to this way of managing uncertainty. It is my contention that this conversion method is bound to fail to convince the spokespersons of new conceptions of the rule of law that do not yet find expression in the rules and doctrines that are prevalent at the time. Also, the conversion of ideals into doctrines and rules prematurely ossifies the rule of law into an authority argument, while what is needed is a reflective understanding of the dynamics of changing interpretations of the master ideal itself. The conversion method is also unable to throw much light on problems in the relationship between the ideal and the practices and institutional arrangements supposed to be its concrete manifestation; the latter are legitimized by fiat. For a better response to these problems, awareness is needed of the interpretive predicament of the members of the democratic polity aspiring, in some way, to live under the rule of law. I will argue that for this both idealism and realism are needed, fostering an attitude that can be termed *realist idealism*.

---

[5]  This discussion is summarized in M.A.P. Bovens, *De digitale rechtsstaat*, Alphen aan den Rijn, Samsom, 1999.

In elaborating on this idea, I take my lead from Wibren van der Burg's argument for realist idealism in ethical and political controversies. Van der Burg argues that idealism is a dynamic force orienting our practices on a never fully attainable level of aspiration. This idealist orientation enables us to be critical of existing arrangements and practices. In order to prevent idealism from becoming a perfectionist or utopian ideology, however, it must be kept in check by realism. Van der Burg expects this realism to be a reminder of the precariousness of our achievements and wants it to foster non-ideological thinking and normative pluralism. He recognizes inherent tensions in the combination of idealism and realism, but argues that these can be productive. 'Realist idealism requires an attitude in which someone is fully idealist and fully realist, shifting again and again between both perspectives. In a dialectical process, both perspectives will correct each other, criticize each other, but they can never completely coincide. Only by keeping the tension present is mutual correction and inspiration possible.'[6]

As my own contribution to the idea of realist idealism, I will probe two intellectual traditions: political realism – which more or less started with Machiavelli but itself builds on the rhetorical tradition of Aristotle and Cicero – and American legal realism (Llewellyn). Interestingly, some of the best work done in these traditions has recognized idealist motivations and allows insights into the interactions between realism and idealism. But first I will discuss a 'case of trouble', in which the conversion method shows its inherent limitations.

## 2. *Pikmeer*: A 'Case of Trouble'

As an example of the conversion method in action, I will discuss the way the Supreme Court of the Netherlands handled a new problem relating to the rule of law in the *Pikmeer* case of 1996. The fundamental issue is this: Are municipal governments bound by criminal law? In the light of the master ideal of the rule of law, this does not seem an impossibly hard question to answer: if municipal governments are free to disobey criminal law as enacted in formal statutes by the highest legislative authority (consisting of Parliament and the Cabinet), how can we still hold that the rule of law means that government is always bound by the law? Is it conceivable that a municipal authority, which is bound to follow the rules of private law and of administrative law, is above the dictates of criminal law? It sounds like a rhetorical question. Yet, the surprising answer of the Supreme Court is that municipal authorities are

---

[6] Wibren van der Burg, *De verbeelding aan het werk*, Kampen, Agora, 2001, p. 161 (my translation).

indeed sometimes (not in the case of crimes of office, such as bribery or corruption) free to disobey the law. Of course, this judgment in cassation is confined to the facts of the case, which are as follows.[7] The municipal authority of Boarnsterhim in the Province of Friesland allowed the 'Grontmij' company to dump a large amount of polluted materials in lake 'Pikmeer'. The permission to do so is given by the civil servant in charge of building permits and the environment; the municipal authority acts through him. The permission is, however, contrary to penal environmental rules declared by the national authorities. The legal issue is whether it is possible to bring a criminal prosecution against both the municipal authority and the civil servant who supervised the illegal activities.

The Supreme Court denies both claims. Under the Dutch Constitution, municipal authorities have the legal status of 'public bodies'. The Supreme Court has developed a doctrine about their immunity, stating that these public bodies are exempt from judicial scrutiny when they act within their administrative competence. It is a fact that the municipal authority was acting within its administrative competence when it granted the permission for dumping materials in the Pikmeer (albeit that it used this competence contrary to criminal law). The civil servant who gave the permission – and so can be said to have supervised an illegal activity – cannot be prosecuted either because his legal position is intimately bound up with that of the municipality.

The Supreme Court does not refer explicitly to the line of previous decisions in this area. These previous cases do not involve violations of the criminal law, however. The Supreme Court does not give arguments sustaining its judgment either; its reasoning has to be inferred from the conclusion of the Advocate General and from comments by legal scholars. In a civil law system following to a large extent the French model, this is not an unusual state of affairs, but it has to be noted that there are many cases in different fields of law in which the Supreme Court has been willing to provide more extended arguments supporting its decisions, especially when a new development is announced. Reviewing these additional materials, the reasoning of the Supreme Court can be reconstructed up to a point. As in the previous cases, the Supreme Court relies on the separation of powers doctrine, stating that all acts that are within the competence of the administration cannot be reviewed by the courts as criminal acts. Under the separation of powers, it is proper for judges to regard the actions of government authorities as manifestations of a wish to serve the general interest. The decision to provide permis-

---

[7] Hoge Raad (Strafkamer), 23 April 1996, no. 102100E, DD 96.279, annotated by 't Hart.

sion to pollute may then hypothetically be motivated by the general interest (as is the decision to enact environmental prohibitions of water pollution); it may also be counter to the general interest, but this falls outside the scope of what judges can legitimately decide upon. The absence of judicial control is compensated for, however, by the presence of a political control mechanism. This is the political control by democratically legitimate bodies to which the municipal authorities are accountable. The municipal council, elected by the voters, is able to take corrective measures when civil servants or the municipal authority itself acts contrary to criminal law, for instance by dismissing from office the mayor or the alderman who is responsible for the action of the civil servant. Sometimes national authorities, such as the Ministry of the Interior and Kingdom Relations or the Ministry of Housing, Spatial Planning and the Environment, can bring some political influence to bear on decisions by municipal authorities, providing a kind of check. Another argument that is mentioned is that, as an interpretation of the separation of powers, the government as a whole must be conceived as indivisible. National and municipal authorities are parts of a larger whole (the organic theory of the state). The public prosecutor is also a part of this larger whole of the government as such. When he prosecutes the government, the government is prosecuting itself and the fines it imposes in punishment will have to be provided from public funds; there is thus no point in this kind of prosecution.

All in all, the Supreme Court has created a doctrine which looks very much like a local and limited variant of the political question doctrine.[8] When the democratic process can in theory check authorities and their representatives who act contrary to criminal law, it is a political matter which a court of law is not to pronounce upon.

## 3. The Story Line of the Conversion Method

We can summarize the conversion method the Supreme Court used in the *Pikmeer* case in narratological terms as the telling of a 'doctrinal story'.[9] The reconstructed argument projects a kind of scenario that the actors in the theatre of politics are supposed to enact in their processes of democratic governance. This scenario combines the notion of the

---

[8] Justice Brennan in Baker v. Carr, 369 US 186, 1962. See also Edward McWhinney, *Supreme Courts and Judicial Lawmaking*, Dordrecht, Martinus Nijhoff, 1986, and T. Koopmans, *Vergelijkend publiekrecht*, 2nd ed., Deventer, Kluwer, 1986, pp. 51-56.

[9] Willem J. Witteveen, 'Doctrinal Stories', *International Journal for the Semiotics of Law* VI (1993) 17, 179-202.

separation of powers with a conception of democratic politics that is exclusively representational in character. What the Court in effect says to its audience is this: the approved way of governance draws a sharp distinction between the roles of public bodies charged with tasks of governance (such as the municipal authorities) and the democratic assemblies of representatives to which they are accountable and it draws another sharp distinction between these bodies and the courts; the only role for citizens in this process of governance is as voters setting the machinery of representation in motion. What the authorities do in furthering the general interest is beyond the competence of courts and citizens alike; the determination of public policy falls to the representatives and to office-holders together. The role of the civil servant is that of an instrument of the public body, no more and no less, which excludes personal responsibility or culpability when the civil servant is playing his legitimate part (in the eyes of his superiors).

This compact doctrinal story fails to convince as an interpretation of the ideals of the rule of law on three counts, which will be considered separately even though they are interrelated. The conversion method fails as constitutional rhetoric, as constructive interpretation and as guidance for democratic governance.

## 3.1 Failing as Constitutional Rhetoric

As we have seen, in the *Pikmeer* case the conversion method produced a very concisely motivated judicial decision in which a question about the meaning of an ideal or a set of ideals (the rule of law) was reduced to an authoritative assertion of a constitutional doctrine. Interestingly, this strategy failed to work as constitutional rhetoric. The reactions in the media immediately were negative. While the municipal authorities of Boarnsterhim and the anonymous civil servant remained silent, academic lawyers wrote articles for newspapers and environmental organizations expressed their disappointment in public declarations. While the latter deplored the decision because it meant that all municipal authorities would now be free to disregard environmental protection law when they saw fit to do so as part of their official duties, the academic lawyers concentrated on the doctrinal story that was at the basis of the judicial decision. They argued that it is morally unacceptable that the government cannot be convicted for committing certain criminal acts for which citizens and companies are prosecuted and convicted; this is a form of unreasonableness that offends the equality principle. There were also arguments to the effect that every person in every office of the government should in some way be accountable for breaking the law, because these persons in their official capacities (also as civil servants) use their power to affect the interests of the citizens, of the community and of the environment and that all these acts of power must be publicly accounted for; this is an argument for transparency and for public responsibility. In this additional perspective, accountability should not only be located in the forums of representative democracy, such as the municipal council, but it should be extended to the courts, especially when the representative public bodies do not act effectively in checking digressions. (As a matter of fact, the record shows that only very rarely have municipal councils sanctioned their own officials upon disobeying national environmental rules; they tend to prefer considerations of economic interest and tend to protect 'their own people'.)[10]

Soon a parliamentary debate was held. In Parliament, two government parties (the social-democrats and the liberals) took up the arguments of the critics and concluded that in the light of the undesirable effects of the Supreme Court's decision, the legislation concerning public bodies would have to be changed to end the criminal immunity of municipal authorities and civil servants. The then Minister of Justice, Winnie Sorgdrager, did not agree. She stressed the remaining possibilities, viz. to prosecute whenever municipal authorities or their civil servants act beyond their administrative competences; but this rejoinder did not convince the critics who wanted to put an end to the 'unequal treatment' of government agencies and officials compared with citizens and companies. Sorgdrager emphasized her allegiance to the ideal of the rule of law, which also in her view requires that government is under the law, not above it, and then she referred the matter to her department for further investigation, promising to present a new initiative in the matter.[11]

While this debate started to get momentum, the Supreme Court itself seems to have realized that it had failed to convince a wider audience of the correctness of its doctrine. The official secretary of the Supreme Court, Van Nispen tot Sevenaer, wrote an article for *NRC Handelsblad*, in which the decision of the Court in *Pikmeer* was explained and defended as merely the logical consequence of a line of established precedents, all offering the government immunity against criminal charges. This was a remarkable move, since usually the Supreme Court does not react to criticism and does not take part in the debate even in the academic legal journals; an article by its official secretary is the closest one can get to an official interpretive pronouncement on a case. This inter-

---

[10] See, e.g., the articles by Richard van Elst in *NRC Handelsblad* of 10 September 1996 and by Peter Rehwinkel and Willy Swildens in *NRC Handelsblad* of 28 September 1996.

[11] *NRC Handelsblad*, 19 February 1997.

vention did not have the effect of ending the debate; it merely exacerbated it.[12]

## 3.2 Failing as Constructive Interpretation

The conversion method also failed as an act of constructive interpretation of the ideal of the rule of law. An interpretation of the ideal of the rule of law can be called constructive when it does not pretend to be based on a tradition of interpretations alone but also purports to extend the tradition into the future by constructing a new doctrine from the materials available; the impetus for doing this is an actual problem in the practices that orient themselves to the ideal.[13] For evidence hereof, we have to leave the public debate in the media aside, and focus on comments by two distinguished jurists on the case.

In the conclusion of Advocate General Van Dorst we find an indication of the interpretation of the ideal of the rule of law that the Supreme Court is turning into a doctrine. It is the ideal of the separation of powers. Van Dorst notes that in previous cases the Supreme Court has oriented its decision to a passage in the legislative texts concerning Article 51 of the Dutch Penal Code, where the government literally states that 'civil servants who supervise illegal activities have the same immunity as public bodies acting in their official capacity'.[14] Van Dorst regards this passage as the basis for acceptance by the Supreme Court of the separation of powers and remarks that also in the *Pikmeer* case this line of reasoning is presupposed.

In his annotation concerning the *Pikmeer* case, 't Hart on this point takes issue with Van Dorst. In the first place, 't Hart argues that it depends on the interpretation of the separation of powers what consequences follow for the immunity of the state or of governmental bodies. There is a plausible interpretation of the separation of powers to the effect that all three powers – the executive power no less than the others – must be subjected to the laws, so that when the rules the legislature has made are breached by the executive, it is the task of the judicial power to ensure compliance with the laws by the executive. In other words, interpreting the separation of powers as a version of the political question doctrine, as the Supreme Court has done, is but one option. It has to be defended against other plausible interpretations and the Supreme Court fails to do this. In the second place, 't Hart attacks the idea

---

[12]  *NRC Handelsblad* of 29 August 1996.

[13]  Willem Witteveen, *De geordende wereld van het recht*, Amsterdam, Amsterdam University Press, 2001, pp. 123 ff.

[14]  My translation.

that the separation of powers is the only ideal that matters in interpreting the rule of law. Referring to the academic debate in the Netherlands since 1970, when Koopmans published his seminal study of the changing role of the legislature,[15] 't Hart notes that there is a virtual consensus that the ideal of the rule of law – when it comes to shaping the relations between the three powers of the trias politica – requires not only a separation but also a balance of powers. The notion of 'checks and balances', developed in the American tradition of the trias politica but going back to Montesquieu, is an attractive interpretation of the ideal. It can even be put into the form of an alternative doctrinal story, projecting a different scenario for the interactions between the three powers.[16] For immunity from criminal charges there is clearly no place in an interpretation of the ideal in terms of the balance of powers. In conclusion of these two arguments by 't Hart, it can be said that the Supreme Court has prematurely ossified the ideal of the rule of law where it pertains to the trias politica by converting it into a doctrine. This doctrine is based only on an authority claim (that is, the authority of the Court itself), and it overlooks the possibility of competing plausible interpretations of the ideal, out of which a better candidate could have been selected providing a different and socially more acceptable version of the rule of law.

't Hart notes that the reasoning of the Supreme Court and of Van Dorst conceives of the state as an organic whole. He rejects this line of thinking as well. Here 't Hart uses a realist argument, pointing out that in practice the state or the government does not appear as a 'monolith', does not act as a unified personality, but is instead a 'diversity of functions and offices of which the actions and the interests are rarely in harmony with each other'.[17] When we shift away from the view of the state as an organic whole and towards a more diversified notion of offices and agencies performing their functions in different ways and reflecting opposed interests (such as economic versus environmental interests), the logic forbidding prosecution because of its financial circularity, also disappears. The point is not so much that the state will have to pay a penalty to itself, but that one branch of government is shamed in public and thereby provided with an incentive to function better when it has to pay a preferably symbolic amount of money to another government agency representing in this instance the general interest. It is not the money that matters but the check on misused

---

[15]  T. Koopmans, 'De rol van de wetgever', in *Honderd jaar rechtsleven*, Zwolle, W.E.J. Tjeenk Willink, 1970, pp. 221-235.

[16]  W.J. Witteveen, *Evenwicht van machten*, Zwolle, W.E.J. Tjeenk Willink, 1991.

[17]  See n. 7 (my translation).

power. As before, the doctrinal story of the Supreme Courts fails to convince as a constructive interpretation.

### 3.3 Failing as Guidance to Democratic Governance

Converting ideals into doctrines is thus not without risks. By avoiding the issue of how the ideal must be interpreted in such a way as to be practically useful in new circumstances that raise the old questions, the whole point of constructive interpretation of shared political and legal ideals is lost from view. No wonder such an approach, manifesting itself in a rhetoric of authoritative proclamation rather than in a more hermeneutic vein, is not very persuasive to a larger audience wanting to know just why government bodies and their employees should be above the law. But there is a related failure of the conversion method. It does not provide guidance for making the problems of democratic governance more manageable. Just what are these problems? Interestingly, neither the Supreme Court nor the Advocate General mentions them but they are present in the considerations of commentator 't Hart. Of course, they are more frequently mentioned in the public and parliamentarian debates about the issue.

The *Pikmeer* case should in the first place provide guidance for the problem of municipal evasion of national (and, increasingly, European) environmental regulations. The events in Boarnsterhim are not an isolated case. In many municipalities environmental rules are disobeyed in order to attract economically interesting projects that are considered to be good for the municipal economy. They are also broken out of a wish to proceed more quickly and efficiently with building operations. It is sometimes felt that neighbouring municipalities would have a competitive advantage if the rules are being followed too strictly. A relaxed attitude towards these rules has the advantage of being better able to compete with more legalistic neighbours. The whole culture of municipal governance has changed considerably in the last decades. Municipal governance used to be more rule oriented than it is today. Rules are now often seen as an obstacle rather than as a necessity. There is massive acceptance of rule evasions by citizens and companies when there are socially useful reasons for doing so. Out of this tolerant attitude, the uniquely Dutch concept of *gedoogbeleid* developed, which can be translated with difficulty only: the official recognition of the non-enforcement of certain rules and regulations. *Gedoogbeleid* first developed in the areas of soft drugs and... environmental regulations. Many municipalities view these environmental protection rules as rigid demands coming from The Hague or Brussels; they do not constitute pressing concerns for the local citizens and the civil society one caters for.

Seen from the national and the European levels of government, the situation is not so positive. The environmental norms are intended to increase safety and prevent health risks, and they are to contribute to long-term goals concerning environmental quality. They are definitely not intended to be applied selectively. That is why, at the behest of national authorities, the public prosecutors wanted to act against municipalities that break the law in this field; many other cases were kept on file while the Supreme Court considered *Pikmeer*. As a result of the 'negative' outcome for the national policy, these cases had to be abandoned.

But the *Pikmeer* case is expressly not limited to environmental law. The Supreme Court presents a doctrine that is as general as it can be, covering all instances in which a public body acts on the basis of an administrative task. The problems of democratic governance the rule of law must deal with are similarly not confined to environmental problems.

Here, some additional developments come into view. As a result of changing management philosophies, many executive agencies have been placed at a greater distance from representative councils; strengthening their expertise and giving them more independence is hoped to make them more client oriented. The question then is how to guarantee that these agencies that are no longer under strict scrutiny by democratic bodies can still be brought under the rule of law. It is a development that points towards more extensive judicial control rather than less. A second development, which only just started at the time of the *Pikmeer* case, concerns an increase in negotiated decision-making. This is a form of public administration 'in which the decision-making process, as far as the preparation, approval, and execution of policy is concerned, is dependent on the result of deliberation and negotiation... between public authorities (or their staff) and private organisations or groups of people'.[18] Especially in the field of environmental policy and in land use planning, administration increasingly consists in more consultation and negotiation between government agencies and other interested parties (such as firms) rather than in one-sided determinations of policy. As Verschuuren and De Waard remark in a study of this phenomenon, this new development, which promotes the ideal of consensus in democracy,

---

[18] André Hoekema, quoted in Jonathan Verschuuren and Boudewijn de Waard, 'Introduction', in Boudewijn de Waard (ed.), *Negotiated Decision-Making*, Den Haag, Boom Juridische Uitgevers, 2000, pp. 1-9, at p. 1.

raises serious questions about its compatibility with traditional notions of legality, democracy, the protection of weak or excluded interests, transparency, participation and judicial protection.[19] All of these notions are part of the family of ideals of the rule of law. Both the distancing of agencies from representative bodies and the distancing of representative bodies from negotiated decision-making pose challenges to the rule of law ideals. Practices of governance are seen to emerge that are thought to be desirable but cannot easily be brought under the old constitutional doctrines. The doctrine of the *Pikmeer* case does not address these challenges as it does not respond to changing realities in environmental regulation or in regulation generally. Of course, one court case could never address such a vast range of constitutional issues concerning the continuing practicality of the ideals of the rule of law. In a line of cases much more could be done, especially when a reflective attitude is taken towards the problems of governance. But it is not even evident that the Supreme Court is at all aware of the problem. Perhaps this is also a consequence of its conversion of the separation of powers from an open-ended ideal into a closed doctrine; this doctrine, after all, shifts the responsibility for the well-functioning of the democratic system as a whole to the legislature.

## 4. Towards an Attitude of Realist Idealism

How to avoid these pitfalls? The conversion method in the case of the rule of law has not been a great success when it comes to persuasiveness, constructive potential and normative guidance. An alternative method can be envisaged, however: judges do not engage in an exercise in authoritative promulgation of doctrines, but would take a leading role in developing a reflective discourse about the rule of law conceived as an open-ended complex of ideals. This would require recognising of the rule of law not as a constitutional doctrine in itself, but as a master ideal capable of generating many doctrinal interpretations. It would also mean rejecting a perfectionist attitude towards the ideal: it can be sought, but never fully attained; it can be realized only up to a certain point, but there is always the risk of regression; it may legitimately mean different things to different interpreters. Above all, this reflective discourse concerning the rule of law must be open to sharp empirical analyses of changing social circumstances and of the rise of new challenges that offer both new possibilities for extension of the ideal and threats to its manifestations now taken for granted. Clearly, such a reflective discourse concerning the rule of law in a democratic society is itself an

---

[19] Verschuuren and De Waard, 'Introduction', pp. 5-6.

important achievement that already would be a sign of the vitality of the system. This is why it should never be the task of just one institution. The meaning of the rule of law should be debated in Parliament, in governmental agencies and in the courts; it should be the subject of media attention and of academic debates; and it should be contemplated by ordinary citizens as they find the power of the government affecting their lives.

There is a common element to this undertaking that ideally connects all participants in the dialogue about the changing meaning of the rule of law. Idealist and realist considerations must be joined in the effort to achieve constructive interpretations of the ideals of the rule of law. In the *Pikmeer* case, we see that throughout the discourse generated by the controversy, realist and idealist considerations indeed come forward, but that they are not integrated into sustained arguments. To achieve this desirable effect, an attitude of realist idealism (or idealist realism) is needed. In this attitude different strands of reasoning come together. How this could be done in the *Pikmeer* case will be shown below, taking idealism and realism in turn as starting points for the argument.

## 4.1 Idealism Meets Realism

What happens when the rule of law is seen as a complex of ideals? A standpoint is taken from which it is justified to aim high, to really project a morality of aspiration[20] in which a very high degree of conformity to the rule of law is imagined. 'A rule of measures, not of men.' This high standard is then used as a standard for existing practices and from this confrontation a more realist consideration is born: the understanding that the perfection of the ideal can only imperfectly be attained.

In the *Pikmeer* case, we have discerned two interpretations of ideals belonging to the complex of the rule of law which can be taken in this idealist sense and then lead to sobering, realist reflections. The interpretation of the trias politica most relevant to the problem of municipal authorities that disobey national laws, is the ideal of the balance of powers. It can indeed be taken to a high level of aspiration, demanding a perfect balance (and what is more perfect than balance?) between all state bodies performing the functions of legislating, governing and judging. Power must limit power, ambition must be made to counteract ambition; out of the frictions between powerful agents, a measure of freedom for the citizens will result. But this idealist formula is clearly open to a more realist understanding. It demands a realistic assessment

---

[20] Lon L. Fuller, *The Morality of Law*, rev. ed., New Haven, Yale University Press, 1969, ch. 1.

of the actual power relationships in democratic politics and when important changes occur in these power relationships – sometimes introducing new powerful actors, sometimes making traditional authorities obsolete – the balance of powers will have to be adjusted accordingly. Also, an ideal that relies on power and ambition cannot be too highly strung, it has to be down to earth.

The other rule of law ideal in the *Pikmeer* case that lends itself to an idealist interpretation is the demand that power must be transparent and must be accounted for. Power implies responsibility, the argument goes, and responsibility extends to all persons and organizations wielding power, especially since acts of power affect interests of the members of the community and of the community as a whole (the 'general interest'). This is a strongly idealist formula since the demand that power be accountable is unrelated to legal recognition of this power; also, acts of power that fall outside the scope of the law are in principle open to inspection and criticism. But also, in this example, the realist urge immediately asserts itself. What can a principle requiring responsibility be without effective institutions in which the principle can be acted upon? And this leads inexorably to the question what attributes institutions must possess in order to perform this function. This question, in its turn, leads to empirical investigations relating to the actual working of democratic institutions and it requires normative attention to the particulars that make institutions into effective ones. Idealism, imagined as pure, soon leads into the reality of practices and institutions in which the ideal can at least to a certain degree be realized.

What this interdependence of idealist and realist motives shows is that there is not a Great Chain of Being in which the master ideal is the highest source from which lower-order ideals, middle-level principles and operational rules can be logically deduced. It also shows that the ideals cannot best be inferred from valid rules and principles. The image is not that of a ladder with its movement upwards and downwards. Rather, idealist considerations meet realist ones halfway; the intelligibility of the one kind of consideration depends on the understanding of the other kind. By exploring ideals, principles, rules, institutions and practices for useful arguments, in the end a vast amount of motives for action become available,[21] out of which new constructions can be made in a tradition that in the process is established as still tenable and valuable. The driving force of the idealist approach to the rule of law is a

---

[21] Kenneth Burke, *A Grammar of Motives*, Berkeley, Cal., University of California Press, (1945) 1969.

sober constructivism. Maybe the metaphor of the rule of law as a house for a democratic polity is an apt one here.[22]

### 4.1.1 The Enduring Problem of Institutionalization

When idealism meets realism, it becomes possible to confront an enduring problem: that of the partial institutionalization of the ideal. Not only can ideals never be fully attained and not only are all institutional arrangements aspiring towards ideals open to criticism, the institutions that are supposed to embody certain ideals may over time come to capture the ideal in a less convincing or productive way, even degenerating into caricatures of themselves; making the original ideals seem distant indeed, as a perversion of themselves. For the rule of law, the most frequently mentioned slide downwards is into bureaucracy. In a bureaucratic regime there are plenty of rules and they do indeed govern, but the rules and regulations have lost their point, they are enforced in unjust ways that run counter to ideals of liberty, equality and solidarity. When bureaucratization makes a caricature of the ideal of legality, it is sometimes found necessary to reframe the animating ideal in an entirely new way. Nonet and Selznick have tried to save the ideal of the rule of law from bureaucratic parody by articulating an ideal of 'responsive law'. This is explicitly meant as a new interpretation of the old master ideal of legality. But, they argue:

> The ideal of legality should not be confused with the paraphernalia of 'legalization' – the proliferation of rules and procedural formalities. The bureaucratic patterns that pass for due process (understood as an 'obstacle course') or for accountability (understood as compliance with official rules) are alien to responsive law. The ideal of legality needs to be conceived more generally and to be cured of formalism. In a purposive system legality is the progressive reduction of arbitrariness in positive law and its administration.[23]

This passage exemplifies the spirit of realist idealism animating the constructive interpretation of the ideal of the rule of law. It acknowledges partial and even perverse institutionalization as an enduring problem and offers a challenge to it. How this mechanism works is also described in Hannah Pitkin's thoughtful book *Wittgenstein and Justice*. She concludes that tensions between substance and purpose on the one hand and institutionalization and conventionalized practice on the other are an important feature of all concepts of action and of social institu-

---

[22] Bovens, *Digitale rechtsstaat*.

[23] Philip Nonet and Philip Selznick, *Law and Society in Transition: Towards Responsive Law*, Berkeley, Cal., University of California Press, 1969, pp. 107-108.

tions in our language. There is a 'duality' of purpose and institutionalization, as follows:

> If our purposes and ideals could not be institutionalized, taught, put into practice in regularized ways, they would remain empty and idle, mysterious blessings which occasionally and inexplicably appear among us, but which we have no power to produce or to prolong. Therefore, their embodiment in social practice or individual action is their realization, truly deserves (almost) the same commitment from us as the initial purpose or ideal, is rightly called by the same name. Yet actions fall short of intention, and institutional practice develops a momentum of its own. We need, always, to hold our concepts partly aloof from the practices and institutions in which they are (supposedly) realized, in order to continue to be able to criticize, to renovate and to revise.[24]

Pitkin here calls for a particular attitude to language, which she derives from Wittgenstein (and Cavell). It attempts to 'hold concepts aloof from practices', imagining them as they are meant to be, and to do this as a precondition for critical reflection. This is what I mean by the attitude of realist idealism.

## 4.2 Realism Meets Idealism

What happens when the rule of law is seen primarily as a realistic motive in political action? The rule of law is then judged on its practical usefulness for politicians and officials in the context of the established institutions of a democratic polity. In former days, this political realism about the rule of law was translated into advice to kings and other office-holders about how to govern the state in such a way as to keep the peace and also attain their political objectives. In this genre, Machiavelli's *The Prince* is a classic example.[25] Machiavelli is perhaps unusual in his strong emphasis on the strategical approach to people, to things (to people as things) and towards purposes and aspirations; he places power and violence at the centre of the political process and thus seems far removed from rule of law idealism. Yet, even with Machiavelli there are some idealist motives at work in his thinking. They show themselves in his commitment to Italian unity as an overriding aim of which in the end all Italians will benefit, and even more in his declared preference for classical republicanism as a normatively superior way of life.

---

[24] Hannah Pitkin, *Wittgenstein and Justice*, Berkeley, Cal., University of California Press, 1972, p. 190.

[25] Quentin Skinner, *The Foundations of Modern Political Thought, Vol. I*, Cambridge, Cambridge University Press, 1978, pp. 33-48.

Political realism in an age of democracy and of the rule of law counsels a strategic use of the ideals of legality. We here encounter the strategy of self-binding. The authorities must keep to the laws they themselves have enacted because only in this way can they convincingly claim the obedience of all those subjected to the laws. Only if public authorities are seen to follow the same rules that are applicable to all, can this claim of authority be meaningful to citizens; there is a constant comparison going on between calculating officials and calculating citizens. The 'government of measures, not of men' is in this way made into a rational contract. Self-binding is a realist strategy for any government needing to establish and maintain relationships of authority with its subjects, because if this authority is not accepted the subjects will not behave like responsible citizens. They will then try to evade the law or openly break it, and soon the government will discover it has only limited means available to force free citizens into compliance. It is all a question of the effective management of reciprocated expectations.

Environmental policy is a modern area of governance where this reciprocity in compliance with the laws is of great importance. Successful environmental policy with desirable long-term effects depends on the active and constructive cooperation of citizens and businesses. Neither sanctions nor incentives can be strong enough as inducements for compliance since economic (short-term) interests are presumably stronger. The prevalence of public relations strategies, and of efforts to stimulate self-regulation by interested parties are indirect evidence of this. The cooperative compliance strategy, seeking the positive participation of many actors not under the control of government agencies, depends crucially on the strategy of self-binding.[26] The symbolic dimension of environmental policy aims to make citizens, and especially polluting organizations and enterprises, into responsible actors. This can only be achieved when the government itself in all its manifestations scrupulously obeys the same laws. And if governments are seen to be above the environmental regulations, so citizens and businesses will feel free to similarly disobey the laws. Authority and norm compliance depend on reciprocity.

Rule of law realism can be summarized in the formula: self-binding of the government is a necessary condition for binding citizens. This maxim is in fact an old one. As part of the rhetoric of advice to kings and office-holders, it originated in the Renaissance and gained prominence in the liberal tradition of political philosophy. Jean Bodin (1529-1596), legal adviser to France's absolute monarchs, developed it in his

---

[26] Jon Elster, *Ulysses and the Sirens*, rev. ed., Cambridge, Cambridge University Press, 1984.

theory of sovereignty. Interestingly, he posited an absolutist notion of sovereignty (to the pleasure of his masters), but argued that once the sovereign claims to be in absolute command over the citizens, prudence dictates the sovereign to voluntarily accept limitations on his absolute power (such as dictates of legality, i.e. respecting the property of the subjects). This self-limitation then enforces the claim to sovereignty. Stephen Holmes, who investigated the liberal tradition following and extending Bodin's insight, states that constitutionalism has two faces: the government that limits itself in the interests of liberty (negative constitutionalism) is at the same time the government that has a correct understanding of the conditions for effective power (positive constitutionalism). 'By restricting the arbitrary powers of government officials, a liberal constitution can, under the right conditions, increase the state's capacity to focus on specific problems and mobilize collective resources for a common purpose.'[27]

While reciprocity is, in the realist perspective, first of all a strategic consideration, it easily extends into the realm of idealism and then acquires normative status. Reciprocity is then seen as one of the fundamental norms for open public deliberation expressing the democratic ideal. In this vein it is, for instance, prominently treated in Gutmann and Thompson's ground-breaking work on deliberative democracy.[28] Before this, the notion of reciprocity as a standard for the interactions between officials and citizens, especially in relation to the institutions of the legal system, already pervaded the writings of Lon Fuller.[29] But with him, reciprocity not only comes into view as a result of an idealist wish to achieve social harmony, suggesting, for instance, that contract – this reciprocal institution *par excellence* – can make cooperation between strangers possible. At the same time, reciprocity expresses the realist stance of free individuals aiming to increase their own welfare and accepting social conditions that are idealistic in nature as part of this effort. Without an idealistic orientation, all realism is doomed to suboptimality. Without the trust needed for contractual relationships, a trust fusing realist and idealist motives, the benefits of a market economy cannot be achieved and all profit-seeking individuals would do much worse without the collective institutions that make markets functional. Just as idealism is incomplete without realism, needing its empirical

---

[27] Stephen Holmes, *Passions and Constraint*, Chicago, Ill., Chicago University Press, 1995, p. 7.

[28] Amy Gutmann and Dennis Thompson, *Democracy and Disagreement*, Cambridge, Mass., The Belknap Press, 1996.

[29] Lon L. Fuller, *The Principles of Social Order: Selected Essays of Lon L. Fuller*, ed. Kenneth I. Winston, Durham, N.C., Duke University Press, 1981.

focus, so realism is in need of idealism, providing it a broader orientation than mere self-serving motivations can provide.

Taking realism as its starting point, the consideration of effective strategies of governance leads to idealist motives implied by realism. This is not so strange when we remember that political realism itself derives from the rhetorical tradition and that, as I have argued elsewhere, the rhetorical tradition (notably in the works of Aristotle, Cicero and Quintilian) combines strategic and communicative motives.[30] All in all, the attitude fostered by realism is one of prudence. Realism holds idealist tendencies in check and so prevents disillusionment; it promotes clear sight. A metaphor expressing this attitude is that of the rule of law as a journey where every new stage in the progression of the travellers brings new challenges, adventures and opportunities and where it is the actual behaviour of the actors which determines the destination reached.

### 4.2.1  The Revival of Juristic Method

When realism meets idealism, citizens and officials have to come to terms with a profound problem of judgement. How sophisticated must our analysis of the empirical circumstances be in order to make correct or at least useful decisions about the constructive interpretation of the ideal? The facts as presented by the two sides in a court of law, the *Pikmeer* case shows, are clearly not sufficient material to work with. Sociologically sound background studies – in *Pikmeer* relating for instance to environmental policy and providing insight into the established interaction patterns between various actors who are supposedly cooperating on environmental themes – should be available for a sound judgment. What is required is a method for bringing a wide range of 'facts' to bear on ideals as expressed in constitutional law. Following Llewellyn, one of the founders of the jurisprudential school of American realism, we can call this *juristic method*.[31]

For studies of realist idealism, Llewellyn is an exceedingly interesting author. He started a movement in legal theory that aimed at greater realism in the study of the legal system, but soon turned this realist impulse into a plea for an ideal of better methods for the handling of 'cases of trouble' that present themselves to judges and to legislators. While his realism is expressed perhaps most clearly in his great anthropological study, together with Hoebel, of the legal culture of the Cheyenne Indians, in *The Common Law Tradition* (1960) Llewellyn

---

30  Willem Witteveen, *De retoriek in het recht*, Zwolle, W.E.J. Tjeenk Willink, 1988.

31  Karl N. Llewellyn and E. Adamson Hoebel, *The Cheyenne Way*, Norman, Okla., Oklahoma University Press, (1941) 1967, p. 292.

makes his realistic approach productive in a study of the decision styles of American appellate judges; in the latter book, the switch is made towards a constructive idealism that even articulates a model for the juristic method in the so-called 'Grand Style' of judging.[32]

Llewellyn surveyed a large number of appellate decisions in various periods of American legal history, and from this survey he derived two models of juristic method opposing one another: the Formal Style and the Grand Style. While the Formal Style can be called authoritarian, formal and logical, the Grand Style seems to be argumentative, factual and rhetorical. These terms of course do not signify very much; Llewellyn's typifications are rich and more complex, sometimes elusive also, but they at least give an indication of the nature of the differences. The 'Grand Style' is an innovative idea. Llewellyn learned from the Cheyenne Indians that their judges deciding 'trouble cases' in the context of an oral culture without written laws, managed to build on the accepted tradition of collective 'wisdom', but at the same time managed to be daringly innovative, providing flexible guidance in pressing social problems (such as crime under the influence of alcohol). Cheyenne judges offered explicit arguments in terms of generally acceptable principles that resonated in the culture and so laid a basis for further development of these principles. Something very similar Llewellyn saw at work in the appellate decisions of American judges using the Grand Style, even though the context now was that of a written legal culture steeped in formalistic juristic method. A judge reasoning according to the Grand Style typically supplies the principles or background considerations or ideals that support the authority of a rule at issue (the rule itself is only of importance in as far as it is the workable expression of a principle of law) and in order to be able to do this, the judge will jump from the small range of legally relevant 'facts' to all the available sources of information that are potentially relevant to the problem at hand; this broad orientation regarding facts is called 'situation sense'. The third element of the Grand Style is that explicit guidelines for future development of the law are given (the 'singing reason').

What to make of the Grand Style? Its most intriguing element is obviously this 'situation sense'. This is also, in my terminology, the locus of realist idealism. Unfortunately, while Llewellyn gives illuminating examples of judicial arguments showing situation sense, his theoretical pronouncements are not very clear and may seem to be contradictory. William Twining has, however, painstakingly reconstructed Llewellyn's

---

[32] Karl N. Llewellyn, *The Common Law Tradition: Deciding Appeals*, Boston, Little Brown, 1960.

intentions.[33] Under the heading of situation sense a complete method of judgment is hidden. I will here present Twining's reconstruction and add my own comments.

1. Situation sense begins with consideration of the 'facts'. As Twining puts it: 'Start by studying the facts as a layman familiar with their general context might see them. Try to grasp what would have happened if things had been working smoothly and what it was that brought the dispute about. Analyse what interests are in conflict and formulate statements of policy that may be relevant.' Llewellyn here advocates a way of working that is now expected more from a manager or a legislator than from a judge. This reflects a pragmatist orientation.

2. The next element is a consideration method. Twining summarizes it as follows: 'Try to fit the facts into some socially significant category or pattern, separating clearly irrelevant "fireside equities" peculiar to this case from potentially relevant elements in the situation. In seeking appropriate categories the following guidelines should be observed: (i) in categorizing the facts choose "situational concepts" – i.e. categories which clearly refer to facts situations only and do not straddle facts and legal consequences; (ii) terms used and distinctions drawn by persons familiar with the context of the dispute (either as experts, observers or participants) may provide appropriate categories; (iii) the practices and expectations of such persons may also be of use; (iv) one aspect of the problem is to characterize the facts at an appropriate level of generality.' What is here recommended is a kind of perspectivist method: the judge must imaginatively enter into the points of view of experts, observers and participants in order to organize his knowledge in such a way as to reflect different viewpoints. Llewellyn here draws on a rhetorical method deeply ingrained in the legal tradition which uses the dynamics of opposing arguments to reach balanced judgements which contain sufficient relevant information.

3. The next phase of the method of situation sense deals with 'values'. Twining's reconstruction again: 'Sometimes it will be found that after the facts have been categorized, there may be a consensus within the affected group or within society as a whole respecting applicable policies or principles. In such cases the selection of an appropriate situational concept may be sufficient to resolve the problem.' In this potential for the generation of consensus, there is an important ground rule: the consensus is not theoretically or normatively presupposed, as so often happens in Dutch legal and political culture; it emanates from

---

[33]  William Twining, *Karl Llewellyn and the Realist Movement*, London, Weidenfeld and Nicholson, 1973, pp. 226-227.

careful consideration of all the facts and only after all relevant perspectives have been activated to generate information. This is an ethical injunction.

4. The consideration of values may lead to complications, however. Twining continues thus: 'In other instances, a conflict of principles or policies may be found. In such cases the process of categorization should have assisted in identification of the issues of policy, etc., but will not in itself resolve such conflict. However, even if reasonable men might disagree on the choice of conflicting policies, they might share common ground in limiting the range of choices.' It is becoming clear that the method of situation sense offers the prospect of agreement on a meta-level of discourse where the field of argument is limited to a small number of well-developed positions; for instance, between separation of powers and balance of powers as relevant constructive interpretations of the rule of law. Agreement on a meta-level of discourse may be a ground on which the debate about conflicting interpretations may be more productive.

5. The final step in the method of situation sense, concerns the 'measures' taken in judgment. Twining succinctly summarizes this aspect as follows: 'Determine what you consider to be the most appropriate line or direction of treatment and only then decide on what specific prescription is appropriate.' It is noteworthy that this is a quite different idea than the Dworkinian notion of a 'right answer' emerging from the hermeneutical circle of considerations about facts and values.[34] Llewellyn demands at this stage in the reasoning a conscious choice about the long-term line of development to precede the actual decision about the issue to be resolved; a new and clearly in some sense political element here enters into the process.

6. As an afterthought, Twining provides an important caveat. 'This procedure provides no cure-all for finding "appropriate" categories or choosing between competing values.' The Grand Style promises a pragmatic way of dealing with trouble cases, but this promise does not include the legal certainty of the 'right answer'. Even though idealism has been included in the dynamics of the process, in the consideration of values and their further development into law, the attitude required remains a realist one, acknowledging the fundamental fact that there will never be full agreement on anything and that perfect solutions for intractable problems are illusory.

---

[34] Ronald Dworkin, *Law's Empire*, Cambridge, Mass., Harvard University Press, 1986.

## 4.2.2   Realist Idealism and the Rule of Law

What contributions can realist idealism make towards better con-structive interpretation of the ideals of the rule of law? We have now identified two areas of activity. An attitude of realist idealism is first of all able to draw attention to the enduring but often overlooked problem of the partial institutionalization of the ideal. The danger of the bureauc-ratization of legality is a real and persistent one; any approach that offers a stance counter to this tendency, is an advantage. But perhaps even more useful is the contribution realist idealism makes towards a method of judgement for citizens and officials grappling with problems of legality. We have seen how Llewellyn (and Twining) develop the notion of situation sense into a juristic method that goes to the heart of the interpretive enterprise. This can be extended to the interpretive enter-prise in which our democratic ideals of a 'government of measures and not of men' must be given fresh meanings and at the same time practical problems must be solved in a changing environment. A Grand Style of rule of law reasoning is at least a possibility.

This idealist conclusion demands realistic qualification. In Dutch constitutional practice, a Grand Style approach is, as yet, no more than a theoretical possibility. Our democratic practices actually seem to be badly organized for reflective discourse about their practical progression towards distant ideals. The citizens and officials debating issues of the rule of law seem unable to bring about explicit changes to the old and worn building of the *rechtsstaat Nederland*, with the history of failed attempts to introduce a modest variant of the statutory referendum as a telling example.

The aftermath of the *Pikmeer* case provides evidence in point. After the criticisms in the media, in academia and in the forums of democratic politics, the Supreme Court retraced its steps; it did not officially defend its doctrinal story with arguments. Due to the rules of criminal proce-dural law, the *Pikmeer* case actually reached the Supreme Court a second time. As the first case had been referred back to another Court of Appeal for the settlement of the factual issues (something which the Supreme Court in cassation is unable to do), a new chance to go to the Supreme Court presented itself. In the second *Pikmeer* case, a much more elaborate line of reasoning is followed.[35] The Court acknowledges some of the criticisms, especially on the idealist side of the equation. It even agrees that there are, under its own doctrine, too few effective action possibilities to prosecute a municipal authority that contravened criminal law. Then it reverses its own decision in the earlier *Pikmeer*

---

[35]   Hoge Raad (Strafkamer), 6 January 1998, no. 106160.E.

141

case. As a result, the immunity of municipal authorities as 'public bodies' is limited to a degree. Immediately after the decision, the Supreme Court provides guidelines for the public prosecutors and the lower courts that continue to award a privileged position for municipal authorities. Their immunity actually remains intact in all situations where the administrative task of the public body can only be fulfilled by a government agency and cannot be relegated to private initiatives. (As an example of a municipal task that can be handed over to a private organization, think of the collection of refuse.) Thus, all policy-making tasks and all tasks relating to the execution of the laws (such as the supervision of environmental regulations) are still within the sphere of immunity. All in all, this was a partial review at best; it looks like a doctrinal compromise. The Supreme Court does not enter into the argument on self-binding; it does not take a realistic look at the established patterns of interaction in practices of (environmental) governance and it does not go into the problem of the reciprocity of expectations and its impact on the effectiveness of environmental regulation.

So, even though the doctrine in *Pikmeer* was partially adapted in view of criticisms emanating from the democratic process and, beyond this, from public debate, we cannot conclude that the method the Supreme Court used resembles the Grand Style. It more closely resembles the Formal Style, especially in its proceduralism. And the second *Pikmeer* case was, in the public eye, not much more successful than the first one. It did not provide a convincing constitutional rhetoric, it did not appear to be a constructive interpretation of an underlying ideal of legality, it failed to give guidance to democratic governance in municipal politics. Small wonder then that the debate continued. In the end, the government had to give in to repeated statements by a parliamentary majority and appointed a state commission to investigate the desirability of new rules. This commission has since then advised to do away with the special protection for municipal authorities; they should not be above the law. At the time of writing of this text, seven years after the first litigation in *Pikmeer*, it is still unclear what will happen with these recommendations.[36]

And so, *Pikmeer* as a 'case of trouble' for a democratic polity aspiring to live under the rule of law, is open-ended.

---

[36] For academic comments on the *Pikmeer* cases, see W.J. Witteveen *et al.*, *Strafbaarheid van overheden*, Publikaties van de staatsrechtkring 15, Deventer, W.E.J. Tjeenk Willink, 1998.

# 5. Conclusion

In this chapter, an effort has been made to shed light on the dynamics of interpretations of the rule of law. As a result of the complexity of the master ideal in its relation to actual practices of governance, the *attitude* of the interpreters of the rule of law is a crucial factor. In Dutch debates a legalistic attitude often prevails, even when this is no more than a rhetorical pretence suggesting a greater degree of certainty than is really present in the mind of the interpreter. Courts and legislatures are drawn towards what I have termed the *conversion method*, which attempts to hide the ambiguities and antinomies of the ideal under rules and doctrines presented as precise and uniformly applicable. The conversion method facilitates a rhetoric of authority arguments, as exemplified in the *Pikmeer* cases. An alternative style of interpretation, manifesting a more reflective and hermeneutic understanding of the nature of the ideal, would employ a contrasting rhetoric of balancing arguments. This requires *an attitude of realist idealism*, in which the tension between idealist and realist perspectives is openly acknowledged and made productive through a comparison of opposing argumentations.

How would a realist idealist judge have reasoned in the *Pikmeer* case? While different lines of reasoning would no doubt be available, it seems to me that in all of them the constant switching of perspectives would be at the forefront. An interpretive rhetoric of balancing could, for instance, go like this. The starting point would be an idealist reading of the requirements of the rule of law, placing the decision in the tradition of earlier decisions under the master ideal. As a realist, the judge would then consider the likely effects of the proposed interpretation on practices of governance and rule-following as they have manifested themselves in the case at hand. (Already at this point the conversion method has reached its limits.) Knowing this, the judge turns again to an idealist perspective, asking whether the moral claims of reciprocity militate against placing local authorities above the law. Being realist again, the answer to this question is confronted with the judge's estimation of the disruptive effects resulting from not honouring the moral claim or of the positive symbolic effects of accepting it.

This leads to a still wider circle of interpretive arguments, including the second-order question of the proper role of the judge in relation to representative bodies. Inclining, for instance, in an idealist vein to the idea that democratically elected representatives are better placed to call their authorities to account than are appointed judges, this inclination is tempered, and perhaps even offset, by a realist consideration of the limited effectiveness of the control exercised by local authorities in this regard, given the way this actually functions. This would naturally promote the idealist aspiration to outline a way of judicial control that interferes as little as possible with the ordinary channels of democratic procedure, remembering the rule of law ideal of the balance of powers, which encourages just such an effort. In the end, both the idealist and the realist perspectives complement each other. They lead to a reaffirmation of the master ideal, to an acknowledgment of its antinomies and ambiguities, to an exploration of its potential in new conditions. At the same time, they provide a grounding of the ideals in practices of governance already thought to be in accord with the rule of law.

An attitude of realist idealism, using the potential of perspectival switches, becomes possible once realism and idealism are conceived as complementary rather than as opposing forces. The relationship between idealism and realism must then be thought of as at most antinomical, not antithetical. At this point, there is an interesting asymmetry. It is in our culture much easier to see that an idealist attitude needs to be tempered with a good dose of realism than that a realist attitude needs to be corrected by some higher aspiration. Somebody professing idealist motives will easily be taken to be an optimist or even a utopian, while someone propounding a realist world view is not confronted with the immediate response that she must be more imaginative or even hopeful. While idealism seems limited in its emphasis of constructive potential, realism appears to be its own justification. Idealists are not allowed to forget the imperatives of practice while realists may harbour secret dreams of a better world.

# References

Berlin, Isaiah, 'The Originality of Machiavelli', in Isaiah Berlin, *Against the Current*, London, Hogarth Press, 1980, pp. 25-79.

Böhtlingk, F.R., *De rechtsstaat Nederland*, Alphen aan den Rijn, Samsom, 1958.

Bovens, M.A.P., *De digitale rechtsstaat*, Alphen aan den Rijn, Samsom, 1999.

Burke, Kenneth, *A Grammar of Motives*, Berkeley, Cal., University of California Press, (1945) 1969.

Dworkin, Ronald, *Law's Empire*, Cambridge, Mass., Harvard University Press, 1986.

Elster, Jon, *Ulysses and the Sirens*, rev. ed., Cambridge, Cambridge University Press, 1984.

Fuller, Lon L., *The Morality of Law*, rev. ed., New Haven, Yale University Press, 1969.

————, *The Principles of Social Order: Selected Essays of Lon L. Fuller*, ed. Kenneth I. Winston, Durham, N.C., Duke University Press, 1981.

Gutmann, Amy, and Dennis Thompson, *Democracy and Disagreement*, Cambridge, Mass., The Belknap Press, 1996.

Holmes, Stephen, *Passions and Constraint*, Chicago, Ill., Chicago University Press, 1995.

Koopmans, T., 'De rol van de wetgever', in *Honderd jaar rechtsleven*, Zwolle, W.E.J. Tjeenk Willink, 1970, pp. 221-235.

————, *Vergelijkend publiekrecht*, 2nd ed., Deventer, Kluwer, 1986.

Llewellyn, Karl N., *The Common Law Tradition: Deciding Appeals*, Boston, Little Brown, 1960.

————, and E. Adamson Hoebel, *The Cheyenne Way*, Norman, Okla., Oklahoma University Press, (1941) 1967.

McWhinney, Edward, *Supreme Courts and Judicial Lawmaking*, Dordrecht, Martinus Nijhoff, 1986.

Nonet, Philip, and Philip Selznick, *Law and Society in Transition: Towards Responsive Law*, Berkeley, Cal., University of California Press, 1969.

Pitkin, Hannah, *Wittgenstein and Justice*, Berkeley, Cal., University of California Press, 1972.

Radbruch, Gustav, *Rechtsphilosophie*, Stuttgart, Koehler Verlag, 1973.

Rehwinkel, Peter, and Willy Swildens in *NRC Handelsblad* of 28 September 1996.

Skinner, Quentin, *The Foundations of Modern Political Thought, Vol. I*, Cambridge, Cambridge University Press, 1978.

Twining, William, *Karl Llewellyn and the Realist Movement*, London, Weidenfeld and Nicholson, 1973.

Van der Burg, Wibren, *De verbeelding aan het werk*, Kampen, Agora, 2001.

Van Elst, Richard, in *NRC Handelsblad* of 10 September 1996.

Verschuuren, Jonathan, and Boudewijn de Waard, 'Introduction', in Boudewijn de Waard (ed.), *Negotiated Decision-Making*, Den Haag, Boom Juridische Uitgevers, 2000, pp. 1-9.

Witteveen, Willem, *De retoriek in het recht*, Zwolle, W.E.J. Tjeenk Willink, 1988.

————, *Evenwicht van machten*, Zwolle, W.E.J. Tjeenk Willink, 1991.

————, 'Doctrinal Stories', *International Journal for the Semiotics of Law* VI (1993) 17, 179-202.

————, *De geordende wereld van het recht*, Amsterdam, Amsterdam University Press, 2001.

————, *et al.*, *Strafbaarheid van overheden*, Publikaties van de staatsrechtkring 15, Deventer, W.E.J. Tjeenk Willink, 1998.

# Ideals of Doing Political Philosophy:
# From the Perspective of Eternity
# to Hermeneutical Perspectivism

Bert VAN DEN BRINK*

## 1. Introduction

All political philosophers have their own ways of approaching the object of their studies – political life. Some aim for something like a view from nowhere;[1] the 'God's eye' point of view from which it becomes possible to determine what, for instance, social cooperation, democratic deliberation, and justice are, and what they require from us. Others opt for a more situated, hermeneutical approach to deal with such questions.[2] And there are, of course, many other approaches still. Whatever approach is taken, it will always presuppose a specific ideal of doing political philosophy.

Ideals of doing political philosophy tend to comprise both substantive and deliberative ideals. As one recent definition puts it, substantive ideals 'present models of excellence against which things in a relevant class can be assessed, such as models of the just society or the good person'. Deliberative ideals, on the other hand, 'present models of excellent deliberation, leading to correct or warranted ethical conclusions'.[3] If being a good political philosopher were about reaching cor-

---

* For their comments on an earlier draft of this paper I thank Wibren van der Burg, David Owen and Sanne Taekema. The usual disclaimer applies. I should like to thank the Royal Netherlands Academy of Arts and Sciences for its generous support of my work.

[1] Thomas Nagel, *The View from Nowhere*, New York, Oxford University Press, 1986.

[2] For a thorough discussion of these two competing approaches, see Georgia Warnke, *Justice and Interpretation*, Cambridge, Mass., MIT Press, 1993.

[3] Both definitions are from Connie S. Rosati, 'Ideals', in Edward Craig (ed.), *Routledge Encyclopedia of Philosophy, Vol. 4*, London [etc.], Routledge, 1998, p. 672. Let me note that I see no reason why the adjective 'ethical' should be considered part of the general definition of a deliberative ideal. Not all types of deliberation aim at ethical conclusions.

rect conclusions by way of excellent deliberation alone, then substantive ideals of doing political philosophy would coincide with deliberative ideals of doing political philosophy. But as I hope to show in this chapter, there is more to being a political philosopher than excellent deliberation. Most importantly, a political philosopher will often work with a certain controversial ethical, political, or methodological programme in mind, such as reinstating a certain understanding of ethics,[4] or enlightenment or critique,[5] or an aspect of a particular political tradition that has been lost from view.[6] This often quite systematic concentration on certain *aspects* of doing philosophy rather than on doing philosophy per se (whatever that may mean) is captured by substantive ideals of doing political philosophy. The concentration on aspects to a large extent determines the way in which philosophers approach the object of their studies. From a methodological angle, this helps explain why there are analytical (the aspect of conceptual clarification), critical theoretical (the aspect of ideology), hermeneutical (the aspect of intercontextual understanding), and genealogical (the aspect of the historicity of our self-understandings) approaches to political philosophy.[7] From a normative theoretical angle, it helps explain why there are liberal (the aspect of individual liberty), republican (the aspect of political freedom), and communitarian (the aspect of primordial ties) traditions in political philosophy. Substantive ideals of the good philosopher are normatively 'thick', and therefore controversial. They do not just stand for general criteria of good deliberation, but for certain controversial answers to the

---

[4]  Alasdair MacIntyre, *After Virtue: A Study in Moral Theory*, Notre Dame, Ind., Notre Dame University Press, 1981.

[5]  Jürgen Habermas, *The Philosophical Discourse of Modernity*, tr. F. Lawrence, Oxford, Polity Press, 1987; Michel Foucault, 'What is Enlightenment?', in Foucault, *Ethics, Subjectivity and Truth*, ed. Paul Rabinow, New York, The New Press, 1997, pp. 303-320.

[6]  See, e.g., Peter Berkowitz, *Virtue and the Making of Modern Liberalism*, Princeton, N.J., Princeton University Press, 1999.

[7]  For the sake of the clarity, I assume that not all methodological issues concern first-order questions of correct deliberation, understood narrowly as questions concerning the process that leads to correct or warranted conclusions. Michel Foucault's concentration on an enlightened attitude of doing philosophy which is both methodological and ethical in nature, for instance, is not directed towards the goal of understanding normative requirements of the first-order process of deliberation. Foucault is rather interested in the second-order or meta-issue as to the kind of perfectionist *ethos* one needs in order to be sufficiently equipped to deliberate on first-order practical questions in an adequate way (see Foucault, 'What Is Enlightenment?', *passim*). This focus escapes the definition of the deliberative ideal from the main text and makes it clear that questions of methodology can concern substantive as well as deliberative aspects of the ideal of doing political philosophy.

questions philosophers tend to deliberate *about*. Where we make ideals of doing political philosophy thinner, we first take away the aspect of political ideology and subsequently filter out all controversial methodological choices. The thin model of doing political philosophy is a model of doing deliberation according to minimal demands of rationality.

In this chapter, I am interested in substantive ideals of doing political philosophy – especially in ideals as to how the philosopher should approach the object of his studies. I will start by looking at a well-known approach that concentrates on the aspect of foundations of practical reasoning *sub specie aeternitatis*. It is characterized by a cognitivistic, proceduralistic, and universalistic orientation in determining firm principles of practical reasoning that can instruct human beings about the legitimacy of concrete social and political ideas and actions. This ideal is found in the work of philosophers such as John Rawls and Jürgen Habermas.[8] It takes its lead from the analytical method mostly (in Habermas's case joined to a 'critical theoretical' approach),[9] and it concentrates on deliberative issues, although it cannot avoid to be seen as a substantive model as well. I will point to two serious problems with this ideal, which both concern the one-dimensional way in which it inspires the philosopher to search for foundational principles and rules implicit in political practices. I will then go on to sketch the contours of a more situated and historically sensitive alternative ideal, which I will label hermeneutical perspectivism. The most distinctive feature of this ideal is that it inspires philosophical perception to always remain open to other aspects of political life than its supposed foundations in principles of practical reasoning. This ideal does not reject the attempt to search for principles and rules for specific political practices. It does, however, reject the unnecessarily restrictive tendency to reduce the philosophical study of political practices to an exercise in the articulation of foundational rules and principles. Although this approach has many problems of its own, I will not discuss them in depth here. My aim is purely to show that the model of hermeneutical perspectivism fares better with respect to the problems I identify for the other model. The task of identifying the problems of the ideal of hermeneutical perspectivism must wait for another occasion.

---

[8]   John Rawls, *A Theory of Justice*, Cambridge, Mass., Harvard University Press, 1971; Jürgen Habermas, 'Philosophy as Stand-In and Interpreter', tr. Christian Lenhardt, in Habermas, *Moral Consciousness and Communicative Action*, Cambridge, Mass., MIT Press, 1987.

[9]   See Thomas MacCarthy, *The Critical Theory of Jürgen Habermas*, Cambridge, Polity Press, 1984.

## 2. The Perspective of Eternity

So let me start with a well-known ideal of doing political philosophy that aims for knowledge from a perspective *sub specie aeternitatis*. As John Rawls famously put it on the last page of *A Theory of Justice*, the aim of this approach to doing political philosophy is 'to regard the human situation not only from all social but also from all temporal points of view'.[10] This ideal of reaching general, comprehensive conclusions about a specific issue – in Rawls's case, social justice – is at the core of this understanding of doing philosophy. According to Rawls, the 'perspective of eternity' he sketches does not require a viewpoint that is itself 'beyond the world', or is the viewpoint of a 'transcendent being'.[11] Regulative principles of practical reasoning are always already built into practice. But we need a very specific kind of detached and impartial perspective to recognize them as the ones that should guide us in practice. This is the 'perspective of eternity', central to Rawls's philosophical ideal, the requirements of which are described in the famous thought experiments of the original position and the veil of ignorance. This perspective of eternity is

> … a certain form of thought and feeling that rational persons can adopt within the world. And having done so, they can, whatever their generation, bring together into one scheme all individual perspectives and arrive together at regulative principles that can be affirmed by everyone as he lives by them, each from his own standpoint. Purity of heart, if one could attain it, would be to see clearly and to act with grace and self-command from this point of view.[12]

'Purity of heart' and 'a certain form of thought and feeling' are at the core of what Rawls considers to be the motivating disposition for thinking, acting, and indeed *living* from the point of view of timeless principles of practical reasoning. The ideal of doing political philosophy here is to approach questions of political philosophy from this point of view. Understandably, Rawls stresses that it is not easy to acquire the philosophical attitude that makes it possible to work from this ideal. However, once acquired, it will motivate all those who aim for genuine knowledge about the basic rules of our moral and political practices to 'arrive together at regulative principles that can be affirmed by everyone'. As long as their hearts are pure, *all* reasonable people can take on the required stance – based in the philosophical perspective of eternity – and

---

[10]  Rawls, *Theory of Justice*, p. 587.

[11]  *Ibid.*

[12]  *Ibid.*

arrive at the *telos* of engaging in philosophy from this stance – finding regulative principles for practical reasoning that can be affirmed by all. This ideal of doing philosophy is mainly deliberative in orientation. It aims to tell us something about how we should deliberate on questions of political philosophy. Still, in aiming for the ideal of correct deliberation, a substantive ideal of doing philosophy must be guiding too. This is the ideal of concentrating, in one's approach to the object of one's studies, mainly on one specific *aspect* of political practices: that of the general principles of practical reasoning, i.e. of rational and reasonable rules for deliberation that are supposed to be implicit in our practical actions and utterances.

## 3. Enlightenment and the Perspective of Eternity

The idea that our ideal of doing political philosophy should be guided by the perspective of eternity is very old. For our purposes, it is interesting to look at a debate that started at the end of the eighteenth century with regard to the question 'What is enlightenment?' From the beginning, one camp in that debate held that thinking 'for oneself', looking 'within oneself... for the supreme touchstone of truth' was the prime sign of enlightenment. That radical attitude – the quotation is from Kant's 'What Is Orientation in Thinking?' – looked for principles of reason 'within oneself', i.e. in the universal conditions of rational thought that, by means of a transcendental method, could be made visible in one's own thought (as well as in everybody else's). The attitude of enlightenment necessarily had to reject the notion that the directives of tradition, religion, or political authority could in any way be more authoritative than the critical thought of individuals.[13] Of course, tradition, religion, and political authority can be right about things. Ultimately, however, the prejudices inherent in unquestioned traditions and practices, to the extent that they cannot withstand the critical scrutiny of rational inquiry, are 'the ball and chain of an everlasting minority'.[14] Those who dare to make use of their own

---

[13] For the discussion that follows I have benefited from James Schmidt, 'What is Enlightenment? A Question, Its Context, and Some Consequences', in James Schmidt (ed.), *What is Enlightenment? Eighteenth-Century Answers and Twentieth-Century Questions*, Berkeley, University of California Press, 1996, pp. 1-44. The quotation from Kant is taken from Schmidt's article, p. 17.

[14] Immanuel Kant, 'An Answer to the Question: What is Enlightenment?', in Kant, *Practical Philosophy*, ed. Allen Wood, tr. Mary J. Gregor, Cambridge, Cambridge University Press, 1996, p. 17 (8:36).

understanding will stand up and test and reject them through the public use of reason.[15]

Give and take some considerable revisions, the use of reason as Kant thought of it is still very much a guiding principle in the work of contemporary philosophers such as Rawls and Habermas. This approach to practical reasoning and to political philosophy is, among other things, cognitivistic, proceduralistic, and universalistic. It is cognitivistic because it looks for principles from which the legitimacy of given norms and practices can be investigated in a mode that is analogous to the way we test truth claims. The idea is that we can have firm *knowledge* of the exact criteria by which such tests of legitimacy should be run. The approach is proceduralistic because the tests of legitimacy are phrased in terms of procedures, i.e. rules and principles that tell the actor how to act. Kant's categorical imperative, Rawls's method of reflective equilibrium, and Habermas's principles of discourse and universalization tell us which rules we have to follow in order to find out whether concrete directives and practices we are faced with are legitimate. Finally, this approach to practical philosophy is universalistic insofar as it looks for principles of practical reasoning that do not simply express the intuitions and prejudices of a specific culture or historical era, but that express a guide for thinking and acting that every reasonable person will affirm.[16]

This approach to doing practical philosophy has resulted in some of the most impressive and influential political theories we know. Philosophical theories such as those of Rawls and Habermas construct or reconstruct very clear and morally highly appealing principles of reasoning and of justice – and do so against the background of rather fuzzy practices of reasoning and justice. They are thought to be able to play a role in making these practices less fuzzy, better ordered, and legitimate. And there is no doubt that a more Rawlsian or Habermasian approach to *some* of the social and moral problems of our time would result in great practical improvements – Rawls's theory is as relevant as ever with regard to questions of distributive justice in capitalist societies, and a careful application of Habermas's democratic theory to the rules of debate in many parliaments would not exactly weaken the idea of democracy. Yet, that circumstance does not answer the question whether the philosophical ideal behind these approaches is always the right one. The practical value of the normative recommendations of these theories

---

[15]   *Ibid.*, p. 17 (8:35).

[16]   See Jürgen Habermas, 'Morality and Ethical Life: Does Hegel's Critique of Kant Apply to Discourse Ethics?', in Habermas, *Moral Consciousness and Communicative Action*, tr. Christian Lenhardt and Shierry Weber Nicholson, Cambridge, Polity Press, 1990, pp. 195-215.

does not imply a clear answer to the question whether our philosophical ideal should necessarily be inspired by the perspective of eternity.

I see various reasons to doubt that it should. Let me discuss the two that I consider most important. The first concerns the limits of accounts of practical reasoning in terms of rules and principles. It will be discussed in section 4. The second concerns the limits of the systematic normative theories that result from such accounts. I will discuss it in section 5.

## 4. Why Rules and Principles Do not Provide Foundations to Practical and Theoretical Knowledge

Well-known critics of especially the Kantian strand of the Enlightenment tradition such as Hans-Georg Gadamer, Richard Rorty, and Charles Taylor have expressed their doubts on the assumption that reason should be thought of as an *independent* critical instance *vis-à-vis* our prejudices, traditions, and unreflected beliefs and practices. Accounts of practical reasoning in terms of rules and principles tend to oppose claims from reason to claims from prejudice and tradition, and equate the latter with false belief. Against this view, Gadamer has held that 'Enlightenment itself rests on a fundamental prejudice' – a 'prejudice against prejudice itself'.[17] Gadamer's perhaps most famous argument states that without prejudices – *Vorurteile* – we would not be able to make sense of the world at all. As seen from this view, principles of practical reasoning that are said to be developed from a purely formal or transcendental reflection on practice will, in some way or other, always turn out to be tied to a specific set of prejudices from specific social and historical contexts and its problems. Of course, these prejudices may well be in need of critical scrutiny, and an appeal to systematized principles of practical reasoning will often be helpful in this. But the circumstance that we often want to appeal to such principles in order to gain a critical perspective on our practices and prejudices does not in any way make them fully independent of those practices and prejudices – or the true yardsticks of understanding.

Understanding, says Gadamer, is not primarily a theoretical activity, but a practical one. A normative theory that claims to be the true and independent yardstick of practical understanding runs the risk of forgetting that it was born from and is still a part of – i.e. a specific form of reflection on – situated contexts of practical knowledge. As seen from this view, we might want to say that not just the motivation but also the

---

[17] Hans-Georg Gadamer, *Truth and Method*, 2nd rev. ed., New York, Continuum, 1989. Quoted from Schmidt, 'Enlightenment', p. 19.

normative substance of Rawls's theory was not born from a truly ahistorical thought experiment that did away with the substantive se- diments from earlier ages in the contract theories of Hobbes, Locke, and Rousseau. Rather, his age drove Rawls to construct, in the face of pressing questions of intolerance, economic justice and equal citizenship of the 1950s and 1960s, a situated theory of what justice means – collecting strong intuitions, rules, principles, and background theories of justice that echoed the political aspirations for freedom and equality, and bringing them in reflective equilibrium. Note that this interpretation is not just born from my desire to strengthen my own argument. For what I have just said reproduces in a nutshell Rawls's reworked position on the status of his theory from his 1985 article, 'Justice as Fairness: Political not Metaphysical', onwards.[18]

Let me try to make the same point in a different way. In recent years, political theorists inspired by Wittgenstein's *Philosophical Investigations*[19] have questioned the assumption that our political practices *always already* harbour essential rules and principles for action coordination that can be articulated in a cognitivistic, proceduralistic, and universalistic fashion and that can be made central to a theoretical account of such practices. That assumption suggests that social practices have firm foundations that are always already there in practice and that are looking for a complete articulation. In a recent article,[20] James Tully singles out two Wittgensteinian points in order to argue against this view. The first point says that 'understanding general terms – such as freedom, equality, democracy, reason, power, and oppression – is not the theoretical activity of grasping and applying a definition, rule, or theory that states the necessary and sufficient conditions for the application of such general terms in any case'.[21] According to Wittgenstein, understanding the meaning of a general term is not a reflective and theoretical, but rather an unreflected pre-theoretical and practical activity. As seen from such a perspective, my belief that I am a free human

---

[18]  In John Rawls, *Collected Papers*, ed. Samuel Freeman, Cambridge, Mass., Harvard University Press, 1999, pp. 388-414.

[19]  James Tully, 'Wittgenstein and Political Philosophy', *Political Theory* 17 (1989), 172-204; Chantal Mouffe, 'Wittgenstein, Political Theory and Democracy', in Mouffe, *The Democratic Paradox*, London, Verso, 1989, pp. 60-79; David Owen, 'Wittgenstein and Genealogy', *SATS: Nordic Journal of Philosophy* 2 (2001), 1-28.

[20]  James Tully, 'Political Philosophy as a Critical Activity,' *Political Theory* 30 (2002), 533-555.

[21]  *Ibid.*, p. 542.

being is not caused by my 'operating a calculus according to a rule'[22] that defines what it is to be a free human being. The application of the term 'being a free human being' is, to use Wittgenstein's famous phrase, 'not everywhere bounded by rules'.[23] My understanding is given with and witnessed by my actually experiencing myself as and acting like a free human being *in practice*, not with some kind of theoretical reflection on – or interpretation of – what it means to be a free human being. Of course, reflection on or interpretation of what it means to be free may very well become necessary, for instance when you and I come to disagree about the question whether my not having effective democratic control over some of the laws I live under affects my freedom. But from the fact that such reflections are possible and sometimes necessary one cannot conclude that someone's understanding of what it means to be free is necessarily dependent on some kind of theoretical knowledge that can be captured in general terms, definitions, or rules.[24]

This brings us to a second Wittgensteinian point that Tully highlights. It says that if a general political term is being used among speakers, its criteria for application will often be too strongly contested 'to be explicated in terms of a fixed rule or theory, no matter how complex'.[25] This idea of essentially contested concepts is already expressed in Wittgenstein's thesis that there are no complete sets of rules or prescripts that make us use a particular term in similar but not exactly equal cases. Rather, there are 'family resemblances... a complicated network of similarities overlapping and criss-crossing: sometimes overall similarities, sometimes similarities in detail'.[26]

Think about freedom again. A liberal defender of a 'negative' concept of freedom[27] and a republican defender of the concept of freedom as 'non-domination'[28] will readily agree that, in the abstract, interference with a person's activity always harbours a danger of loss of freedom for that person. In that respect, their understandings of what it means to be free are similar. However, when it comes to determining under what

---

[22] Ludwig Wittgenstein, *Philosophical Investigations*, Oxford, Oxford University Press, 1953, s. 81.

[23] *Ibid.*, s. 84.

[24] For a good discussion of this question about freedom see Philip Pettit, 'Freedom as Antipower', *Ethics* 106 (1996), 576-605.

[25] Tully, 'Political Philosophy', p. 546.

[26] Wittgenstein, *Philosophical Investigations*, ss. 65-67.

[27] Isaiah Berlin, 'Two Concepts of Liberty', in Berlin, *Four Essays on Liberty*, Oxford, Oxford University Press, 1969, pp. 118-172.

[28] Pettit, 'Freedom as Antipower'.

conditions interference with a person's activity should be considered an actual threat to the person's freedom, they disagree. The liberal will consider any form of interference a threat to individual freedom. As John Stuart Mill put it: 'All restraint, qua restraint, is evil'.[29] The republican, on the other hand, will say that only arbitrary interference, interference that is not backed up by legitimate law, is a breach of freedom. Still, although the liberal and republican do not employ the same conceptions of freedom, there seems to be no problem for them to accept that they are genuinely talking about the same concept of freedom and about a range of practices, competencies, virtues that, depending on the conception used, may or may not be included in their understandings of freedom. Although they do not share a finite and fixed set of principles of freedom, they recognize that the family resemblances between the conceptions of the practice of freedom they are employing warrant the conclusion that they are roughly talking about the same thing.

If this view is sound, then we must conclude that 'foundational' rules and principles are not complete, unequivocal, and unshakable reconstructions of rules and principles always already implicit in practice. At best, they capture certain important *aspects of* our political practices; aspects that play a role in practices of lending authority to claims about the social and political world. As such, we may hold on to them for a while because this is in our best epistemological, moral, or political interest. We may appeal to theories such as those of Rawls and Habermas because they illustrate a point about justice or fair deliberation we want to make. But shortly after we may find ourselves criticizing such theories for being too narrow in focus, for forgetting their origins in time and place, for making too comprehensive claims about what it means to be reasonable, etc.[30]

What does all this mean for the ideal of doing philosophy? We may conclude that rules and principles of practical reasoning are at best no more than partial and incomplete constructions of non-foundational aspects of our political practices. For our ideal of doing philosophy, this means at least two things. First, it must mean that instead of the perspective of eternity from which we can see what lies behind the contingency of political practices, we are in need of a more situated perspective from which we can take seriously the priority of practice to rules and principles, of contingency to (supposed) eternity. Second, from such a situated

---

[29] John Stuart Mill, *On Liberty*, in Mill, *On Liberty and Other Essays*, ed. John Gray, Oxford, Oxford University Press, 1991, pp. 5-128, here quoted from Pettit, 'Freedom as Antipower', p. 577.

[30] On the problem of forgetting, see Owen, 'Wittgenstein and Genealogy'.

perspective, it should become possible to study political life from a broader philosophical ideal, i.e. one that does not try to reduce the essence of our practices to a calculus of rules but that remains open to a broad range of aspects of practice that may, at any given time, become central to practice – many of which (such as the channelling of political passions through parties, action groups, or social movements; the ironic use of language; culturally situated symbolic action; the exercise of culturally specific virtues and competencies; creative action, etc.) escape the cognitivistic, proceduralistic, and universalistic approach. Our ideal needs to be more flexible and situated in order for it to remain possible to study political life as the complex and often muddled practice it is.

## 5. A Danger of Searching for a Timeless Perspective

Let me illustrate one consequence of what has been said above by means of pointing to a frequently made mistake. When philosophical theories about politics forget that they were born from a reflection on certain aspects of situated practices of reasoning, they frequently claim interpretative and prescriptive authority over practices and problematics that do not resemble those that the theory was initially developed from. Michael Walzer, in his book *Spheres of Justice*, has convincingly shown what such blindness as to the legitimate scope of one's theory can amount to.[31] He argues that the egalitarian, rights-based way of looking at justice of mainstream modern liberalism was developed against the background of a very specific theory of the nation state, society, and citizenship. For that reason, it is well suited to help us reflect on, for instance, the rule of law, or social benefits provided by the state. It cannot, however, say much about what it means to act from justice in relationships of love and friendship, in private organizations, or in hierarchical relationships of, say, master and pupil. Neither can it inform us much about future-oriented political initiatives that might want to do away with nation-based ideas of political cooperation. If a theory of justice forgets that different social goods and social spheres are characterized by different ways of distributing benefits, recognition, and opportunities, it runs the risk of imposing its own distributive criteria – which are taken from a theory about a specific (set of) practice(s) – on social spheres to which those criteria are really quite foreign. Particularly when backed up by state power, such a theory may do considerable damage to the social fabric of social relations. The examples are well known, and have in the last decades been phrased by communitarians, feminists, conservatives, multiculturalists, and many other critics of

---

[31]    Michael Walzer, *Spheres of Justice*, New York, Basic Books, 1989.

egalitarian liberalism. If we come to think about love and friendship in terms of rights and entitlements, then we import to those goods a type of relationship that stems from moral and legal, not emotional and ethical relations. If we come to think about civic responsibility largely in terms of making judgments from a socially detached perspective, then all traditional, local forms of dealing with the problems and possibilities of civic interaction fall from view. If we come to think about agents on the market in terms of their individual ability to redistribute opportunities and gains, then we mistake the perspective of the entrepreneur for that of the welfare state. If we come to think about the relationship between master and pupil, professor and student in too egalitarian terms, then the in many ways inegalitarian conditions of learning and conveying knowledge come under threat. A normative theory, or a state ideology for that matter, that forgets where it is coming from, cannot judge whether it is applicable to specific social contexts.

Now, I do not mean to suggest that theorists who work from a proceduralist and cognitivistic perspective of eternity are, by definition as it were, unaware of these dangers. Theorists such as Habermas and Rawls continuously stress the limits to their formal, minimalistic theories about the basic structure (Rawls) or the basic rules for deliberation (Habermas). They would be among the first to admit that there are specific practices of distributive justice or communication that are not captured by their theories. Still, although they admit this, they do suggest that a concentration on the structures for political interaction they sketch are foundational, in the sense that they provide the ultimate anchors of normative action in liberal-democratic societies.[32] We have already seen that this foundationalist view should be abandoned. Once that has been done, there is no reason why the ideal of doing philosophy cannot be broadened to include aspects of political interaction that do not fall under supposedly rule-governed practical behaviour.

## 6. Interlude: Consequences for the Ideal of Doing Political Philosophy

We have seen in section 4 that there are strong indications that rules and principles of practical reasoning cannot be arrived at from a perspective *sub specie aeternitatis*. At best, such principles are illuminating *constructions* of how we may think about the requirements of practical reasoning. When applied to appropriate contexts and problematics, they can be of enormous value. In section 5 we have briefly touched upon

---

[32]  Of course, in Rawls's case, this goes only for *A Theory of Justice*, not for his work since 'Justice as Fairness'.

one danger of not acknowledging the problematic issue of application in our ideal of doing political philosophy: it may lead to normative recommendations that affect the integrity of social practices since they were taken from settings of normativity that are foreign to the practice in question. In both cases, the idea that the ideal of doing political philosophy should be joined to the perspective of eternity becomes problematic. If, as philosophers, we aim to remain responsive to the multifaceted and continuously changing nature of political life, then it seems that we are in need of a serious reformulation of the ideal of doing political philosophy.

In what follows I want to discuss three aspects of an alternative ideal of doing political philosophy that I think follows from what has been said in my critique of the perspective of eternity. The first concerns the importance of the value of *civility* I will argue that, given the 'loss' of the perspective of eternity as the anchor of philosophical reasoning, it can help us cope with the difficulties given with finding workable principles of practical reasoning that are fair to all. I will discuss this in section 7. In section 8, I will look at a value that I consider to be important as a counterweight to the danger of the philosopher becoming caught up in a proceduralistic system of ideas that is only seemingly complete: the value of *creativity*. In section 9, I will label my approach *hermeneutical perspectivism*. It can help the philosopher to remain realistic in staying aware of the many limitations to her idealistic search for philosophical truth.

## 7. An Ethos of Civility

To start with, I propose that we introduce to the ideal of doing political philosophy a value that we know both from political and academic practice: the value of *civility*. Civility is an ethical code that helps participants in social practices to remain respectful of each other while engaging in normative conflicts over their respective understandings of aspects of these practices and options for action. If we act on our findings from the previous sections, then we must admit a degree of *uncertainty* into our philosophical approach. The main attraction of the perspective of eternity is that it suggests an Archimedean point from which we can reach certain and timeless knowledge about the 'essence' of politics. The philosopher who, for good reasons, rejects the perspective of eternity does not have that advantage. This does not in any way imply that he must let go of the ideal of truth. After all, there is a truth claim behind the rejection of the perspective of eternity. It says that, given the way in which principles and rules are always incomplete articulations of multifaceted, complex, situated practices and problematics, it is *true* that

159

human beings cannot regard the human situation from all social and temporal points of view. Based on this truth claim, this approach goes on to look for a way of learning to deal with one important consequence of this, i.e. the consequence that political practice and political philosophy cannot be guided by unshakable rules and principles that are external to and at the same time foundational of political and academic practice. As they are laid down in constitutions, in moral systems, in professional codes, practical rules and principles are results rather than foundations of social practices – and by their very nature contested. Indeed, testing the efficacy and justification of practical rules and principles is an integral part of any flourishing practice.[33] In order for participants to test such rules and principles in a productive and respectful mode, they need a code that warrants stability and mutual respect in the required deliberative contestations in political and academic arenas. Civility is the ethical code that does that job.

In political and academic settings which are sufficiently well organized and decent, we experience that we can, without any dangers of importing instability or injustice to them, *disagree* with each other's exact views as to both quite abstract principles for reasoning and action and all kinds of more detailed issues concerning political problems and scientific and intellectual queries as long as we do so in a *civilized* manner. When we start from that experience, we may want to say that the disposition towards *civility* is more basic to a political and philosophical ethos than a disposition towards *substantive agreement* on shared rules and principles – at least in the sense that the disposition towards *civility* is needed to maintain the conditions under which substantive agreement – or an agreement to disagree – can be achieved. In order to be good citizens of a democracy, we do not have to *agree* with each other's exact ideas as to what constitutes, for instance, justice or freedom. And in order to be good political philosophers, much the same is true. However, in politics, we do need to participate actively in a practice of civility. We have to regard each other as free and equal citizens, respect each other's rights, be willing to listen to each other's political claims, accept arguments that are better than ours, be responsive to each other's urgent political needs, yield to majority democratic decisions as long as they remain responsive to dissident views, and tolerate or even endure many of each other's peculiarities or even repugnant views.[34]

---

[33] See MacIntyre, *After Virtue*, passim.

[34] Russell Bentley and David Owen, 'Ethical Loyalties, Civic Virtue and the Circumstances of Politics', *Philosophical Explorations* IV (2001), 223-239; Bert van den Brink, 'Politischer Liberalismus und ziviler Perfektionismus', *Deutsche Zeitschrift für Philosophie*, 50 (2002), 907-924.

Again, in academic life, much the same is true. We have to regard each other from a presumption of equal competence, respect each other's academic freedoms, be willing to openly review the merits of each other's views, accept arguments that are better than ours, and find constructive and creative ways of dealing with our many disagreements about our profession and its subject matter. If we fall short of the willingness to engage in those practices in this way, we fall short of what, for both contexts, I would like to call an ethos of civility. Again, note that this does not imply that we need to agree with each other's exact understandings of *what it means* to recognize each other as free and equal citizens, or as academics working on the same kinds of questions. Our everyday practices show that what binds us is often not the circumstance that we are in total agreement on these things, but rather that we are in an ongoing debate about them.[35]

It is important to stress that, both in politics and in academia, deliberation over questions of common concern does not just occur because, as an ethical defence of dialogue would have it, it is good to be engaged in debate, or, as an aesthetic defence would hold, because there is beauty in keeping the conversation going. Although I think that there are compatible truths in these views, we should not forget that our ongoing conversations are primarily triggered by the practical circumstance that we are constantly in need of political and intellectual visions and institutional forms that can function, if only for a while, as the *unquestioned background* against which we try to increase our knowledge and improve our social practices. The circumstance that we cannot build our practices of doing political philosophy on a perspective of eternity does not imply that we can, for any given context, do without a firm background against which our debates take place at all. The difference with the perspective of eternity is that according to the situated view there is no ultimate foundation or anchor of practical reasoning in the unquestioned background, i.e. a foundation or an anchor that is itself beyond dispute. Rather, the unquestioned background – which may be a constitution, a moral theory, a political theory – is a necessary aspect of what Jeremy Waldron has aptly labelled the 'circumstances of politics': '... the felt need among the members of a certain group for a common framework or decision or course of action on some matter, even in the face of disagreement about what that decision or action should be...'[36]

---

[35] James Tully, 'The Agonic Freedom of Citizens', *Economy and Society* 28 (1999), 161-182, here pp. 170-171.

[36] Jeremy Waldron, *Law and Disagreement*, Oxford, Oxford University Press, 1999, p. 102.

Similarly, in political philosophy, we need dominant theories about power, democracy, freedom, citizenship, equality, etc., in order to structure and keep open the conversation about the best account of these values and practices. Under fair academic conditions, dominant theories will be convincing in many respects. However, they will hardly ever be uncontested. Furthermore, in fair academic conditions, their falsification will lead to their rejection as dominant theory or theories. Again, allowing disagreement to be a major force in a specific practice is not necessarily a sign of the weakness of that practice. Often – under conditions of civility as sketched above – it will rather be a sign of its strength, i.e. of its integrity as a practice that allows of open contestations over perspectives on the truth about facts and norms in a democratic society.

We may conclude that given these 'circumstances of political philosophy' an ethos of civility must be central to the ideal of doing political philosophy too. As a form of reflection on the irreducibly pluralistic, multifaceted, and contestatory practice of politics, political philosophy itself becomes an arena in which pluralistic, multifaceted, and contestatory debates about politics take place. Therefore, just as in political practice, the conduct of disagreement becomes a central aspect of the practice of political philosophy. Dogmatism is one answer to this. Engaging in political philosophy from a perspective of eternity is another. Both answers deny that the civil conduct of disagreement is a normal circumstance of the practice of political philosophy. Truthfulness and respect to theoretical opponents in the face of undecided philosophical debates demand that we introduce an undogmatic and situated dialogical ethics of civility into the ideal of doing political philosophy. Political philosophy is as much a political as it is a philosophical genre.

## 8. The Importance of Creativity

From the perspective of eternity – if it could be reached – one would hardly see anything new. Rather, one would see what has always been true about human interaction; one would see laws, principles, categorical imperatives, etc. Behind this lies the strange assumption that, ultimately, the normative core of human conduct can be captured in laws and principles carved out in stone. Yet, the competencies and virtues of great political figures are hardly ever described in such terms. Rather, they are described in terms of their originality, their creativity, their judgment, or their being in touch with the signs of the times, their recognizing the specific political challenges before them and their showing, in a brilliant and unexpected manner, the strength, the *virtu* needed to benefit the welfare of the polity. As we have noted earlier, although it is true that no polity can exist without laws, principles, and rules, their importance lies not at the level of foundations but at the level of the unquestioned authority – if only for a while – they bring in the face of disagreement. Against this background, the interpretative struggle among opponents with different political or indeed political philosophical views takes place. In this struggle, creativity, the bringing into debate of a new perspective on a debated issue, is a highly important moment. By testing – in an experimental, future-open mode – rules, procedures, routines, beliefs, traditions, and ideologies with respect to their adequacy to guide us through practical situations, we often stumble upon new ways of seeing and organizing things. This attests to what Hans Joas calls 'the creativity of action'.[37] With this term, he refers to the practical skill to see things differently, to judge not exclusively from familiar frameworks of perception and judgment, but to let human intelligence find, by means of social, political, cultural, legal, economic, and artistic experiments, new ways of looking at, dealing with, judging about, and understanding the world. The core of this approach is summarized in the following lengthy quotation from Joas – which echoes the spirit of American pragmatism by which it is inspired:

> … creativity is more than merely one of the necessities for the survival of an organism. A problem of action is not only given when the organism is in fundamental danger. Action constantly encounters unexpected obstacles: goals show themselves to be unattainable; simultaneously pursued goals prove to be mutually exclusive; attainable goals have doubts cast upon them by other actors. In these various crises of habitual action, the action situations have to be redefined in a new and different way. This involves defining that which is as yet undefined, rather than simply making a different selection from a reservoir of situation components that are already defined or have no need of definition. … [A]ction consists not in the pursuit of clear-cut goals or in the application of norms, and creativity is not the overcoming of obstacles along these prescribed routes. Anchoring creativity in action allows [us] to conceive of creativity precisely as the liberation of the capacity for new actions.[38]

Joas goes on to quote John Dewey, the originator of this aspect of pragmatist thought, on this:

> The pragmatic theory of intelligence means that the function of mind is to project new and more complex ends – to free experience from routine and from caprice. Not the use of thought to accomplish purposes already given either in the mechanism of the body or in that of the existent state of society,

---

[37] Hans Joas, *The Creativity of Action*, Chicago, University of Chicago Press, 1996.

[38] *Ibid.*, p. 133.

but the use of intelligence to liberate and liberalize action, is the pragmatic lesson.[39]

In Western political philosophy of the twentieth century, one can reconstruct a scattered counter-tradition to rule-oriented Enlightenment thought that constantly stresses this point. Central to the tradition is the idea that political freedom consists neither in the enjoyment of individual rights that protect one from unlawful interference by others, nor in following perfectly reasonable principles of practical reasoning or just procedures of democratic lawmaking, but in the capacity to question and, if necessary, go beyond the limits imposed on us by the many different mechanisms of social and political power that have made us into the subjects that we are. I put the point here in highly Foucaultian terms,[40] but the counter-tradition includes many others, for instance John Dewey, Theodor W. Adorno, Hannah Arendt, Jacques Derrida, Stanley Cavell, and James Tully. What unites these otherwise very different authors is that they all stand for a philosophical ethos that sees creativity, making a new beginning, learning to see things differently, raising a new voice *vis-à-vis* dominant practices of power and identity formation as the kernel of the political action and political freedom of individual citizens.

So next to an ethos of civility, stressing the importance of creativity, of trying to see things differently in order to possibly revise and change one's perspective, is central to the ideal of doing political philosophy I am sketching. The importance of this is not stressed for the value of creativity per se, but because experimentation, bringing new and uncertain perspectives to the world because they may help us cope better with practical problems before us, is a necessary element of human thought and action.

## 9. Hermeneutical Perspectivism

In engaging in political philosophy from a stance that aims to be both civilized and creative, the philosopher plays a particular role in the political community. This is a role of description, reconstruction, deconstruction, and recommendation with respect to all possible aspects of our political practices and our political theories that in some way cause

---

[39] John Dewey, 'The Need for a Recovery of Philosophy', in *The Essential John Dewey, Vol. 1 Pragmatism, Education, Democracy*, Bloomington and Indianapolis, Ind., Indiana University Press, 1998, pp. 46-70, p. 67.

[40] See Foucault, 'What Is Enlightenment?', and 'The Subject and Power', in Foucault, *Power: Essential Works of Foucault 1954-1984, Vol. 3*, ed. James D. Faubion, New York, New Press, 2000, pp. 326-349.

problems as to the felt needs and interests of members of the polity. Our political theories do not radically transcend our practices but are an integral part of them; they are a political genre, a certain way of thinking, speaking and acting with respect to political practices.

Because of this, engaging in political philosophy presupposes a certain modesty with regard to the more comprehensive, practice-transcending theoretical claims one might want to make in political debates. Since theoretical knowledge is born from practice and tends to originate in specific problematizations on the one hand and is hardly ever complete and will often tend to grow outdated on the other, the political philosopher will constantly be on the lookout for new and alternative perspectives on political issues that come from different and unexpected directions. Such perspectives – historical examples are perspectives born from the experience of subjugation by women, cultural minorities, etc. – will look at problems in different ways, contain alternative problematizations, interpretations of civility, creative solutions, and, undoubtedly, blind spots. Charles Taylor has recommended that, in encountering different perspectives, i.e. different practical and theoretical approaches to political questions, we should work from a hermeneutical 'presumption of equal worth',[41] so that we remain responsive to legitimate needs and interest that are threatened by current social and political relations. As Gadamer does, Taylor proposes to look at alternative perspectives as different but not necessarily less valuable ways of approaching practice. The point of stressing the importance of what I call hermeneutical perspectivism is one I have stressed before: if we look at practice from a theory that has forgotten about its initial situatedness in a concrete problematic and is now seen by many as an independent yardstick for the justification of social and political claims, then the unfamiliarity of new voices and new perspectives in political debate will often be mistaken for their unreasonableness.[42] The political claims of, for instance, indigenous peoples, representatives of immigrant cultures, and religious minorities may often rest on rhetorical strategies and notions of political power and rights that do not sit easily with mainstream Western liberal constitutionalism.[43] In itself, this is not sufficient reason for not taking them seriously. They can inform us about the often

---

[41]  Charles Taylor, 'The Politics of Recognition', in Amy Gutmann (ed.), *Multiculturalism*, Princeton, N.J., Princeton University Press, 1994, pp. 25-74; here pp. 66 ff.

[42]  See Bert van den Brink, *The Tragedy of Liberalism: An Alternative Defense of a Political Tradition*, Albany, N.Y., State University of New York Press, 2000; Bentley and Owen, 'Ethical Loyalties'.

[43]  See James Tully, *Strange Multiplicity: Constitutionalism in an Age of Diversity*, Cambridge, Cambridge University Press, 1995.

unintended or relatively invisible consequences of dominant modes of political thought and organization for various groups within society. For some of us, dominant political modes of thought and organization simply reinforce existing identities, for others they undermine or even destroy existing identities and replace them with something new. This may be for better or for worse. The political philosopher investigates such developments in the light of a set of political and philosophical values and orientations such as the one I have sketched thus far. None of the variables involved in this simple example, which could be further illustrated by looking at philosophical literature on multiculturalism, can be held steady all of the time, i.e. is beyond critique. A minority perspective and political claim may be reasonable or unreasonable in many of its aspects, and the same is true of claims from dominant political culture. As philosophers, we may see, think, and judge from values and beliefs that are or are not sound. The only way of testing this is by starting from our own prejudices and firm beliefs and confronting them with those of others. Theories that claim to build upon unshakable, eternal principles of practical reasoning will have a hard time at this. And that is probably why they are losing their relevance in contemporary debates in political theory. If we want to gain knowledge of relatively new or renewed, fiercely debated political phenomena like globalization, cosmopolitanism, multiculturalism, economic and political migration, anti-democratic terrorism, etc., then holding steady familiar ways of thinking about politics is not always the most productive way to proceed. The question is not whether the many life worlds in our societies are responsive to our abstract theories of practical reasoning. Rather, the question is whether our theories are responsive to the many different life worlds and modes of experiencing political reality in our societies.

## 10. On the Standards of Criticism

According to the ideal of doing political philosophy I have sketched, the critical standards against which aspects of problematic political practices are measured are not external to those practices. Critique is an aspect of any political practice that deserves that name. And hermeneutical perspectivism vehemently stresses that critique can take on many forms. We can criticize existing power relations by confronting them with a theory of justice or undistorted communication; we can also criticize it by giving a painfully detailed description of how power is being exercised over subjects; how subjectivity is being formed and subjugated; by confronting existing social and political forms with alternative forms that have existed in the course of history or which are coming into being through the creative use of action and language. The need for hermeneutical perspectivism to reject the perspective from eternity is born from the circumstance that this latter perspective is not flexible enough to acknowledge the multiplicity of ways in which both philosophical and political critique can be engaged in.

Still, it would be wrong to assume that hermeneutical perspectivism is interested in opening up new ways of thinking and acting just for the sake of plurality. A plurality of perspectives in society is not good in itself, but good insofar as it serves the needs of well-being of the subjects who are formed by and in their turn form the conditions under which they live. The well-being of the subject is the most important standard of criticism, but again it should be stressed that, informed as it is about the dangers of all-too-abstract philosophical approaches, hermeneutical perspectivism avoids thinking about the subject in a one-dimensional way. Indeed, hermeneutical perspectivism's openness to many different kinds of organizing political life vehemently denies that philosophers should repeat in theory what the exercise of political power has so often done in practice: force the plurality of social, ethical, and political perspectives in society in a monocultural form, thereby robbing many citizens of the opportunity to relate in their own civilized and creative manner to the sources of their identity and well-being. In the light of that insight, Stanley Cavell phrases the relevant question for political philosophy accurately: 'How do we attend to the strange multiplicity of political voices and activities without distorting or disqualifying them in the very way we approach them?'[44]

There is something more to be said about the type of subjectivity that hermeneutical perspectivism, despite its pluralism, has in mind. We might label it 'agonistic subjectivity'; a form of subjectivity that resists, in the name of the freedom to make a new beginning, to depart from pre-established rules and procedures of thought and action where this is necessary, its being captured in practices that do not test their own boundaries. The agonistic subject is the struggling subject, the subject that finds its dignity in testing and – where necessary criticizing and, together with other citizens, changing the social and political structures that codetermine its identity. In doing so, the agonistic subject at the same time tests its own social en political ideas and performance in a self-critical mode. In short, this notion of agonistic subjectivity, which I cannot look at in depth in this article,[45] is characterized by the same insight that guides hermeneutical perspectivism: because there can be no

---

[44] Stanley Cavell, *Conditions Handsome and Unhandsome*, Chicago, University of Chicago Press, 1990, pp. 101-126. Quoted from Tully, 'Political Philosophy', p. 537.

[45] See Tully, 'Agonic Freedom'; David Owen, *Nietzsche, Politics and Modernity*, London and Thousand Oaks, Sage, 1995; Van den Brink, 'Politischer Liberalismus'.

end to the process of making sense of our ever-changing social and political practices, which codetermine our identities as subjects, there can also be no end to the process of coming to terms with our own social and political ideas, performance, and desire for social and political freedom. The most important standard of criticism for hermeneutical perspectivism is given with the ideal of agonistic political freedom of the subject.

## 11. Conclusion

I have argued that if we want to understand what it means to engage in political philosophy, we may benefit from investigating the *ideals* of doing political philosophy that can be found in the field. My argument has been that such ideals do not just sketch pictures of deliberative excellence, but also tell a story about the way in which a political philosopher might approach the object of his studies: political life. I have looked at two such ideals. One is inspired by the idea of attaining philosophical knowledge from a perspective *sub specie aeternitatis*. The other is inspired by the idea of attaining philosophical knowledge from a hermeneutical perspective that is situated in place and time. I have tried to show how doubts as to the feasibility of the first model's understanding of the role of rules and procedures in theory construction as well as the application of rules and principles to practice may lead us to opt for the second model, which I have labelled *hermeneutical perspectivism.*

Hermeneutical perspectivism is an ideal of doing political philosophy that is broad enough to function as a model for various philosophical traditions on the one hand and narrow enough to evade the dangers of the approach *sub specie aeternitatis* on the other hand. Although it leaves room for disagreement over every philosophical issue, it is characterized by an argument for 1) acceptance of the value of civility in the conduct of philosophical disagreement, 2) acknowledgment of the role of creativity in human thought and action, 3) acknowledgment of the perspectival nature of philosophical knowledge as a reminder of the situatedness of this type of knowledge in specific problematics, and 4) defence of an agonistic understanding of subjectivity. Hermeneutical perspectivism reminds us of the circumstance that doing political philosophy is not just a technical matter of reaching valid conclusions to processes of deliberation, but of reaching such conclusions from a standpoint that is itself an ethical-political one. The substantive character of this political philosophical stance is both its strength and its weakness. On the one hand, its partiality to substantive interpretations of, for instance, the value of civility, enables it to develop a critical analysis of political practices that is developed from and remains tied to these practices. Such an approach is more flexible, more in tune with the many aspects of any political practice than a perspective of eternity could ever be. On the other hand, its being firmly tied to given traditions of interpretations within political communities makes it impossible to develop the truly general answers to classical questions of political philosophy that are so often expected to be the result of philosophical investigations, such as what is freedom?, what is equality?, what is solidarity?, etc. In order to gain the former advantage, it seems that hermeneutical perspectivism's way of approaching political practice has to accept that it has not much to offer in that latter kind of philosophical conversation. An investigation into the question whether that circumstance should be held against the sketched account of the ideal of doing political philosophy must wait for another occasion.

# References

Bentley, Russell, and David Owen, 'Ethical Loyalties, Civic Virtue and the Circumstances of Politics', *Philosophical Explorations* IV (2001), 223-239.

Berkowitz, Peter, *Virtue and the Making of Modern Liberalism*, Princeton, N.J., Princeton University Press, 1999.

Berlin, Isaiah, 'Two Concepts of Liberty', in Berlin, *Four Essays on Liberty*, Oxford, Oxford University Press, 1969, pp. 118-172.

Cavell, Stanley, *Conditions Handsome and Unhandsome*, Chicago, University of Chicago Press, 1990.

Dewey, John, 'The Need for a Recovery of Philosophy', in *The Essential John Dewey, Vol. 1 Pragmatism, Education, Democracy*, Bloomington and Indianapolis, Ind., Indiana University Press, 1998, pp. 46-70.

Foucault, Michel, 'What is Enlightenment?', in Foucault, *Ethics, Subjectivity and Truth*, ed. Paul Rabinow, New York, The New Press, 1997, pp. 303-320.

———, 'The Subject and Power', in Foucault, *Power: Essential Works of Foucault 1954-1984, Vol. 3*, ed. James D. Faubion, New York, New Press, 2000, pp. 326-349.

Gadamer, Hans-Georg, *Truth and Method*, 2nd rev. ed., New York, Continuum, 1989.

Habermas, Jürgen, *The Philosophical Discourse of Modernity*, tr. F. Lawrence, Oxford, Polity Press, 1987.

———, 'Philosophy as Stand-In and Interpreter', tr. Christian Lenhardt, in Habermas, *Moral Consciousness and Communicative Action*, Cambridge, Mass., MIT Press, 1987.

———, 'Morality and Ethical Life: Does Hegel's Critique of Kant Apply to Discourse Ethics?', in Habermas, *Moral Consciousness and Communicative Action*, tr. Christian Lenhardt and Shierry Weber Nicholson, Cambridge, Polity Press, 1990, pp. 195-215.

Joas, Hans, *The Creativity of Action*, Chicago, University of Chicago Press, 1996.

Kant, Immanuel, 'An Answer to the Question: What is Enlightenment?', in Kant, *Practical Philosophy*, ed. Allen Wood, tr. Mary J. Gregor, Cambridge, Cambridge University Press, 1996.

MacCarthy, Thomas, *The Critical Theory of Jürgen Habermas*, Cambridge, Polity Press, 1984.

MacIntyre, Alasdair, *After Virtue: A Study in Moral Theory*, Notre Dame, Ind., Notre Dame University Press, 1981.

Mill, John Stuart, *On Liberty*, in Mill, *On Liberty and Other Essays*, ed. John Gray, Oxford, Oxford University Press, 1991, pp. 5-128.

Mouffe, Chantal, 'Wittgenstein, Political Theory and Democracy', in Mouffe, *The Democratic Paradox*, London, Verso, 1989, pp. 60-79.

Nagel, Thomas, *The View from Nowhere*, New York, Oxford University Press, 1986.

Owen, David, *Nietzsche, Politics and Modernity*, London and Thousand Oaks, Sage, 1995.

————, 'Wittgenstein and Genealogy', *SATS: Nordic Journal of Philosophy* 2 (2001), 1-28.

Pettit, Philip, 'Freedom as Antipower', *Ethics* 106 (1996), 576-605.

Rawls, John, *A Theory of Justice*, Cambridge, Mass., Harvard University Press, 1971.

————, *Collected Papers*, ed. Samuel Freeman, Cambridge, Mass., Harvard University Press, 1999.

Rosati, Connie S., 'Ideals', in Edward Craig (ed.), *Routledge Encyclopedia of Philosophy, Vol. 4*, London [etc.], Routledge, 1998, p. 672.

Schmidt, James, 'What is Enlightenment? A Question, Its Context, and Some Consequences', in James Schmidt (ed.), *What is Enlightenment? Eighteenth-Century Answers and Twentieth-Century Questions*, Berkeley, University of California Press, 1996, pp. 1-44.

Taylor, Charles, 'The Politics of Recognition', in Amy Gutmann (ed.), *Multiculturalism*, Princeton, N.J., Princeton University Press, 1994, pp. 25-74.

Tully, James, 'Wittgenstein and Political Philosophy', *Political Theory* 17 (1989), 172-204.

————, *Strange Multiplicity: Constitutionalism in an Age of Diversity*, Cambridge, Cambridge University Press, 1995.

————, 'The Agonic Freedom of Citizens', *Economy and Society* 28 (1999), 161-182.

————, 'Political Philosophy as a Critical Activity', *Political Theory* 30 (2002), 533-555.

Van den Brink, Bert, *The Tragedy of Liberalism: An Alternative Defense of a Political Tradition*, Albany, N.Y., State University of New York Press, 2000.

————, 'Politischer Liberalismus und ziviler Perfektionismus', *Deutsche Zeitschrift für Philosophie*, 50 (2002), 907-924.

Waldron, Jeremy, *Law and Disagreement*, Oxford, Oxford University Press, 1999.

Walzer, Michael, *Spheres of Justice*, New York, Basic Books, 1989.

Warnke, Georgia, *Justice and Interpretation*, Cambridge, Mass., MIT Press, 1993.

Wittgenstein, Ludwig, *Philosophical Investigations*, Oxford, Oxford University Press, 1953.

# The Ideal of Equality
# in Political Philosophy

Roland PIERIK

## 1. Introduction

From all the disciplines in the humanities, political philosophy seems to be the natural home base for ideals. History provides us with several appealing examples: The French Revolution took place in the name of 'Liberty, Equality, and Fraternity', while Marxists were united under the slogan 'From each according to his ability, to each according to his needs'.[1] Of course, such ideals are never fully realizable. Nevertheless, they are essential notions in political philosophy because they enable us to extend '... what are ordinarily thought of as the limits of practical political possibility'.[2] As such, ideals provoke our imagination and function as guiding ideas in the transition from the status quo towards an ideal state of the world. Indeed, especially within political philosophy, ideals are helpful tools because they 'transcend concrete formulation and implementation by way of principles and rules, they are open to continuous reformulation in the light of new circumstances'.[3]

This chapter discusses the ideal of equality in political philosophy. Equality can be discussed at different levels of abstraction, following the distinction between 'concept' and 'conception'.[4] At a high level of abstraction, we refer to equality as a *concept*; at a lower level of abstract-

---

[1] Karl Marx, 'Critique of the Gotha Programme', in *Marx/Engels Selected Works in One Volume*, ed. Karl Marx and Friedrich Engels, London, Lawrence and Wishart, 1875, p. 321.

[2] John Rawls, *The Law of Peoples*, Cambridge, Mass., Harvard University Press, 1999, p. 6.

[3] Wibren van der Burg, 'The Importance of Ideals', *The Journal of Value Inquiry* 31 (1997), 23-37, p. 29.

[4] Ronald Dworkin, *Taking Rights Seriously*, London, Duckworth, 1977, pp. 134-136; John Rawls, *Political Liberalism*, New York, Columbia University Press, 1993, p. 14, n. 15; Wibren van der Burg, *Het democratisch perspectief: Een verkenning van de normatieve grondslagen der democratie*, Arnhem, Gouda Quint, 1991, p. 125.

tion, we refer to the *conception* of equality as a particular interpretation of that concept. As Dworkin explains: 'At the first level agreement collects around discrete ideas that are uncontroversially employed in all interpretations; at the second the controversy latent in this abstraction is identified and taken up.'[5] Concepts are phrased in such a high level of abstraction that possible disagreements about their interpretation and implementation are concealed. Only when they are made more concrete, that is, translated into conceptions, these disagreements come to the fore. Argued the other way around, two conceptions of justice that look different at first sight, might share one underlying concept. This is the line of thought that I shall follow in this paper, bridging two strands of thought in contemporary political philosophy: liberal egalitarianism and multiculturalism. Liberal egalitarianism focuses on welfare-state redistribution whereas multiculturalists focus on accommodation of social and cultural diversity. Although both strands of thought are dominant in contemporary political philosophy, there has been little cross-boundary public debate. They are generally seen as distinct paradigms, with different (and possibly contradicting) assumptions and methods – aptly summarized by Nancy Fraser as the dilemma between redistribution and recognition.[6] Although one of the classics in multiculturalism, Kymlicka's *Multicultural Citizenship*, is defended as *A Liberal Theory of Minority Rights*, liberals have not been too enthusiastic to allow multiculturalists in their midst.[7] Brian Barry, for example, claims: 'I have found that there is something approaching a consensus among those who do not write about it that the literature of multiculturalism is not worth wasting powder and shot on.'[8]

Instead, I shall argue that these two approaches have more in common than the liberal-egalitarian critics of multiculturalism, the 'doctrinaire liberals' like Barry, are willing to admit.[9] Moreover, I shall argue that an ideal-oriented approach enables us to find this shared basis. The concept of equality will be interpreted as an ideal that can bridge the

[5] Ronald Dworkin, *Law's Empire*, Cambridge, Mass., The Belknap Press, 1986, p. 71.

[6] Nancy Fraser, 'From Redistribution to Recognition? Dilemmas of Justice in a "Post-Socialist" Age', *New Left Review* 212 (1995), 68-93.

[7] Will Kymlicka, *Multicultural Citizenship: A Liberal Theory of Minority Rights*, Oxford, Oxford University Press, 1995.

[8] Brian Barry, *Culture and Equality: An Egalitarian Critique of Multiculturalism*, Cambridge, Mass., Harvard University Press, 2001, p. 6.

[9] Cf. the title of David Miller's review of Barry's book, 'Doctrinaire Liberalism versus Multicultural Democracy: Review of Brian Barry's *Culture and Equality*', *Ethnicities* 2 (2002) 2, 261-265.

divide between adversaries in this political-philosophical debate.[10] Both approaches share the concept of equality as the underlying ideal and they can be seen as consistent, equivalent, and non-conflicting conceptions thereof.

## 2. The Liberal Concept of Equality: Equal Respect and Concern

We can find a first formulation of the concept of equality in Ronald Dworkin's work, namely his 'abstract egalitarian claim':

> I presume that we all accept the following postulates of political morality. Government must treat those whom it governs with concern, that is, as human beings who are capable of suffering and frustration, and with respect, that is, as human beings who are capable of forming and acting on intelligent conceptions of how their lives should be lived. Government must not only treat people with concern and respect, but with equal concern and respect.[11]

This claim sums up three important elements of Dworkin's approach. Firstly, *moral individualism*. In our evaluation of government and its institutions, we should only focus on the interests of the members of the community.[12] Only persons are seen as 'ends in themselves' unlike, e.g. tradition, the family, tribe, or ethnic, cultural, or religious communities. Secondly, *impartiality*. From a moral point of view, there are no privileged persons: everyone's life has the same value.[13] Therefore, each individual's interests are equally important in our evaluation of institutions. Finally, Dworkin focuses on the role of government: the abstract egalitarian claim starts from the standpoint of *politics*. Government has an important role in providing the basic conditions necessary for the well-being of its citizens: '[E]quality, as a political virtue, demands... not only an attitude, but concrete institutions.'[14]

---

[10]  Wibren van der Burg and Sanne Taekema, 'Introduction' to this volume.

[11]  Dworkin, *Taking Rights Seriously*, pp. 272-273.

[12]  Ronald Dworkin, *Sovereign Virtue: The Theory and Practice of Equality*, Cambridge, Mass., Harvard University Press, 2000, p. 5.

[13]  James Rachels, *The Elements of Moral Philosophy*, 4th ed., New York [etc.], McGraw-Hill, 2003, p. 13.

[14]  Ronald Dworkin, 'Do Liberty and Equality Conflict?', in Paul Barker (ed.), *Living as Equals*, Oxford, Oxford University Press, 1996, pp. 39-57, at p. 44.

## 3. A First Conception of Equality: Equality of Resources

From 1981 onwards, Ronald Dworkin published four articles under the title 'What Is Equality?', which have become classics in the literature on distributive justice. They are reprinted as the first four chapters of *Sovereign Virtue*. Dworkin provides a defence of the welfare state, and his work has generated a rich literature on economic justice.[15] Besides the abstract concept of equality – the abstract egalitarian claim – his work on redistributive justice also gives a conception thereof, namely equality of resources.

Dworkin develops his theory of distributive justice from a counterfactual example, an imaginary story in which a group of people is shipwrecked on a desert island with abundant resources. Dworkin seeks to demonstrate the role and effects of the abstract egalitarian claim in a 'state of nature', a situation in which immigrants have to make decisions about the design of their societal institutions. This detour via 'ideal theory' is a common element in political philosophy.[16] The idea is that one has to abstract from concrete situations in society to be able to formulate principles of justice. One starts by describing a hypothetical situation in which contingent and unjust institutional heritages of our actual world do not exist (e.g. accumulation of wealth in specific families, history of slavery, the feudal system). Moreover, other interfering issues of injustice are removed to focus only on the issue at hand. Such abstractions '... are justified only because they enable us to focus on certain main questions free from distracting details'.[17] Moreover, ideal theory can help us to formulate the line of action we should undertake, given the ideals we are committed to. Any observation of a gap between our ideals and political practice should not be seen as a critique of our ideals to be 'unduly demanding in practice'; instead, it should be seen as 'a critique of our practice as insufficiently attentive to our principles'.[18]

Once the 'principles of justice' have been formulated in this ideal situation, they are used as criteria in our evaluation of justice in the real world. Ideal theory should 'provide some guidance in thinking about

---

[15] It is therefore important to distinguish Dworkin's work and reputation in jurisprudence from his work and reputation in political philosophy – especially in the field of distributive justice. Here Dworkin inspired G.A. Cohen, John Roemer, Eric Rakowski, Richard Arneson, Derek Parfit, and Philippe van Parijs, to name a few.

[16] Of course, Thomas More's *Utopia* and John Rawls's *Veil of Ignorance* are the most notorious examples of the use of ideal theory in political philosophy.

[17] Rawls, *Political Liberalism*, p. 12.

[18] Quentin Skinner, *Liberty before Liberalism*, Cambridge, Cambridge University Press, 1998, p. 79.

non-ideal theory, and so about difficult cases of how to deal with existing injustices. It should also help to clarify the goal of reform and to identify which wrongs are more grievous and hence more urgent to correct.'[19] The inherent hypothetical character of ideal theory is not a disqualifier by default.

Dworkin assumes that the shipwrecked people on the utopian island agree that 'no one is antecedently entitled to any of these resources, but that they shall instead be divided equally among them'.[20] Their deliberation proceeds in two steps. The first contains an auction in which the resources available on the island (ground, animals, etc.) are divided equally amongst the shipwrecked.[21] In the second stage, institutions are developed to preserve this equal distribution of resources in a dynamic economy with labour, investment, and trade.[22] Dworkin asserts that the deliberations of the immigrants will result in a rule of fair distribution, which he summarizes as follows:

> [W]e must... recognize that the requirements of equality pull in opposite directions. On the one hand we must... allow the distribution of resources at any particular moment to be (as we might say) ambition-sensitive. It must, that is, reflect the cost or benefit to others of the choices people make so that, for example, those who choose to invest rather than consume, or to consume less expensively rather than more, or to work in more rather than less profitable ways, must be permitted to retain the gains that flow from these decisions in an equal auction followed by free trade. But on the other hand, we must not allow the distribution of resources at any moment to be endowment-sensitive, that is, to be affected by differences in ability of the sort that produce income differences in a laissez-faire economy among people with the same ambitions.[23]

This formulation exemplifies again Dworkin's statocentric approach. Since a distribution of resources in a *laissez-faire* society is not choice sensitive and endowment insensitive by default, the implicit argument here is that the ideal of equality presupposes a clear role for government. The government should aim at a choice-sensitive distribution of resources, for example by supporting personal autonomy, fighting monopolies, and drawing up anti-trust laws.[24] Moreover, it should strive for

---

[19] John Rawls, *Justice as Fairness: A Restatement*, ed. Erin Kelly, Cambridge, Mass., Harvard University Press, 2001, p. 13.

[20] Dworkin, *Sovereign Virtue*, pp. 66-67.

[21] *Ibid.*, pp. 65-71.

[22] *Ibid.*, pp. 66-67.

[23] *Ibid.*, p. 89.

[24] *Ibid.*, ch. 3.

endowment insensitivity of the distribution of resources. Dworkin focuses on two unchosen endowments in particular: handicaps and lack of talents. His redistributive approach focuses on the limited individual earning capacities resulting from these endowments. To this effect, Dworkin proposes a 'periodic redistribution of resources through some form of income tax'.[25] Moreover, this formulation of the conception of equality is entirely phrased in terms of distribution of resources; it is essentially a theory of distributive or economic equality.[26] Dworkin simply takes for granted that justice requires the equal distribution of *something.*[27] 'Our final aim is that an equal share of resources [is] devoted to the lives of each person.'[28] Dworkin's preoccupation with distributive justice can be understood in the light of the circumstance that the paper was written in the mid-1970s, as a defence of welfare-state arrangements against attacks inspired by libertarians.[29] As a result, Dworkin's theory is (generally interpreted as) primarily a defence of distributive justice. However, as I shall argue, distributive justice is only one interpretation of and is anchored in the more general ideal of equality.

## 4. A Reformulation of the Liberal Concept of Equality

I have described Dworkin's work in terms of a concept of equality – claiming that government should treat its citizens with equal respect and concern and a conception thereof – his assertion that government should strive for a distribution of resources in society is both choice sensitive and endowment insensitive. Although the maxim of equal respect and concern is clear in its intention, it does not give much direction.[30] In this section I will reformulate the concept of equality by including elements of its conception as presented in section 3, without also including its distributive focus. The concept of equality can be formulated as follows:

> Inequalities in the advantages people enjoy due to choices about the good life are seen as part of the personal autonomy and responsibility and there-fore morally legitimate. Inequalities in the advantages people enjoy that de-rive from unchosen features of their endowments are seen as morally arbi-

---

[25] *Ibid.*, pp. 90-91; see also pp. 92-109.

[26] Dworkin, *Taking Rights Seriously*, p. 135.

[27] Samuel Scheffler, 'What Is Egalitarianism?', paper presented at the *Centre for Politics, Law, and Society Seminar Series*, University College London, 23 January 2002, p. 11.

[28] Dworkin, *Sovereign Virtue*, pp. 84-85.

[29] E.g. Robert Nozick, *Anarchy, State and Utopia*, New York, Basic Books, 1974.

[30] Dworkin, *Taking Rights Seriously*, p. 135.

trary and therefore generate a responsibility for government to remedy this inequality.

The assertion that government should distinguish in its policies between choice sensitivity and endowment insensitivity is implicit in the abstract egalitarian claim, given the emphasis on respect *and* concern. The idea that government should treat citizens with *equal respect* demands that choice involves personal responsibility. Government should respect the autonomy of individuals and therefore not interfere with personal preferences or ambitions by force or manipulation. As a result, persons themselves are responsible for (the formation of) their aims, ambitions, and decisions and, therefore, the consequences thereof. Therefore, equal respect implies that government should make a big effort to ensure that citizens bear the true costs and benefits of their choices and decisions.

The idea that government should treat citizens with *equal concern* demands that endowments induce collective responsibility. In the case of endowments, there is no moment at which a person, through choosing, can make a difference; instead, endowments simply involve brute bad luck. The concept of equality demands that government has a duty to act to compensate adverse consequences of unchosen endowments – e.g. limited individual earning capacities resulting from handicaps or lack of talent. Of course, not every inequality can be rectified, or only at too high a cost. The paradigmatic example is the forced transfer of body parts, e.g. when a sighted person has to donate one eye to a blind person. In this case, the remedy is seen as worse than the disease because it wrongfully interferes with the bodily integrity of the sighted person.

In this way, the abstract egalitarian claim implies a division of responsibility between individuals and government. It is a formulation of equality as an ideal: it is a 'value that is never completely realizable',[31] because it is a 'compromise of two conflicting requirements of equality, in the face of both practical and conceptual uncertainty how to satisfy these requirements'.[32] Moreover, this ideal of equality plays 'a role in justifying decisions and opinions', since it is the background against which equality of resources is defended.[33]

Moreover, this formulation of the ideal of equality is a concept in the concept/conception distinction as described in the introduction to this

---

[31] Van der Burg and Taekema, 'Introduction' to this volume.
[32] Dworkin, *Sovereign Virtue*, p. 91.
[33] Van der Burg and Taekema, 'Introduction' to this volume.

chapter, because it is abstract enough to generate general support.[34] 'The best, perhaps the only, argument for the egalitarian principle lies in the implausibility of denying any of the components that make it up...'[35] Indeed, only racists might be capable of doing so.[36]

## 5. Is Socioeconomic Distribution the Only Valid Conception of Equality?

The importance of the conceptual contribution by liberal-egalitarians to distributive justice is undisputed. However, they have been criticized for limiting the ideal of equal respect and concern to this narrow scope of distributive justice. Doing so, they ignored many issues central in current political debates, such as social and cultural diversity and multiculturalism. Iris Marion Young claims that, although '... distributive issues are crucial to a satisfactory conception of justice, ... it is a mistake to reduce social justice to redistribution'.[37] Elisabeth Anderson claims that Dworkin and other liberal-egalitarians neglect 'the much broader agendas of actual egalitarian political movements' discussing, for example, racial and gender inequality, etc. Therefore, she claims that they have a flawed understanding of equality and precisely miss 'the point of equality'.[38] Kymlicka argues that most countries today are culturally diverse and that this diversity gives rise to a series of important and potentially divisive questions. 'Finding morally defensible and politically viable answers to these issues is the greatest challenge facing democracies today.'[39] However, this challenge is not answered by contemporary liberal egalitarians, because they 'have operated with an idealized model of the polis in which fellow citizens share a common

---

[34] Will Kymlicka uses the abstract egalitarian claim as the founding idea of his textbook on contemporary political philosophy; Will Kymlicka, *Contemporary Political Philosophy: An Introduction*, 2nd ed., Oxford, Oxford University Press, 2002, ch. 1, esp. pp. 3-4. It should be seen as an egalitarian plateau against which differential theories can be compared. Libertarians, e.g., could argue that the interests of the members of society are best guaranteed by an extensive interpretation of equal self-ownership rights.

[35] Ronald Dworkin, 'In Defense of Equality', *Social Philosophy and Policy* 1 (1983) 1, 24-40, p. 32.

[36] But, again, racists presuppose equality amongst 'whites' and 'blacks', so even racists cannot escape the egalitarian logic.

[37] Iris Marion Young, *Justice and the Politics of Difference*, Princeton, N.J., Princeton University Press, 1990, p. 15.

[38] Elisabeth Anderson, 'What Is the Point of Equality?', *Ethics* 109 (1999), 287-337, at p. 288.

[39] Kymlicka, *Multicultural Citizenship*, p. 1.

descent, language, and culture'. Moreover, they seem to assume that 'the culturally homogeneous city-states of Ancient Greece provided the essential or standard model of a political community'.[40] Indeed, the issue of distributive justice has dominated current liberal egalitarianism whereas the issue of cultural diversity has long been ignored. I agree with Samuel Scheffler's conclusion that:

> [U]nless the relations between distributive norms and broader ideals of equality are kept firmly in view, the putatively artificial device of treating distributive equality as an independent topic can all too easily take on a life of its own, and the inquiry can lose touch with what is ultimately at stake when questions of distribution are debated. The trajectory of the luck-egalitarian literature over the years seems to me to provide a clear illustration of this danger.[41]

Socioeconomic redistribution has dominated liberal egalitarianism while other conceptions of equality have been ignored. Multiculturalism, for example, has also been an important strand in political philosophy, but was excluded from the egalitarian circle. One may doubt whether this exclusive attitude by luck egalitarians is justified. Dworkin explicitly acknowledges that distributive equality 'is only one aspect of the more general problem of equality, because it sets aside a variety of issues that might be called, by way of contrast, issues about political equality'.[42] He also argues that:

> Distributional equality, as I describe it, is not concerned with the distribution of political power, for example, or with individual rights other than rights to some amount or share of resources. It is obvious, I think, that these questions I throw together under the label of political equality are not so independent from issues of distributional equality as the distinction might suggest... But it nevertheless seems likely that a full theory of equality, embracing a range of issues including political and distributional equality, is best approached by *accepting initial, even though somewhat arbitrary, distinctions among these issues.*[43]

The application of the abstract egalitarian claim in the imaginary story of the shipwrecked is a helpful ideal-theoretical tool to illustrate the intuitive strength of the choice/endowment distinction. In this hypothetical society, Dworkin tailors his cases and argues from trivial examples. This enables him to demonstrate the logic of the choice/endowment distinction. In his examples, the endowment element is so evident

---

[40]  *Ibid.*, p. 2.
[41]  Scheffler, 'What Is Egalitarianism?', pp. 25-26.
[42]  Dworkin, *Sovereign Virtue*, p. 12.
[43]  *Ibid.*, p. 12 (emphasis added).

that the choice element is locked out and vice versa. So, equality of resources is not a set of first principles. Instead, it is one conception of equality, an important one, that is also used as an example to spell out the more general concept of equality.[44]

Brian Barry, on the other hand, is convinced that equality and multiculturalism have nothing in common. He argues that multiculturalism takes away the attention from the really important issue, namely socioeconomic inequalities.[45] He warns us that the 'whole thrust' of multiculturalism is '... that it seeks to withdraw from individual members of minority groups the protections that are normally offered by liberal states'.[46] And indeed, some multicultural claims might be focused on cultures themselves and may therefore be inconsistent with moral individualism.[47] But, as I will argue in the next section, there is no *intrinsic* incompatibility between multiculturalism and liberal egalitarianism.

# 6. Multiculturalism as a Second Conception of Equality

Dworkin simplified the examples in the 'fable of the shipwrecked' to clarify the choice/circumstance distinction. However, outside ideal theory, and especially in the context of multicultural societies, the choice/endowment distinction, which is so clear in ideal theory, gets blurred. I will discuss the notions of the choice and endowment concepts in turn.

## 6.1 Reconsidering Endowments

Iris Marion Young argues that liberal-egalitarians have focused too much on the question *what* should be distributed equally – resources, welfare, opportunities for welfare, access to advantage, etc.[48] The result is that liberals neglected the flip side of the egalitarian coin, namely, the question of *equality of whom*. If we claim that people should be treated with equal respect and concern, what categories or groups of people are we discussing? Precisely this question, ignored by liberal egalitarians, is central to many actual political debates in multiculturalism. These

---

[44] Scheffler, 'What Is Egalitarianism?', p. 25.

[45] Barry, *Culture and Equality*, pp. 63-64.

[46] *Ibid.*, p. 326.

[47] Examples are Charles Taylor, 'The Politics of Recognition', in Amy Gutmann (ed.), *Multiculturalism and the Politics of Recognition*, Princeton, N.J., Princeton University Press, 1994, pp. 25-73; Avishai Margalit and Moshe Halbertal, 'Liberalism and the Right to Culture', *Social Research* 61 (1994) 3, 491-510.

[48] Iris Marion Young, 'Equality of Whom? Social Groups and Judgments of Injustice', *The Journal of Political Philosophy* 9 (2001) 1, 1-18.

debates start by comparing actual social and cultural groups: women and men, whites and people of colour, members of minority and majority religious groups, etc. In these discussions, the language of the redistribution of resources is not very helpful. Young seeks to provide an alternative approach and therefore she focuses on the question '… whether and how such group-conscious practices of assessing inequality are justified'.[49]

In her evaluation of liberal-egalitarians, Young focuses on the individualistic character of their approach. On the one hand she endorses the statement that 'the ultimate purpose of making assessments of inequality is to promote the well-being of individuals considered as irreducible moral equals'.[50] That is, she shares liberal-egalitarian moral individualism (see section 2). Moreover, she endorses the intuitions as regards endowments and choices as conceptualized in the ideal of equality and the importance of their distinction in a normative framework.[51]

However, she criticizes liberal-egalitarian methodological individualism, that is, the claim that only individual choices and endowments can cause morally relevant inequalities. Indeed, Dworkin's conceptualization of endowment is very individualistic, concentrating only on physical and mental characteristics of the person: physical and mental powers, genetic predisposition to particular diseases, and personal resources of health, strength, and talent.[52] For this reason, we could call them natural endowments. Young argues that many other instances of injustice cannot be understood if one only focuses on individual attributes such as a person's handicaps. 'Instead, the causes of many inequalities of resources or opportunities among individuals lie in social institutions, their rules and relations, and the decisions others make within them that affect the lives of the individuals compared.'[53] Evaluating inequality in terms of social groups enables us to claim that some situations are unjust, although they cannot be recognized as unjust in the framework of distributive justice. Also Kymlicka argues that since no one *chooses* to be born in a minority culture, the choice/endowment logic demands that they should somehow be seen as an endowment. Therefore, the

---

[49]   *Ibid.*, p. 1.

[50]   *Ibid.*, p. 6.

[51]   *Ibid.*, pp. 6-8.

[52]   Dworkin, *Sovereign Virtue*, pp. 81, 287 and 322.

[53]   Young, 'Equality of Whom?', p. 8.

concept of endowments should not only include natural endowments but also elements of one's social environment.[54]

Group-based evaluations are helpful because they reveal inegalitarian effects of institutional relations and processes in society.[55] To acknowledge these (inegalitarian) effects of institutions, we have to understand social mechanisms and social structures. Social mechanisms are well-established and recurring patterns of behaviour in society.[56] The working of social mechanisms cannot be reduced to discernable individuals and their considerations and preferences. Instead, it must be understood in terms of interpersonal processes, conventions, social norms, and herding. Over time, these social mechanisms have resulted in social structures. A social structure can be described as the way in which social life is organized into predictable relationships and patterns of social interaction – including social positions and the related status and role differentiation between them. Social structures are the inevitable result of living together and social cooperation. Results of social structures are social institutions such as the educational system, the welfare state, legal, economic, and political institutions, and the geographical layout of cities. The complex of social structures in society can be brought together under the name of basic structure of society.

The options and possibilities available to individuals are not only determined by their natural endowments – as discussed by liberal-egalitarians – but also by the way society is organized. John Rawls argues that the basic structure of society

> ... contains various social positions and... men born into different positions have different expectations of life determined, in part, by the political system as well as by economic and social circumstances. In this way the institutions of society favor certain starting places over others. These are especially deep inequalities. Not only are they pervasive, but they affect men's initial chances in life.[57]

Rawls mainly focuses on socioeconomic inequalities between classes, whereas multiculturalists broaden the analysis to group differen-

---

[54]   Will Kymlicka, *Liberalism, Community, and Culture*, Oxford, Clarendon Press, 1989, pp. 186-188. In this book, Kymlicka attempts to defend attention for cultural difference by adjusting Dworkin's model of the shipwrecked immigrants in such a way that not one but two – culturally different – groups of shipwrecked arrive at the island simultaneously. See also pp. 192-194.

[55]   Young, 'Equality of Whom?', p. 2.

[56]   Although they do not necessarily have a law-like causal necessity.

[57]   John Rawls, *A Theory of Justice*, rev. ed., Oxford, Oxford University Press, 1999, p. 7.

tiations of gender, ethnicity, sexual preference, and other 'ascribed characteristics that historically served as markers of inferiority and exclusion. ... Categories such as these name groups [that] are positioned by social structures that constrain and enable lives in a way that is largely beyond their individual control.'[58] These inequalities are caused by social mechanisms and social structures and are structural inequalities because '[t]hey describe a set of relationships among assumptions and stereotypes, institutional policies, individual actions following rules or choosing in self-interest, and collective consequences of these things, which constrain the options of some at the same time as they expand the options of others.'[59]

The resulting inequalities are not reducible to individual characteristics, since they typically affect individuals *because* they are members of a specific group. They 'are positioned by social structures that constrain and enable individual lives beyond their individual control'.[60] Understanding behaviour in terms of social mechanisms reveals that 'people themselves treat others as group members, and that the product of many such actions sometimes results in structural inequalities'.[61] Social structures make that individuals, 'despite any good intentions they might have, act and react in a way that has the aggregate effect of structural inequality'.[62]

So, besides inequalities caused by natural endowments, such as handicaps and lack of talent, we can identify inequality caused by what we could call societal endowments.[63] They are called societal endowments because someone's gender, colour of skin, etc., are unchosen elements of one's being that affect one's options and chances. A societal endowment does not *in itself* determine someone's life inescapably, in the way natural endowments do – e.g. the inability to see. Societal endowments affect the situation of persons via 'social structures that involuntarily position people, constraining some more than others and privileging some more than others'.[64]

---

[58]  Young, 'Equality of Whom?', pp. 4, 6.

[59]  *Ibid.*, p. 11.

[60]  *Ibid.*, p. 6.

[61]  *Ibid.*, p. 17.

[62]  *Ibid.*, p. 9.

[63]  The terms 'natural endowments' and 'societal endowments' are developed in Roland Pierik and Ingrid Robeyns, 'Dworkin on Sen: On the Role of Social Mechanisms in Egalitarian Theory', mimeo, 2001.

[64]  Young, 'Equality of Whom?', p. 7.

This implies that it is very well possible for multiculturalists to start from the ideal of equality and embrace the idea that endowments generate morally relevant inequalities. But they do not use the detour of ideal theory; instead they focus on real-life issues of injustice and broaden the concept of morally relevant endowments, by also acknowledging societal endowments. However, societal endowments are less easy to recognize. Dworkin restricts himself to useful and clear-cut examples of endowments, and his ideal-theoretical approach enables him to argue in a clear deductive cause/effect logic: endowments cause inequality. Once we have discovered the morally relevant endowments, we can identify the correlating categories of persons between whom government should redistribute resources. However, societal endowments cannot be explained in such a straightforward cause/effect logic. Although we can observe clear differential positions of social groups in society – for example, between men and women or people of colour and whites – it is less obvious to recognize the cause of that inequality, and whether this cause is a choice or an endowment. This is not a distinction of strong and weak theories, but a result of differences between ideal theory – deliberately excluding ambiguous cases – and non-ideal theories for the real world. As mentioned above, Dworkin tailored his cases to exemplify the logic of the ideal of equality.

In itself, there is nothing wrong with (starting with) straightforward examples: usually they are the best illustrations of a theoretical position. The multicultural analysis, however, goes one step further, by using the liberal-egalitarian ideal-theoretical framework to evaluate less straightforward cases. In these cases we need an inductive method and arguing in an inverse logic: from an evident result, namely inequalities, to possible causes, namely societal endowments. To be sure that these inequalities are morally relevant, we have to formulate some requirements to confirm that they are really caused by unchosen societal endowments.[65] Firstly, it should be observable that a specific category of individuals is unequal to others on certain important measures of well-being. The groups evaluated should be 'generally recognized social positions' in the basic structure of society. Second, we need to give a plausible explanation for the observed inequality in terms of societal endowments, 'about how the relations, rules, expectations, and cumulative consequences of collective action specifically condition the lives of that group.' Finally, we need a plausible explanation of the way in which the social mechanisms and the social structures account for observed inequalities.

---

[65] *Ibid.*, pp. 15-16.

We must explain how institutional rules and policies, individual actions and interactions, and the cumulative collective and often unintended material effects of these relations reinforce one another in ways that restrict the opportunities of some to achieve well-being in the respect measured, while it does not so restrict that of the others to whom they are compared, or even enlarge their opportunities. This story will be aided, moreover, by evidence that the basic configuration of the patterns shows little change over decades.[66]

Let me conclude. In section 4, I formulated the endowment part of the ideal of equality as follows: Inequalities in the advantages people enjoy that derive from unchosen features of their endowments are seen as morally arbitrary and therefore generate a responsibility for government to remedy this inequality. Besides morally relevant inequalities generated by natural endowments as discussed by liberal egalitarians, in multicultural societies we may also encounter morally relevant inequalities generated by societal endowments. The latter are unchosen features of a person's circumstances too and are in line with the concept of equality as presented in section 3.

## 6.2 Reconsidering Choices

In section 4, we saw that the notion of equal respect is strongly connected to choice. It was argued that government should respect personal autonomy and not interfere with the relations between preferences, ideas about the good life, the successive choices made, and the effects of these choices. Although choice is an important element in Dworkin's theory, the concept itself is hardly elaborated. It can be described in three features.[67] First, choosing requires a choice set: a number of options (at least two) from which to choose. Secondly, choosing depends on preferences: '... comparative evaluative attitudes that permit the agent to rank the various elements in the choice-set in terms of their relative desirability.' Thirdly, choosing consists in a selection process: ranking the options and picking out the most preferred option.[68]

---

[66] *Ibid.*, p. 16.

[67] Meir Dan-Cohen, 'Conceptions of Choice and Conceptions of Autonomy', *Ethics* 102 (1992), 221-243, at p. 222; John Rawls, *A Theory of Justice*, Oxford, Oxford University Press, 1971, p. 124.

[68] Dan-Cohen also describes a fourth feature: 'Finally, choosing involves opportunity costs, roughly, the value to the agent of the opportunities forgone in favor of the selected option'; Dan-Cohen, 'Conceptions of Choice', p. 221. This element is less important for our discussion because it is not an element of the process of choosing, but a result of that process.

In ideal theory, individual choice is – by default – unproblematic. However, the capacity to make choices in a rational and informed way is not innate; it has to be developed in the course of one's upbringing and education. This raises questions of social and cultural preconditions of choice, which are dealt with in Will Kymlicka's *Multicultural Citizenship*. His aim is 'to show that the liberal value of freedom of choice has certain cultural preconditions, and hence that issues of cultural membership must be incorporated into liberal principles'.[69] The theoretical background against which Kymlicka develops his *Liberal Theory of Minority Rights* is liberal egalitarianism, as defended by Dworkin and Rawls.[70] Moreover, he endorses the choice/endowment distinction as described by Dworkin and formulated here as the ideal of equality.[71]

To what extent are choice and culture related? 'Put simply, freedom involves making choices amongst various options, and our societal culture not only provides these options, but also makes them meaningful to us.'[72] Individuals make choices on the basis of their preferences: beliefs about the value of several options. But where do these beliefs come from? The freedom of choice is not 'free-floating in the void', Kymlicka states. 'To have a belief about the value of a practice is, in the first instance, a matter of understanding the meaning attached to it by our culture.'[73] And: 'The availability of meaningful options depends on access to a societal culture, and on understanding the history and language of that culture – its "shared vocabulary of tradition and convention".'[74] So both individual preferences and the selection process are influenced by upbringing and socialization in a societal culture, defined by Kymlicka as: 'A culture which provides its members with meaningful ways of life across the full range of human activities, including social, educational, religious, recreational, and economic life, encompassing both public and private spheres. These cultures tend to be territorially-concentrated, and based on a shared language.'[75] This societal culture serves as the context of individual choice, and therefore provides the institutional background for individual freedom of choice.

---

[69] Kymlicka, *Multicultural Citizenship*, p. 76.

[70] *Ibid.*, ch. 5.

[71] Kymlicka, *Liberalism, Community, and Culture*, pp. 38, 186; *Multicultural Citizenship*, ch. 5, esp. pp. 80-82; *Contemporary Political Philosophy*, ch. 4.

[72] Kymlicka, *Multicultural Citizenship*, p. 83.

[73] *Ibid.*, p. 76, referring to Dworkin.

[74] *Ibid.*, p. 83, referring to Dworkin.

[75] *Ibid.*, p. 76.

Liberal-egalitarians do not disagree here.[76] Dworkin, for example, argues that culture 'provides the spectacles through which we identify experiences as valuable',[77] and, therefore, '[w]e inherited a cultural structure, and we have some duty, out of simple justice, to leave that structure at least as rich as we found it.'[78] Kymlicka and Dworkin disagree, however, about the question whether this societal culture is equally available. Dworkin assumes the borders of the societal culture overlap with the borders of nation states. He tends to think of culture as a kind of societal 'public good' – important but equally available to all members of society, and therefore unproblematic from an egalitarian point of view. Dworkin never makes this assumption explicitly, but it seems implicit throughout his work, and this could explain why he never discusses the potential for inequality stemming from cultural differences. It is reflected in several passing references he makes to citizens sharing a common language and culture, having 'a shared vocabulary of tradition and convention'.[79] He also suggests that the United States contains a single 'cultural structure' based on and related to a 'shared language'.[80] Kymlicka emphasizes the multicultural character of contemporary liberal democratic societies. He distinguishes two main sources of cultural diversity. The first is multi-nationality, which refers to the coexistence of more than one nation within a state, where 'nation' means a historical community more or less institutionally complete, occupying a given territory or homeland, sharing a distinct language and culture.[81] Examples of multi-national states are Belgium (inhabited by Walloons, Flemish, and a small German nation) and, of course, Canada (inhabited by an Anglophone and a Francophone nation, and indigenous groups). The second form of cultural diversity is poly-ethnicity, which refers to a diversity in society as a result of immigration of individuals and families from other states (and cultures) and who are allowed 'to maintain some of their ethnic particularity'.[82] Examples of immigration countries are Canada, the United States, and Australia. Described this way, states can be both multi-national and poly-ethnic – as for example Canada is.

---

[76] Dworkin discusses this subject in 'Liberal Community', *California Law Review* 77 (1989) 3, 479-504, and 'Can a Liberal State Support Art?', in *A Matter of Principle*, Cambridge, Mass., Harvard University Press, 1985, pp. 221-233.

[77] Dworkin, 'Can a Liberal State Support Art?', p. 228.

[78] *Ibid.*, pp. 232-233.

[79] *Ibid.*, p. 231.

[80] *Ibid.*, pp. 231-233; Dworkin, 'Liberal Community', p. 488.

[81] Kymlicka, *Multicultural Citizenship*, p. 11.

[82] *Ibid.*, p. 14.

Culture as a context of choice is not a matter of course for national minorities and ethnic minorities. Kymlicka asserts that governments should support national minorities which seek to preserve their distinct societal culture and support ethnic groups that seek to integrate into the dominant societal culture of their new state, while maintaining their ethnic distinctiveness. Kymlicka discusses three sorts of rights to support the culture as a context of choice for these minority groups.[83] Kymlicka's work is in line with the choice element of the ideal of equality: 'Inequalities in the advantages people enjoy due to choices about the good life are seen as part of the personal autonomy and responsibility and therefore morally legitimate.' Kymlicka emphasizes the fact of cultural diversity in contemporary societies as a potential cause for inequality that is ignored by Dworkin and other liberal egalitarians. Multi-nationality and poly-ethnicity undermine the liberal assumption that all members of society share a context of choice. Since choices are made in a cultural environment and since these contexts of choice differ in multicultural societies, the choice/endowment distinction, so clear as an analytical device, is complicated outside the context of ideal theory in real multicultural societies. Therefore, Kymlicka uses Dworkin's emphasis on choice to defend group-specific rights for minority groups.

## 7. The Relation between the Two Conceptions of Equality

Let me recapitulate the argument so far. I have presented a concept of equality – the ideal propagating that government should protect individual autonomy and responsibility and eliminate unchosen inequalities – and two conceptions thereof: socioeconomic redistribution in the welfare state and the accommodation of cultural difference in the multicultural society. The latter conception proposes some adaptations of the former. In a multicultural context, the term 'endowment' should not only include natural endowments but also societal endowments, whereas 'choice' presupposes a cultural context and that therefore the acknowledgement of cultural diversity generates unchosen inequalities between members of different cultural groups.

Let me discuss a potential argument against my analysis. One could object that my interpretation of the liberal-egalitarian conception of equality is too narrow in terms of socioeconomic redistribution. Dworkin, for example, is not only well known for his 'What Is Equality?' articles, but is also one of the most prominent defenders of the legality and justifiability of race- and gender-conscious policies of

---

[83]  *Ibid.*, pp. 27-33.

affirmative action.[84] One could argue that I overstate the dichotomy between liberal egalitarianism and multiculturalism by interpreting liberal egalitarianism too narrowly. Let me discuss this argument by evaluating Dworkin's work. Within the context of redistributive justice, Dworkin firmly holds on to methodological individualism. Equality of resources (willfully) ignores socially generated inequalities, because

> [i]t aims to provide a description of (or rather a set of devices for aiming at) equality of resources person by person, and the considerations of each person's history that affect what he should have, in the name of equality, do not include his membership in any economic or social class. ... [Therefore, equality of resources] proposes that equality is in principle a matter of individual right rather than one of group position.[85]

He also emphasizes the strict individualist considerations underlying the choice/endowment distinction since it is based on 'judgments about particular people's particular tastes and ambitions, in the interests of giving them what they are, as individuals, entitled to have, rather than as part of any premise that equality is the matter of equality between groups'.[86] One could thus argue that equality of resources is insensitive to issues of cultural diversity.

In his work, Dworkin draws a principled and hierarchical distinction between equality of resources and affirmative action, based on his distinction between 'policy' and 'principle'. For Dworkin, a policy is a standard that sets out a goal to be reached, which is to be evaluated (only) in terms of the common good. A principle is a standard that is to be observed, not because enforcing it promotes the common good, but, instead, because it is a requirement of justice or fairness.[87] Policy decisions, on the other hand, might have unfavourable effects on persons, but do not violate their rights. For example, the rights of a passionate swimmer are not violated if a city council, having to make a policy decision on spending money on a swimming pool or an opera house, chooses to subsidize the latter. In general, policy decisions can only be assessed in consequentialist terms: Which policy does the best job in increasing the common good? Dworkin claims that affirmative action programs, that is, issues of cultural diversity, are not a matter of princi-

---

[84] See, e.g., Dworkin, *Taking Rights Seriously*, ch. 9; *A Matter of Principle*, chs. 14 and 15; Ronald Dworkin, *Freedom's Law: The Moral Reading of the Constitution*, Cambridge, Mass., Harvard University Press, 1996, ch. 6; Dworkin, *Sovereign Virtue*, chs. 11 and 12.

[85] Dworkin, *Sovereign Virtue*, p. 114.

[86] *Ibid.*, pp. 114-115.

[87] Dworkin, *Taking Rights Seriously*, pp. 22-23.

ple but of policy.[88] The rights of whites, disadvantaged by affirmative action programs, are not infringed by that policy; on the other hand, blacks do not have the right to compel government to adopt such policies. This explains why Dworkin treats these issues separately: the issue of resource equality is seen as a requirement of justice and affirmative action as a matter of policy.

Andrew Altman has argued that Dworkin does not offer enough good reasons to maintain this distinction and claims that affirmative action should also be interpreted in terms of principles.[89] I agree with Altman; as I have argued in this chapter, socioeconomic redistribution and accommodation of cultural difference share the concept of equality as the underlying ideal and can be seen as consistent and equivalent conceptions thereof. It is interesting that Dworkin now accepts – in his own ambiguous way – that the distinction can no longer be maintained. In his reply to Altman, Dworkin writes:

> I agree that government has an obligation to treat all those subject to its dominion with equal concern, and that a government that does nothing to redress structural discrimination fails in that obligation. ... It is true... that without some direct and positive action the American governments fail in their responsibilities to treat all citizens as equals, and that is a matter of principle and not just policy.[90]

This seems to be an indirect way for Dworkin to admit that cultural difference is of normative importance and should be included in the normative framework of liberal egalitarianism.

## 8. Conclusion: Is an Ideal-Oriented Approach Helpful in Normative Debates?

In this chapter, I have used an ideal-oriented approach to discuss the contemporary debate on equality. I followed the assertion of the editors of this book that we can understand normative debates as debates between different interpretations of the same ideal. At first sight, there is a vast difference between the redistributive and the multicultural conception of equality. However, after distilling the more general ideal of

---

[88] Dworkin, *Freedom's Law*, p. 155; *Taking Rights Seriously*, p. 22; Andrew Altman, 'Policy, Principle, and Incrementalism: Dworkin's Jurisprudence of Race', *The Journal of Ethics* 5 (2001), 241-262, at pp. 242 and 254.

[89] Altman, 'Policy, Principle, and Incrementalism'.

[90] Ronald Dworkin, 'Replies to Endicott, Kamm and Altman', *Journal of Ethics* 5 (2001), 263-267, at p. 267.

equality, it is very well possible to understand the connection between the two theories.

Although we should not overstate its effect, I think an ideal-oriented approach is helpful in analysing debates in political philosophy. This chapter makes clear that an ideal-oriented approach is very helpful in reflecting on relations between theories. Young and Kymlicka use the concept of equality to defend their positions; however, their approaches are very different from the mainstream liberal-egalitarian defences. An ideal-oriented approach is a helpful conceptual tool in analysing debates in political philosophy because in this debate it provides a common frame of reference. I therefore assume that the editors mean *conceptual* improvement when they argue: 'In normative theory, recognition of the role of ideals is basically recognition of room for improvement.'[91]

The strength of the ideal-oriented approach is its ability to clarify ongoing debates by separating the abstract concepts and ideals from their application in actual policy debates. In the case of liberal egalitarians, the emphasis on the underlying ideal of equality enables us to criticize their single-minded focus on socioeconomic redistribution: Why would this be the only legitimate interpretation of the maxim of equal respect and concern? In this sense, an ideal-oriented approach is helpful for separating the rhetoric from the content. In the case of multiculturalism, this emphasis on the abstract egalitarian claim as the maxim of Young's and Kymlicka's claims is helpful in distinguishing their claims from more communitarian defences of the recognition of identity groups, based on Hegel's work, as presented by, for example, Charles Taylor and Axel Honneth.[92] Moreover, it shows the relations between Young and Kymlicka on the one hand, and liberal-egalitarians on the other. So, an ideal-oriented approach is helpful because it elucidates a debate, clarifies the diverse positions, and reveals differences and (unlooked-for) similarities between different positions.

The question remains, however, what the 'ideal'-component adds to the more general idea of 'concept'. The distinction between concept and conception is the cornerstone of my paper, however, one could ask why this would support the claim that *ideals* are important. My answer is twofold. For one thing, the notion of 'concept' is more appropriate in conceptual and descriptive theories, whereas the notion of 'ideal' better fits in normative theories. Moreover, concepts can be formulated and

---

[91]  Van der Burg and Taekema, 'Introduction' to this volume.

[92]  Taylor, 'The Politics of Recognition'; Axel Honneth, *The Struggle for Recognition: The Moral Grammar of Social Conflicts*, tr. Joel Anderson, Cambridge, Polity Press, 1995.

defined very precisely – if so desired, provisionally or formally. Concepts refer to agreements to formulate specific issues within a theory in a specific way. Ideals, on the other hand, always refer to substantive ideas and transcend every attempt to enclose them in one formulation.[93] Ideals can only be formulated *within* a specific context, e.g. the context of socioeconomic redistribution or the context of cultural diversity. None of these conceptions is a complete interpretation of the general ideal, and together they do not exhaust all possible interpretations of the ideal. To conclude: the concept of 'ideal' differs substantively from the concept of 'concept', and my discussion in this chapter shows the value of the former in debates in normative political philosophy.

# References

Altman, Andrew, 'Policy, Principle, and Incrementalism: Dworkin's Jurisprudence of Race', *The Journal of Ethics* 5 (2001), 241-262.

Anderson, Elisabeth, 'What Is the Point of Equality?', *Ethics* 109 (1999), 287-337.

Barry, Brian, *Culture and Equality: An Egalitarian Critique of Multiculturalism,* Cambridge, Mass., Harvard University Press, 2001.

Dan-Cohen, Meir, 'Conceptions of Choice and Conceptions of Autonomy', *Ethics* 102 (1992), 221-243.

Dworkin, Ronald, *Taking Rights Seriously,* London, Duckworth, 1977.

————, 'In Defense of Equality', *Social Philosophy and Policy* 1 (1983) 1, 24-40.

————, 'Can a Liberal State Support Art?' in *A Matter of Principle*, Cambridge (Mass.), Harvard University Press, 1985, pp. 221-233.

————, *A Matter of Principle*, Cambridge, Mass., Harvard University Press, 1985.

————, *Law's Empire*, Cambridge, Mass., The Belknap Press, 1986.

————, 'Liberal Community', *California Law Review* 77 (1989) 3, 479-504.

————, 'Do Liberty and Equality Conflict?', in Paul Barker (ed.), *Living as Equals*, Oxford, Oxford University Press, 1996, pp. 39-57.

————, *Freedom's Law: The Moral Reading of the Constitution*, Cambridge, Mass., Harvard University Press, 1996.

————, *Sovereign Virtue: The Theory and Practice of Equality*, Cambridge, Mass., Harvard University Press, 2000.

---

[93] Wibren van der Burg, 'The Morality of Aspiration: A Neglected Dimension of Law and Morality', in Willem Witteveen and Wibren van der Burg (eds.), *Rediscovering Fuller: Essays on Implicit Law and Institutional Design*, Amsterdam, Amsterdam University Press, 1999, pp. 169-193, at pp. 177-178.

————, 'Replies to Endicott, Kamm and Altman', *Journal of Ethics* 5 (2001), 263-267.

Fraser, Nancy, 'From Redistribution to Recognition? Dilemmas of Justice in a "Post-Socialist" Age', *New Left Review* 212 (1995), 68-93.

Honneth, Axel, *The Struggle for Recognition: The Moral Grammar of Social Conflicts*, tr. J. Anderson, Cambridge, Polity Press, 1995.

Kymlicka, Will, *Liberalism, Community, and Culture*, Oxford, Clarendon Press, 1989.

————, *Multicultural Citizenship: A Liberal Theory of Minority Rights*, Oxford, Oxford University Press, 1995.

————, *Contemporary Political Philosophy: An Introduction*, 2nd ed., Oxford, Oxford University Press, 2002.

Margalit, Avishai, and Moshe Halbertal, 'Liberalism and the Right to Culture', *Social Research* 61 (1994) 3, 491-510.

Marx, Karl, 'Critique of the Gotha Programme', in Karl Marx and Friedrich Engels (eds.), *Marx/Engels Selected Works in One Volume*, London, Lawrence and Wishart, 1875.

Miller, David, 'Doctrinaire Liberalism versus Multicultural Democracy: Review of Brian Barry's *Culture and Equality*', *Ethnicities* 2 (2002) 2, 261-265.

Nozick, Robert, *Anarchy, State and Utopia*, New York, Basic Books, 1974.

Pierik, Roland, and Ingrid Robeyns, 'Dworkin on Sen: On the Role of Social Mechanisms in Egalitarian Theory', mimeo, 2001.

Rachels, James, *The Elements of Moral Philosophy*, 4th ed., New York [etc.], McGraw-Hill, 2003.

Rawls, John, *A Theory of Justice*, Oxford, Oxford University Press, 1971.

————, *Political Liberalism*, New York, Columbia University Press, 1993.

————, *The Law of Peoples*, Cambridge, Mass., Harvard University Press, 1999.

————, *A Theory of Justice*, rev. ed., Oxford, Oxford University Press, 1999.

————, *Justice as Fairness: A Restatement*, ed. Erin Kelly, Cambridge, Mass., Harvard University Press, 2001.

Scheffler, Samuel, 'What Is Egalitarianism?', paper presented at the *Centre for Politics, Law, and Society Seminar Series*, University College London, 23 January 2002.

Skinner, Quentin, *Liberty before Liberalism*, Cambridge, Cambridge University Press, 1998.

Taylor, Charles, 'The Politics of Recognition', in A. Gutmann (ed.), *Multiculturalism and the Politics of Recognition*, Princeton, N.J., Princeton University Press, 1994.

Van der Burg, Wibren, *Het democratisch perspectief: Een verkenning van de normatieve grondslagen der democratie*, Arnhem, Gouda Quint, 1991.

————, 'The Importance of Ideals', *The Journal of Value Inquiry* 31 (1997), 23-37.

————, 'The Morality of Aspiration: A Neglected Dimension of Law and Morality', in W. Witteveen and W. van der Burg (eds.), *Rediscovering Fuller: Essays on Implicit Law and Institutional Design*, Amsterdam, Amsterdam University Press, 1999, pp. 169-192.

Young, Iris Marion, *Justice and the Politics of Difference*, Princeton, N.J., Princeton University Press, 1990.

————, 'A Multicultural Continuum: A Critique of Will Kymlicka's Ethnic-Nation Dichotomy', *Constellations* 4 (1997) 4, 48-53.

————, 'Equality of Whom? Social Groups and Judgments of Injustice', *The Journal of Political Philosophy* 9 (2001) 1, 1-18.

# An Interactionist View on the Relation between Law and Morality

Wibren VAN DER BURG[1]

## 1. Introduction

The claim of this book is that many issues may be put into a new light if we analyse them with explicit attention to the role of ideals. The relation between law and morality is one of these themes; indeed, my claim is that we will not only be able to understand the debate between natural law theory and legal positivism better, but also to construct a defensible third theory.

In recent decades, the debate between natural law theory and legal positivism has lost most of its sharp edges. Some authors, most notably Ronald Dworkin, construct intermediate positions, which are explicitly referred to as a third theory of law. Various authors have tried to modify positivism and include crucial insights from the Dworkinian criticisms, using phrases such as soft or inclusive positivism. Modern natural law theorists similarly present highly attenuated forms of the old strong positions. However, as critics are eager to point out, these intermediate positions and weaker forms of positivism and natural law also remain quite unsatisfactory, often even much more so than the traditional views. Moreover, as a result of these minor and major modifications, it becomes increasingly difficult to understand what the debate is all about – is there still a genuine disagreement?

It seems time for a fresh start. The debate has, in my view, been led onto the wrong track because neither side so far explicitly recognised that law is an essentially ambiguous concept. Once we understand the essential ambiguity, we may be able to comprehend not only some of the misunderstandings in the debate, but also why attempts to create a coherent third position have failed so far. The recognition of the essen-

[1] I would like to thank the other members of the research group on ideals, especially Marc Hertogh, Bertjan Wolthuis and Sanne Taekema, for their helpful comments on earlier versions of this paper, as well as Hildegard Penn for her meticulous care in correcting and improving my English.

tial ambiguity of law is a first step out of the deadlock, but in itself it is not enough to construct a third theory of law. In order to do so, we must take a second step and recognise the crucial role of ideals in law as sources for both the autonomy and the openness of law.

I will start by elaborating the thesis of the essential ambiguity in the concept of law. We may distinguish two models of law, which cannot be reduced to each other and which are mutually incompatible, yet complementary. I call them the practice model and the product model (section 2). The practice model is the more dynamic model and the product model the more static one. Nevertheless, there is also potential for dynamics in the product model. This potential can primarily be found in ideals (section 3). The debate between natural law and legal positivism may be reconstructed in terms of the two models; if we do so, we see that both positions embody an important insight, but also have a blind spot for the most important insight of the other position (section 4). If we combine this with the role of ideals in law, we can develop a third, defensible though not coherent, interactionist position (section 5).

## 2. The Essential Ambiguity of Law

That law is a controversial or even an essentially contested concept, is not a new insight. Many textbooks on legal philosophy or sociology begin with this remark. However, I want to make a claim which goes beyond this: law (and a similar point can be made with regard to morality) is an essentially ambiguous concept. It is not merely that we quarrel about the characteristics of law, the difference goes deeper: there are different perspectives on law, and different, partly incompatible, ways to model law.[2]

Law is a highly complex phenomenon which is difficult to get a good grip on. It does not exist separate from society; on the contrary, it is an intrinsic part thereof. Of course, there are clearly identifiable legal procedures and institutions, such as legislation and adjudication, and there are clearly identifiable products, such as statutes and verdicts, but these are merely the most visible parts of the law. Law is like a mushroom: the most important and enduring part of that organism is hardly visible as it is an underground network which may stretch beneath a large surface and which cannot be separated from the soil. The visible

---

[2]  For a more elaborate discussion of these two models, see my 'Two Models of Law and Morality', *Associations* 3 (1999), 61-82. Lon L. Fuller (*The Morality of Law*, New Haven, Conn., Yale University Press, 1969, pp. 106 and 118-122), makes a similar distinction between law as a purposive enterprise and the legal system as its product.

mushroom is the product of the organism and cannot live without it. A legal scholar who only studies the official law made by the legislature and the judiciary is like a biologist who only studies the visible mushroom and ignores everything underground.

To study law, we have two models at our disposal: the product model and the practice model. Each has its advantages and limitations; each makes it possible for us to understand phenomena that we cannot fully grasp in the other model. Because law is self-reflexive and the result of human interaction, these models are not merely descriptive – they are also models that structure law. In legal practices, we construe law in specific ways, implicitly using either of the two models or trying to combine elements of both. Consequently, the choice of either of the two models has not only academic, but also practical implications.

The product model can be called 'law in books' only in a metaphorical way, because it is common though not necessary that it is put on paper. In this model, we focus on law as a system of normative propositions such as 'Thou shalt not steal' (or as a collection of texts in which these propositions may be found). But these propositions *are* not the law (even though we often treat them as if they are); they are merely attempts to put the law into words. Legislators do this in statutes, judges in verdicts, legal scholars in their textbooks by constructing the law as a system of rules and principles, as a more or less coherent doctrine. And citizens do it too, for example, when they state that it is not allowed to park somewhere. I suggest the name 'law as a product' for this model. The propositions and texts are the product of human activity, and once produced, they get an existence of their own separate from the action from which they emerged and thus become more easily identifiable. We can go to the library to study legal texts, we may discuss whether a certain formulation of a legal rule is correct or whether it is unjust and perhaps should be changed. Even if we can find the law in statute books, in the end we must always remain aware that law is not something we find, but something we construct.

The practice model focuses on law as an interaction or as a dimension of interaction.[3] Usually, law is merely an implicit dimension of our actions; it constitutes part of their meaning or makes them possible. When we buy something, it is the implicit legal dimension which makes this a meaningful exchange. Driving a car in heavy city traffic is only possible because of reasonable mutual expectations about the traffic

---

[3] The perspective offered by this practice model makes it possible for legal scholars to study phenomena such as living law (Ehrlich), implicit law (Fuller) and emergent or incipient law (Selznick). In a product model, these phenomena are difficult to understand, and will at best be regarded as some deficient or underdeveloped form of law.

norms regulating our actions. Only in some specific practices such as adjudication we take a 'legal point of view': we formulate the implicit legal dimension explicitly and make it the subject of discussion, application and change. Again, these actions and practices *are* not the law but they cannot be understood without their legal dimension. The activities involved are diverse. They may be distinctively legal ones such as court room proceedings, but also activities such as buying (or stealing) a bread from the baker's. In some practices, the law is implicitly applied and (re)created as a matter of customary law, in others the content of the law is explicitly debated and may be changed, for example in legislation and adjudication. The model of law as a practice is, therefore, connected with the recognition that there may be many legal practices as well as practices with legal dimensions, in other words with the recognition of legal pluralism.[4] Hence, law as a dimension of our interaction is much less tangible than law as a product, and it is much more difficult to give a stipulative definition, let alone a demarcation of it.[5]

Law can thus be regarded both as a dimension of interaction and the product of that interaction. These two models are not separate realities. They refer to each other, presuppose each other and complement each other. Legal rules are the product of distinctively legal subpractices and of the broader interaction in society. Statutes and case law are the product of the legal practices of legislation and adjudication. Legal doctrine is (at least in some legal systems like the Netherlands) the product of the academic legal practice. Conversely, social reality is influenced in many ways by law as a product. Citizens' actions are partly determined by rules as they are formulated in statutes, by judgments which order them to do or endure something and by the ideas that citizens themselves construct about the demands 'the law' implies for them. Moreover, they are oriented towards law as a product because the production of statutes or judgments is the main purpose of some subpractices. A similar interdependence may be found in theories about law: as

---

[4] On the connection between an interactionist approach to law and the recognition of legal pluralism, see Fuller, *Morality of Law*, pp. 123-129; Philippe Nonet and Philip Selznick, *Law and Society in Transition: Toward Responsive Law*, New York, Harper, 1978, pp. 95-103.

[5] I will not try to give a definition here, because the model as such is neutral and may be combined with a variety of definitions. Most of the available definitions based on a practice view focus primarily on one of the explicitly legal practices, such as legislation or adjudication, and ignore the implicit legal dimensions of other practices. Cf. Fuller for legislation: 'the enterprise of subjecting human conduct to the governance of rules'; and Dworkin for adjudication and academic legal practice: 'an argumentative and interpretative practice'.

I will discuss below, most sophisticated theorists have tried to combine insights from the two models.

But even if the two models are not separable, they cannot be reduced to each other either. It is like physical models of electrons. The latter may be modelled as small particles or as waves. Each model allows us to understand certain phenomena satisfactorily, which cannot be explained in the other model. We may translate many ideas from the wave model into the particle model and vice versa, but usually there will be some loss of meaning and elegance. Every attempt to understand electrons merely in terms of one of the two models will lead to partial and incomplete theories. To get a full understanding of electrons, we must alternate between the two models.

Analogously, there are different ways to understand law and to model it. Depending on the context and the purposes of our involvement with law, we should choose one or the other. For a full understanding of law, we should continuously switch between the two models. This is why law is not merely an essentially contested concept, but an essentially ambiguous one. It is not merely that every conception of law will always be contested as in the continuing debate on the conceptions suggested by authors like Fuller, Hart and Dworkin. We are forced to accept a more radical and perhaps disquieting thesis: Every attempt to construct one coherent conception is intrinsically flawed because the two models are not fully compatible, yet both hold parts of the truth.

## 3. The Dynamics of Law

The distinction between the two models is especially illuminating when we focus on the phenomenon of change. Law is in a process of continuous change, just like society in general. Statutes are changed sometimes quite radically, sometimes only in minor ways; case law usually develops through smaller steps and so does the implicit law regulating commercial practice or medical practice. Changes in legislation and case law may be the most explicit, but are certainly not the only ones.

The question is: How can we understand and explain these changes? The obvious answer is to take an external point of view and analyse the way in which the law changes as a result of social, economic and political developments. But even if this is an important part of the answer, it is still only part thereof. We should also look for the potential for change inherent in law itself. If there were no such potential, it would be much more difficult for external forces to change the law, as law is at least a partly autonomous institution, and is not merely a completely malleable instrument of social and political forces.[6]

The two models are clearly different with regard to change. Law as a practice is a dynamic model, whereas law as a product focuses on the static side of law. It is therefore not difficult to identify the potential for change when we take a practice perspective. It is obvious that law can be changed in processes of explicit lawmaking, such as legislation and adjudication. Similarly, the law changes when doctors discuss euthanasia and practise it, and gradually develop criteria for whether and when it may be considered part of good medical practice. In those practices where law is merely an implicit dimension of interaction, there is a potential for change in the fact that each new interaction implies a recreation of the implicit legal norms.[7] Even if this recreation usually is the mere application and reinforcement of these norms, application of norms is never purely mechanical and always involves a creative act in which these norms are slightly altered.

In the practice model, the potential for change is thus easy to identify. What exactly these changes involve, however, can be better understood within the context of the product model. In the practice model, we can discern changes in interaction patterns or observe that parliament has passed a new statute. To determine more in detail what these changes imply, we should discuss them in terms of legal texts, doctrines or statements of positive law. But positive law is not merely the passive result of changes in legal practices. It has a logic of its own, inherent possibilities and limitations. If there were no potential for change in law as a product, it would be much more difficult to change it. Therefore, we should also look at the legal doctrine, this supposedly more static dimension of law, and determine where its potential for further development lies. This may seem a curious idea. Legal doctrine is often presented in legal textbooks in an ahistorical way, as a coherent system of rules and concepts. Even if it is admitted that there are small gaps and

---

[6]  Alan Watson (*The Evolution of Law*, Baltimore, The Johns Hopkins University Press, 1985) argues that legal development is mainly determined by the resources and limitations inherent in the legal culture and tradition; societal needs and influences only play a minor role. His statement may be too strong, especially for the modern regulatory state, but he is certainly right in emphasising the importance of inherent resources for change.

[7]  Cf. Eugen Ehrlich's famous dictum in the Foreword to *Fundamental Principles of the Sociology of Law*, New Brunswick and London, Transaction Publishers, 2002; orig. English transl. 1936, orig. 1913, p. lix: 'The center of gravity of legal development lies not in legislation, nor in juristic science, nor in judicial decision, but in society itself.'

minor inconsistencies, these can be solved in line with this general system of rules. In such an approach, major changes seem impossible. Law may work itself pure, but it cannot transform itself in more radical ways.

Obviously, this image of limited change does not do justice to reality. Positive law changes in many ways, and not only via legislation. For example, the judiciary obviously changes the law – sometimes very radically – even if in most legal systems there is an ideology that tries to minimise the creative impact of their interventions. What are the sources that the judges can appeal to to change the existing view of law?

Usually, the reason to change the law is that new concrete problems or more general issues arise for which the legal doctrine either offers no clear solution or suggests a solution that is inadequate. This may be the reason why a change of law is required, but it is not a resource for the change. The resource is to be found rather at the other end of abstraction, at the level of purposes, principles and ideals.[8] When confronted with issues regarding HIV tests or information technology, basic notions such as privacy or autonomy provide guidance and inspiration. Not only that, however; we also see new dimensions of those old notions. That autonomy may also be relevant with respect to information connected with one's personality, such as HIV status or even consumer patterns is something new – a new dimension of the old concepts of autonomy and privacy. The ideals behind those concepts may provide inspiration for dealing with new cases.[9] Only in the light of new cases, we see the inadequacy of the current legal doctrine and find recourse to the potential for change implicit in the ideals with their surplus of meaning.

In this way, ideals provide a source of inspiration for change. The need for change lies elsewhere, outside the doctrine, in new cases and

---

[8] The idea that principles play a major role in legal development is not uncommon; the modern classic being R. Dworkin, *Taking Rights Seriously*, Cambridge, Mass., Harvard University Press, 1978. The idea, however, that ideals and purposes also play such a role is perhaps less standard, but has been suggested by various authors including Fuller, *Morality of Law*; Nonet and Selznick, *Law and Society in Transition*; Dworkin, *Law's Empire*, Cambridge, Mass., The Belknap Press of Harvard University Press, 1986; A.A.G. Peters, 'Law as Critical Discussion', in G. Teubner (ed.), *Dilemmas of Law in the Welfare State*, Berlin, De Gruyter, 1986, pp. 250-279. Cf. Nonet and Selznick, *Law and Society in Transition*, p. 81: 'When Fuller underscores the centrality of purpose in the legal enterprise or when Dworkin and Hughes look to principle and policy as foundations of legal reasoning, they express the modern aspiration for a legal order that is effective in dealing with change.'

[9] That abstract ideals need not always be the best possible guide, especially not when they are cut loose from their basis in legal and empirical reality, is nicely illustrated by Peter Blok's contribution to this volume.

issues. But the resources to develop new ideas which may help to deal with these new cases and issues are to be found in ideals. Ideals are, of course, not the only resource – imaginative thinking may, for example, also be inspired by moral theories or even by literature and art and may borrow from other legal systems.[10] But because ideals – and the connected principles and purposes – not only have a surplus of meaning, but (in any case the legal ideals I discuss here) are also part of the law itself and thus share its authority, they are the first resource to turn to when we need internal change.

These ideals may sometimes be codified, directly or indirectly but never completely. The ideals of legality, legal certainty or justice themselves are not codified in Dutch law, but some more specific implications in the form of the principle of legality (Article 1 Dutch Penal Code) and the principle of equality (Article 1 Dutch Constitution) have been laid down. Even if these slightly more specific principles are codified, it does not mean that their meaning is unambiguous and uncontroversial. On the contrary, these principles are essentially contested, and their interpretation is open to development. This is because their meaning can only be determined in the light of both the context and the underlying ideals with their surplus of meaning. A good example of the way in which the codification of ideals and principles may give rise to a continuous evolution of positive law can be found in the European Convention of Human Rights, discussed in the Introduction to this volume.

In the product model, ideals (and principles and purposes) thus provide a source for change in the legal doctrine.[11] When the provisional equilibrium of legal doctrine is disturbed by new problematic cases or more general issues, they may offer guidance and orientation for revision of the doctrine. However, because they do not offer clear and unambiguous answers and always need to be interpreted, when we do appeal to ideals we are forced to leave the safety and certainty of established legal doctrine and enter a practice of normative argument about

---

[10]  For the influence of ethical analysis on health law (and vice versa), see my 'Bioethics and Law: A Developmental Perspective', *Bioethics* (1997), 91-114; for inspiration by literature, see Martha Nussbaum, *Poetic Justice: The Literary Imagination and the Public Life*, Boston, Beacon Press, 1995; for influences by other legal systems, see Watson, *Evolution of Law*.

[11]  I merely identify the potential for change in ideals in general terms here. The questions when and why participants in the legal practice will indeed appeal to ideals, to which ideals an appeal is made and whether this appeal to ideals is successful, cannot yet be discussed in such general terms because there are too many relevant variables. Some of the case studies in this volume shed light on these issues, but of course, they do not add up to a general theory yet.

the best possible solutions of the concrete cases or the legal approach to more general issues in the light of those ideals. To determine the implications of the general ideals and principles, to elaborate a revised legal doctrine and construct solutions to new cases, we have to participate in law as an argumentative practice.[12]

In discussions, ideals may provide a common frame of reference. They are a common starting point in a pluralist practice. They can be catalysts in promoting an open debate. Such a debate may lead to legal change, through judicial interpretation and legislative action, but also because it results in shifting interpretations by society or by specific sectors or professions. The surplus of meaning and the fact that they will never be completely realised even if they are at least partly realised in law, makes different interpretations possible of what the underlying ideals imply for the societal problems we are confronted with, and what would be the best way to realise them more fully.[13]

Ideals thus play a role in both models. In the product model, they are authoritative sources within the legal doctrine that provide inspiration and guidance for reconstructing the doctrine. In the practice model, they offer a frame of reference for discussion, reflection and action. They do not, however, only play a role in the separate models, but also in the continuous interaction between the two models in the social reality of law.

Once we appeal to them in order to provide answers for hard cases for which the present legal doctrine is inadequate, they promote a switch from the product to the practice model. We are forced to leave settled doctrine and reopen the debate about the construction of the doctrine, of law as a product. In fact, lawyers do this continuously when they apply statutes, construct contracts and wills, argue a case in court and so on. In all such cases, they participate in legal practices and reconstruct legal doctrine. However, the orientation towards ideals makes them do this more explicitly, because they bring a clear source of ambiguity and controversy into the practice which cannot be ignored. Whereas lawyers usually construct the doctrine and the various products based thereon as unambiguous and uncontroversial, as settled positive law, the appeal to ideals unsettles this and makes an open discussion about the content of the legal doctrine unavoidable. The openness of ideals leaves room for

---

[12] Cf. Dworkin, *Law's Empire*, p. 14; Peters, 'Law as Critical Discussion'.

[13] We should beware of a simple instrumentalist view of the relation between these ideals and the means. For a good analysis of the dialectic relationship between means and ends, see Pauline Westerman, 'Means and Ends', in Willem J. Witteveen and Wibren van der Burg (eds.), *Rediscovering Fuller: Essays on Implicit Law and Institutional Design*, Amsterdam, Amsterdam University Press, 1999, pp. 145-168.

multiple interpretations and these should be confronted in the discursive practices of law.[14]

When we participate in the various practices that creatively interpret, reconstruct and discuss the law, we cannot go on debating forever. It is essential that law also provides provisional closures. As Selznick has argued throughout his work, we cannot understand law unless we recognise the leading ideals of the practice. Among the leading ideals of law is legal certainty.[15] This ideal influences the practice of law. It reminds us that we cannot debate forever, and reorients us to law as a product. Law is most effective when it is clearly formulated, when there is a provisionally settled doctrine, or an authoritative judicial decision or a contract about our legal obligations. Only if we attempt to formulate rules and principles, law can help us orient our behaviour and offer solutions for concrete problematic cases. Therefore, we must try to reformulate the law, to reconstruct the doctrine, to make verdicts and contracts. There may be a continuous debate about the construction of the law, but this debate should also lead to provisional closures, by legislatures enacting a statute, by judges pronouncing a judgment and by legal scholars formulating a legal doctrine.

So, we switch continuously between the two models. The distinctively legal ideal of legal certainty forces us to reconstruct the legal doctrine and bring the debate to a provisional closure. On the other hand, the same ideals as well as other ideals open legal doctrine to internal criticism, and offer inspiration and guidance for revision. There is thus a dialectical relationship between the two models, which opens the way to legal change without destabilising the law completely. In this dialectical process, ideals provide a bridge between the two models. They force us to open and then again to provisionally close the legal doctrine, thus keeping the change within acceptable limits.

We may conclude that ideals promote the dynamics of law in various ways. First, they offer a potential for ideas, for new principles and practical solutions when the existing doctrine needs revision. Second, they force us to leave the certainty of legal doctrine and enter an explic-

---

[14] Of course, sometimes the debate will end by an authoritative conclusion, e.g., by a judge, ignoring this pluralism, before the debate has really started.

[15] See Sanne Taekema, *The Concept of Ideals in Legal Theory*, The Hague, Kluwer Law International, 2003, pp. 158-166. Selznick suggests that there is only one master ideal in law, legality. Taekema, however, has argued convincingly in favour of a plurality of leading ideals or core ideals as well as a plurality of other ideals which are not distinctively legal. See G. Radbruch, *Rechtsphilosophie*, 8ste Aufl., Hrsg. von E. Wolf und H.-P. Schneider, Stuttgart, K.F. Koehler, 1973, for the suggestion that legal certainty is one of those ideals.

itly argumentative practice. Third, they provide a common frame of reference in the ensuing discussion. And finally, they stimulate us to reach at least provisional conclusions.

## 4. The Debate between Natural Law and Legal Positivism

The distinction between the two models is helpful for a better under-standing of the debate between natural law and legal positivism. This debate is quite confused; in fact, it is often not clear what exactly the debate is about. In its most general form, we can say that it is about the separation between law and morals. Positivists hold some version of the thesis that such a separation is possible, natural law theorists that it is not. However, there are many different versions of this thesis and its counterpart.[16] Taekema makes a distinction between the thesis that the concept of law is morally neutral and the thesis that the content of law need not necessarily meet certain demands.[17] If, for example, as external observers we define law as a system of rules that have been officially recognised by the sovereign, we use a positivist, morally neutral concept of law. If, as participants in judicial proceedings, we argue that a se-verely unjust statute that violates basic moral tenets is nevertheless valid law, we appeal to a positivist view of the content of law. I need not go into the details and merits of the various versions here, because my contention is a general one. The debate, and especially the numerous misunderstandings and the apparent futility of the attempts by parties in the debate to convince each other, can be better understood in terms of the two models.

If we hold a product model of law, it seems easy to construct the concept of law in such a way that the separation is true – in either of its versions. We may, for example, define law as the complete set of nor-mative propositions that are valid because of some institutional test, or because they have been stated authoritatively by some specified sources. We may claim that both in the concept of law and in the content of law there is no necessary connection to morality. In such a concept of law and in such a view of the way in which the content of the law can be determined, positivism is true. However, it is only true by stipulation, by construction, because we have constructed law in a specific way first.[18] Only because the constructive element in law as a product is so often

---

[16]  For a discussion, see David Lyons, *Moral Aspects of Legal Theory*, Cambridge, Cambridge University Press, 1993, pp. 70 f.; Van der Burg, 'Two Models'; Taekema, *Concept of Ideals*, ch. 8.

[17]  Taekema, *Concept of Ideals*, pp. 176-177.

[18]  Dworkin, *Taking Rights Seriously*, p. 47.

neglected and because we act as if law is an objective social fact that can be found in social reality, independent of the way in which we constructed this reality in the first place, may we believe otherwise. Positivists often argue as if their thesis is a general truth corroborated by the facts of life, but this is an illusion. The separation of law and morals only exists in the eye of the beholder, who ignores that law is the product of our construction.

Still, this is not the death blow to legal positivism. Recognising that it is only the result of our human construction need not invalidate it. It can still be the best possible construction. And orthodox legal positivism has some obvious advantages, such as simplicity and offering a high degree of legal certainty (and thus, indirectly, freedom).[19]

On the other side of the debate, natural law theorists criticise the separation thesis.[20] In terms of the product model, they claim, first, that there is some objective morality and, second, that there is some necessary connection between objective moral truths and law. Both of these theses are problematic but need not be indefensible. The idea that there is some objective morality, a moral natural law, may be less popular than it used to be, but the project is, especially in some weaker forms, certainly not completely abandoned. Although I do not believe this project can be successful, I will focus on the strengths and flaws of the second thesis.

Just like in the case of positivism, we can easily construct our concept of law and our idea of how to determine the contents of law in such a way that the second thesis is true by stipulation. If we want to stipulate that some officially declared rules may only be considered law if they have some minimal content of moral natural law, ours is an easy victory if we henceforth conclude that there is some necessary connection between law and morality. In fact, most modern legal systems have partly included this as a criterion of the content of law, by the acceptance of human rights treaties and human rights clauses in their constitutions. But again, this is too easy a victory for natural law, as it wins only by stipulation.

It seems, therefore, that both parties can easily defend their positions by holding on to their implicit stipulations and then accuse the other of not meeting the criteria stipulated. The way out of this deadlock is, I

---

[19]    For a similar point see Dworkin's reply to 'Soper-Lyons positivism' in which he states that this type of positivism loses the traditional advantages claimed by positivism; Dworkin, *Taking Rights Seriously*, pp. 346-349.

[20]    With 'natural law' I refer to the classical natural law thinkers and modern authors such as Finnis, not to authors such as Dworkin, Radbruch, Selznick or Fuller.

suggest, to leave the product model. We should accept that the concept of law and the conception of how to determine its content are constructed ideas, constructed in the practice that we call law in the more general sense and in the more restricted practice of legal scholarship. As long as we restrict ourselves to the model of law as a product without acknowledging its constructive character, the debate will never be won or lost, as both parties can continue to defend their views successfully. In order to go beyond this stalemate, we need to enter the field of legal practice, and acknowledge the element of construction both in the law itself and in our theories of law.

We should therefore try to rephrase the debate between natural law and legal positivism in constructivist terms. How are we going to decide which party has the better argument? I suggest we should choose that position which fits best with what we do in legal practice and which is also the best defensible one from a philosophical point of view.[21]

If we look at law as a practice, the conclusion can only be that both sides fail. Positivism fails, as both Fuller and Dworkin have convincingly argued, because law as a practice cannot be separated from morality. I take the critical edge of both Fuller and Dworkin to be that they focus on law as a practice rather than on law as a product. Dworkin's main point is that law is an interpretative and argumentative practice, and that in this practice we cannot separate moral and political arguments. (In fact, Dworkin focuses only on one legal practice, that of adjudication, but a similar point may be made with regard to various other legal practices, such as legal scholarship and implicit law.) Fuller, focusing on law-making, regards law as the enterprise of subjecting human conduct to the governance of rules, and holds that if we want to do this successfully, we need to respect the internal morality of law. These two theses can be generalised to conclude that in legal practice a full separation of law and its internal morality is impossible. In general practices where the legal is merely a dimension of interaction, an even stronger point can be made, namely that the moral and legal dimensions are intertwined. In the implicit understandings of our contractual obligations, the meaning of contractual terms and legal rules regulating them will usually be infused with moral notions of fairness and equity.

However, this failure of positivism in the light of the facts does not imply that natural law wins. In law as a practice, we aim at the best

---

[21] Cf. Dworkin's criteria of fit and political morality for acceptance of a legal theory; see *Matter of Principle*, p. 143. Although he develops these criteria for the question whether we should accept a theory as an interpretation of the law of a certain jurisdiction at a certain time, similar criteria may also be used for the question whether we should accept a theory as an interpretation of the phenomenon of law in general.

political morality, but we also know that this aim can never be fully achieved. Even if we could uphold the ontological claim that there is an objective morality, there is still the unsurmountable problem of how to know it. Pervasive moral pluralism is a fact of life in our modern societies. The core of truth in natural law is that a legal practice is inherently connected with morality, with underlying values and normative ideas about what the law should be. Law has a partly moral character. But this does not imply that this moral character is connected with some objective morality. It does not even imply that it is connected with one right answer. We should aim at the best possible answer, but a realistic analysis of our practices shows that there are usually strong conflicts between the values at stake and their interpretations. Moreover, even if Dworkin is right in arguing that each individual participant aims at the best possible answer, this does not imply that the practice as such also aims at the best possible answer. Pluralism in the legal practice is so pervasive and deep that the best a practice can hope for is a plurality of legitimate answers from which may be chosen in many legitimate ways, both by judges and by other participants in the practice.[22]

The conclusion is that the debate between legal positivism and natural law is a debate within the context of law as a product, in which both sides defend positions which at least prima facie may seem defensible within that context as long as one makes the correct stipulations. However, it is mainly a non-debate because – at least when entering the discussion – both parties tend to ignore the constructive element and present it as a debate about what the law is rather than as a debate about how it can best be constructed.

If we reconstruct the two views as competing claims about the best possible construction of law, both prove to have fatal flaws. Both theories have one weakness in common: they cannot adequately cope with legal change. Roger Cotterrell presents this as a criticism of positivism, but it can equally be brought forward against natural law theories.[23] This weakness is the result of a one-sided focus on the product model that is characteristic of (at least the orthodox versions of) both theories. Moreover, legal positivism is unable to do justice to the idea that our legal practice is inherently connected with morality in various ways.[24] Natural

---

[22] See also Taekema, *Concept of Ideals*, pp. 189-190; Jeremy Waldron, *Law and Disagreement*, Oxford, Clarendon Press, 1999, pp. 164-187.

[23] Cf. Roger Cotterrell, *The Politics of Jurisprudence: A Critical Introduction to Legal Philosophy*, London and Edinburgh, Butterworths, 1989, p. 127.

[24] Except for forms of soft positivism or inclusive positivism. However, these versions have flaws of their own into which I cannot go here. See Taekema, *Concept of Ideals*, pp. 188-189, for the argument that these positions are internally inconsistent and

law has two flaws connected with its two central theses. It has proven difficult, if not impossible, to establish convincing arguments in favour of an objective ethical theory – just like the law, our morality is a product of our own construction.[25] As a consequence, there are no convincing arguments about the necessary objective moral basis of the law. Even if this philosophical problem of establishing an objective ethical theory could be tackled, an empirical problem would still remain: it does not do justice to the fact of pluralism. Our legal practice is partly moral in character, yet this morality is not connected with one right answer or with some objective morality, but rather with a plurality of moralities. Natural law seems unaware of the essentially contested character of the moral dimension of our legal practice.

The distinction between the two models of law can thus clarify the debate between natural law and legal positivism.[26] It illuminates both why the positions can be successfully defended in the context of the product model and why they fall short in the practice model. This leaves us with the question how to construct a third alternative, a theory of law which can do justice to both models. In order to construct such an alternative, we should return to the role of ideals in law.

## 5. An Interactionist Perspective

Partly in line with Ronald Dworkin's view, I have argued that in as far as ideals and principles are part of legal doctrine, they force us to question settled legal doctrine and open it for normative discussion. In such a normative discussion, political, moral and legal arguments cannot

---

Dworkin, *Taking Rights Seriously*, pp. 345-350, for the argument that they have lost most of the attractiveness of orthodox positivism.

[25] See Taekema, *Concept of Ideals*, p. 189. This criticism does not imply a relativist position, but is consistent with a pragmatist view. See my 'Dynamic Ethics', *Journal of Value Inquiry* 37 (2003), 13-34.

[26] I have greatly simplified the positions of natural law and legal positivism. Every sophisticated legal theory has tried to combine insights from both models. Even if the focus of both natural law and legal positivism is on the product model, they have also tried to integrate elements from the practice model. For example, H.L.A. Hart called his own theory a 'practice theory of law' (in the Postscript to *The Concept of Law*, Oxford, Clarendon Press, 1994, p. 255); his theory starts with the practice model, by analysing rules in terms of rule-following behaviour. However, when it comes to defending his views against those of Fuller or Dworkin, the focus is on rules as linguistic expressions, as normative propositions needing interpretation. For a more extensive analysis of Hart's position and that of other authors in the debate, see my 'Two Models'.

be separated. Ronald Dworkin even speaks of a fusion of moral and legal theory, at least in the context of constitutional issues.[27]

I believe this is overstating the point. There certainly is no complete merger of law and morals. (In fact, Dworkin himself does not support such a view either.) That we cannot separate them does not mean that they cannot be distinguished. That the construction of legal doctrine is a continuous process in which political and moral arguments are integrated into the legal argument does not mean that there is no distinctively legal point of view, distinctively legal practices or distinctively legal doctrine.

In modern Western societies, law has relative autonomy. It is not fully separate from morality and society, neither is it completely integrated in them. This relative autonomy has its primary basis in the institutional dimension of law; an additional basis may be found at the level of ideals. Law involves a connected set of subpractices such as legislation and adjudication. Each of these subpractices has relative autonomy as a result of its specific function, its procedural and substantive norms which shield it from being completely submerged in the larger social context and the larger moral and political arguments. Adjudication, for example, may be open to moral arguments, but this certainly does not lead to a complete fusion of moral and legal arguments. On the contrary, in most Western countries, the institution is highly, though not completely shielded from a direct influence by political and moral beliefs that may dominate society. Even the legislative process does not allow a complete fusion of legal and political arguments, as the discretionary space of the political institutions is regulated by constitutional constraints, international law, by consistency with the system of existing legislation or, in more general terms, by the rule of law. So the institutional setting of legal practices prevents a complete fusion of law, politics and morality, even if it allows substantial intertwining.

Perhaps we could imagine a legal practice in which the secondary rules exclude all reference to morality or politics and in which legal obligations are determined purely by a mechanistic appeal to formal rules or (when they do not apply) by procedures such as pure chance. Such a practice might approximate the ideal type of a complete separation between law and morality. It is, however, obvious that such practices are uncommon in modern societies. As soon as legal practices allow a normative discussion about the interpretation of rules and concepts in order to make them fit complex situations, a strict separation

---

[27] Cf. Dworkin, *Taking Rights Seriously*, p. 149.

between law and morality is impossible. That is, in my view, the central insight we may learn from Ronald Dworkin.[28] So the reality of those practices, especially of the official law-making institutions, is that of relative autonomy.[29] Moreover, legal practices are rarely separate from society in another way: their aim is usually to regulate non-legal practices, such as those of medicine or trade and, as a consequence, they have to be open to those practices and to the normative dimensions inherent in those dimensions.[30]

This relative autonomy is reflected in legal doctrine. Dworkin is right in arguing that we should not regard legal doctrine as something out there, as a 'brooding omnipresence in the sky', as 'existing law'; it is the product of our construction.[31] Nevertheless, in our construction we distinguish between legal doctrine and moral or political views – even if we accept the anti-positivist truth that a strict separation is not possible. The legal doctrine in most modern societies includes many normative standards with an openness to societal views such as fairness and equity, it includes principles and ideals with an openness to moral theory, and we may have to interpret statutes in the light of the political purposes behind them. However, this openness is not complete; a distinctively legal perspective still remains from which we should try to construct a legal doctrine.

Both the autonomy of law and its relative character may also be understood in terms of ideals.[32] On the one hand, ideals and principles may form a bridge between the moral, legal and political discourses, because many ideals and principles are common to these discourses. If we could speak of a fusion of moral, legal and political theory, it would be expected at this level. Nevertheless, ideals are open to interpretation and get part of their meaning from the network of meanings in which they are embedded: the other ideals with which they are connected, the more specific rules and principles which can be regarded as their implementations and the institutional context in which their meaning is con-

---

28  Other authors have made similar points before. One of the reasons why Ronald Dworkin did not cause much debate in Dutch legal philosophy is that the still highly influential Dutch jurist Scholten already developed a similar theory of judicial interpretation in 1931. See Paul Scholten, *Mr. C. Asser's Handleiding tot de beoefening van het Nederlands burgerlijk recht: Algemeen deel*, Zwolle, W.E.J. Tjeenk Willink, 1974, orig. 1931.

29  For a more elaborate discussion see my 'Two Models', pp. 75 f.

30  See Taekema, *Concept of Ideals*, pp. 167-168, for a similar argument.

31  Dworkin, *Taking Rights Seriously*, pp. 293 and 344.

32  The following analysis is based on Taekema, *Concept of Ideals*, pp. 167-173.

structed.[33] This means that ideals of solidarity or privacy get a specific colouring depending on the context – legal, political or moral – in which they are discussed. There may be one common concept, but the conceptions differ. Although it is especially through ideals and principles that the legal doctrine is connected with moral and political argument, and although this is mainly because the same ideals are used in each of these contexts, the meaning of the ideals in each of the contexts is not identical. In this way, the ideals common to law, morals and politics embody a strong tendency to open up law to politics and morals, even if they allow some autonomy of law.

On the other hand, the autonomy of law is supported by distinctively legal ideals. Philip Selznick's idea of master ideals is illuminating here. According to Selznick, every practice is oriented towards some master ideal, which accounts for its distinctive character.[34] In this way, law is oriented towards the master ideal of legality, which Selznick interprets as the progressive reduction of arbitrariness. Sanne Taekema argues convincingly that Selznick's idea of one and only one master ideal for each practice is not adequate and does not do justice to the complex character of practices.[35] Nevertheless, it is possible to distinguish some ideals which have a more important role for specific practices. We may call them the core values or central ideals of that practice. Legality (including legal certainty) and justice are such core values for law, and in this sense may be regarded as distinctively legal ideals. They are not exclusive to law (justice is the first virtue of social institutions in general, according to Rawls), nor are they the only ideals of law. Yet, they have a special role in the practice of law, just as the democratic ideal has a special role in the context of political institutions without being meaningless in other institutions such as universities or companies. Apart from these ideals which are common to all legal subpractices, there may also be more specific legal ideals for specific subpractices or subfields of law. Democracy and human rights are central to constitutional law, and good governance to administrative law. The ideal of due process is just as central to the practice of adjudication as the ideal of intellectual integrity is central to legal scholarship.

The orientation towards distinctively legal ideals is another ground for the relative autonomy of law. They are not exclusive to law, nor is

---

[33] Cf. Anton Vedder, 'Waarden en het web van zin en betekenis', in Wibren van der Burg and Frans W.A. Brom (eds.), *Over idealen: Het belang van idealen in recht, moraal en politiek*, Deventer, W.E.J. Tjeenk Willink, 1998, pp. 39-54.

[34] Cf. Philip Selznick, 'Sociology and Natural Law', *Natural Law Forum* 6 (1961), 84-108.

[35] Taekema, *Concept of Ideals*, pp. 162-166.

their meaning only determined in legal discourse. Yet, the prime importance of these ideals is distinctive for law and is one reason why we may discern relative autonomy for the law.[36]

This relative autonomy of the law is the central thesis of a third theory of law, distinct from natural law and legal positivism. It is distinct from legal positivism because it holds that in law as a practice law and morality cannot be separated, whereas in law as a product a separation may be a choice we make in our construction but is not an essential characteristic of law as such. It is distinct from natural law because it denies that there is any inherent moral quality in law as a practice, whereas in law as a product we can stipulate that law must meet certain moral standards, but this would make the necessary connection between law and morality merely true by stipulation.

This third theory may be named interactionist, because interaction is central to it in various respects. It regards law both as a practice of human interaction (and as a dimension of practices) and as a product of human interaction.[37] Moreover, it accepts that law, with its relative autonomy, can only exist in a continuing process of interaction with morality and politics, and with society at large. Law cannot be separated from morality, nor can it be completely fused with morality. The content of the law cannot be determined without any appeal to moral or political arguments, yet it maintains relative autonomy as regards those arguments by only selectively incorporating them in the law and by transforming them during the process.

The claim of a third theory of law is, of course, not new. Many legal theorists have claimed to provide such a third theory of law or have been classified by others as doing so. It is helpful to analyse why their attempts to construct a coherent third theory of law have failed, and especially why these have often led to such obvious inconsistencies or vagueness. Both Fuller and Dworkin, to mention only two authors whose work has been characterised as a third theory of law (and whose work obviously is a source of inspiration for the approach I propose), have often been accused, and rightly so, that their theories contain many inconsistencies and unsolved ambiguities. Whereas the two traditional parties, natural law and legal positivism, can, in different versions, be

---

[36]  Taekema, *Concept of Ideals*, pp. 203-204.

[37]  Interactionism in a minimal sense might be interpreted as the idea that law is a practice of human interaction. I defend a richer form of interactionism here, because I add that it may also be regarded as the product of that interaction, and that we cannot separate practice and product.

presented as relatively consistent and defensible theories, this has proven to be much more problematic with third theories of law.[38]

My suggestion is that the reason why all these third theories fail is that they try to do justice to the valuable insights we can gain by combining the two models, yet fail to recognise their incommensurability. The example of Dworkin is illustrative. In *Taking Rights Seriously*, he developed convincing arguments against various versions of legal positivism. In this early work, he switched between two lines of argument. One was internal to the product model, arguing that law was more than a body of rules, and that the inclusion of principles in legal doctrine, with their open and contested character, made a simple pedigree test impossible. The other was based on the idea of law as an argumentative practice, in which we should explicitly recognise the constructive character of legal doctrine. As his many critics were eager to point out, the combination of the two lines led to many inconsistencies and ambiguities. In subsequent books, especially *Law's Empire*, Dworkin tried to respond to these critics and elaborate a coherent theory of law. However, what he won in consistency in this book, he lost in convincingness, because he was forced to skip insights which did not fit into this one coherent theory, yet were initially crucial to his critical project.

If my suggestion is correct that we need both models but that they are incommensurable, we have to accept that one coherent theory is impossible. We are bound to end up with theories in which inconsistencies and ambiguities are unavoidable. Of course, this idea seems, at least at first sight, unacceptable to most legal scholars, especially in as far as they have undergone the influence of analytical philosophy. Weeding out inconsistencies and ambiguities seems one of the central methodological requirements of good scholarship. Openly accepting them seems like declaring the breakdown of academic research.

Therefore it is quite understandable that, in the end, almost every author aiming at a third theory of law presented his theory in such a way that it was either easily reducible to one of the traditional alternatives or easily criticisable by both parties as not doing justice to reality. If they wanted to be consistent, they paid the price of not doing justice to the complexities of reality. If they wanted to do justice to reality, they ended up with a theory full of fatal inconsistencies and ambiguities or with a theory which only consisted in a programme and some loosely connected fragments. It seems to me that Ronald Dworkin's development

---

[38] The internal inconsistency of inclusive positivism, an attempt to integrate some insights of anti-positivist authors such as Dworkin into positivism, is another example. See note 24 above.

took the first road towards consistency, ending up with a theory that fails to address legal reality adequately, whereas Lon Fuller took the second road of trying to do justice to the complexity of reality, ending up with an inchoate theory with many ambiguities.

Is there a way out for proponents of a third theory? I think that the only possibility is to accept the incommensurability of the two models and defend this fact as such. Within each of the models, separate theories can be developed as well as possible, but we must always openly acknowledge that, then, each of the two theories has fatal problems when taken in isolation. Only continuously switching between the two models, with all the inconsistencies and ambiguities resulting from such switching, may give us the best possible insight in the phenomenon of law. In order to understand this continuous switching between the two models, we need to focus our attention on the role ideals play as a catalyst in this interaction. The focus on ideals also opens a fresh perspective on the relation between law and morality. This leads to the thesis of the relative autonomy of law, which justifies the claim that the interactionist theory can be regarded neither as natural law nor as legal positivism and thus constitutes a third theory.

The interactionist theory does not focus on one model of law, but continually switches between two models. It is a combined theory, in which two theories continuously interact, without ever reaching the ideal of one grand theory. Intellectually, this may not be very satisfying, particularly not for authors (including myself) with a strong background in analytical philosophy. We will never be able to reach one complete and internally coherent theory of law. But this is the price we have to pay for doing justice to the complexity of reality.

## References

Cotterrell, Roger, *The Politics of Jurisprudence: A Critical Introduction to Legal Philosophy*, London and Edinburgh, Butterworths, 1989.

Dworkin, R., *Taking Rights Seriously*, Cambridge, Mass., Harvard University Press, 1978.

———, *Law's Empire*, Cambridge, Mass., The Belknap Press of Harvard University Press, 1986.

Ehrlich, Eugen, 'Foreword', in *Fundamental Principles of the Sociology of Law*, New Brunswick and London, Transaction Publishers, 2002; orig. English transl. 1936, orig. 1913.

Fuller, Lon L., *The Morality of Law*, New Haven, Conn., Yale University Press, 1969.

Hart, H.L.A., 'Postscript', in *The Concept of Law*, Oxford, Clarendon Press, 1994.

Lyons, David, *Moral Aspects of Legal Theory*, Cambridge, Cambridge University Press, 1993.

Nonet, Philippe, and Philip Selznick, *Law and Society in Transition: Toward Responsive Law*, New York, Harper, 1978.

Nussbaum, Martha, *Poetic Justice: The Literary Imagination and the Public Life*, Boston, Beacon Press, 1995.

Peters, A.A.G., 'Law as Critical Discussion', in G. Teubner (ed.), *Dilemmas of Law in the Welfare State*, Berlin, De Gruyter, 1986, pp. 250-279.

Radbruch, G., *Rechtsphilosophie*, 8ste Aufl., Hrsg. von E. Wolf und H.-P. Schneider, Stuttgart, K.F. Koehler, 1973.

Scholten, Paul, Mr. C. *Asser's Handleiding tot de beoefening van het Nederlands burgerlijk recht: Algemeen deel*, Zwolle, W.E.J. Tjeenk Willink, 1974, orig. 1931.

Selznick, Philip, 'Sociology and Natural Law', *Natural Law Forum* 6 (1961), 84-108.

Taekema, Sanne, *The Concept of Ideals in Legal Theory*, The Hague, Kluwer Law International, 2003.

Van der Burg, Wibren, 'Bioethics and Law: A Developmental Perspective', *Bioethics* (1997), 91-114.

———, 'Two Models of Law and Morality', *Associations* 3 (1999), 61-82.

———, 'Dynamic ethics', *Journal of Value Inquiry* 37 (2003), 13-34.

Vedder, Anton, 'Waarden en het web van zin en betekenis', in Wibren van der Burg and Frans W.A. Brom (eds.), *Over idealen: Het belang van idealen in recht, moraal en politiek*, Deventer, W.E.J. Tjeenk Willlink, 1998, pp. 39-54.

Watson, Alan, *The Evolution of Law*, Baltimore, The Johns Hopkins University Press, 1985.

Westerman, Pauline, 'Means and Ends', in Willem J. Witteveen and Wibren van der Burg (eds.), *Rediscovering Fuller: Essays on Implicit Law and Institutional Design*, Amsterdam, Amsterdam University Press, 1999, pp. 145-168.

# The Ideal of Data Privacy
# and the Development of Law

## Peter BLOK

## 1. Introduction

During the 1970s, a completely new field of law emerged. In response to concerns over misuse of newly developed information technologies, an elaborate system of rules, principles, and guidelines for handling personal data was created. This coming-into-being of the law of data privacy, as it is called, represents one of the most impressive legal innovations of the last decennia. It is, therefore, an excellent case to examine the function of ideals with respect to legal development. In particular, it will be tested in this chapter whether the development of the law in the field of data processing has been enabled or guided by ideals and, if so, whether ideal orientation has been fruitful for the legal developments in this context.

## 2. A Call for Legal Development

In the late 1960s, a series of books was published that has become known as 'the literature of alarm'.[1] This genre included *The Naked Society* by Vance Packard, *The Intruders* by Edward Long, and *The Privacy Invaders* by Myron Brenton.[2] All these books drew attention to the invention of a number of techniques that made the collection and processing of data about persons more efficient.[3] Hidden cameras and

---

[1]  P.M. Regan, *Legislating Privacy: Technology, Social Values, and Public Policy*, Chapel Hill & London, University of North Carolina Press, 1995, p. 13.

[2]  V. Packard, *The Naked Society*, New York, Pocket Books, 1964; E.V. Long, *The Intruders: The Invasion of Privacy by Government and Industry*, New York, Praeger, 1967; M. Brenton, *The Privacy Invaders*, New York, Coward-McCann, 1964; see also A.F. Westin, *Privacy and Freedom*, New York, Atheneum Press, 1967; A. Miller, *The Assault on Privacy*, Ann Arbor, The University of Michigan Press, 1971.

[3]  An often neglected empirical study by Westin and Baker in 1973 showed that the actual developments were not as alarming as the literature had presented them (A.F. Westin and M.A. Baker, *Databanks in a Free Society: Computers, Record-*

snooping devices would record every detail of a person's life. Computers would make the storage and retrieval of personal data uncontrollable. The literature of alarm was to warn the public about the risks that these technological developments would bring along and sketched a frightening picture of a completely transparent society.

The technological developments were thought to be a problem mainly because of the inherent shift in power relations that these developments would bring about. All the books note that information technology is a powerful tool that can be used and abused to control individuals. As Michel Foucault, among others, cogently argued in his book *Discipline and Punish: The Birth of the Prison*, surveillance has a strong disciplinary effect on individuals.[4] Since technological innovations considerably enhanced the efficiency and capacity of surveillance, they would pose a threat to individual liberty. Moreover, the surveillance technologies would be used mainly by governmental organizations and large companies: exactly the entities that already had a powerful position in society. At the same time, the means of the individual to control this 'information power' diminished. The use of technologies made the processing of personal data less transparent. Most individuals did not have the technological knowledge adequate enough to assess the risks posed by certain technologies. Besides, the very amount of records that were kept made it hard to oversee all possible uses. Taken together, these developments tended to increase established power asymmetries. As one commentator sharply summarized the problem: 'It is becoming much easier for record-keeping systems to affect people than for people to affect record-keeping systems.'[5] Therefore, both the media and the politicians called out for legal measures to restore the power balance and

---

*Keeping, and Privacy*, New York, Quadrangle Books, 1973). At that time, a part of the record-keeping was done by computers, but, surprisingly, this increase in efficiency had not led to a significant increase in the amount of personal data that were processed. Moreover, the study made clear that the use of the computer had not made the record-keeping practices unruly. The processing of personal data by means of the computer was regulated by the same norms and procedures that applied to the handling of paper files. These facts have never changed the public perception of the problem.

[4] M. Foucault, *Discipline and Punish: The Birth of the Prison*, New York, Vintage Books, 1979.

[5] U.S. Department of Health, Education, and Welfare, Secretary's Advisory Committee on Automated Personal Data Systems, *Records, Computers, and the Rights of Citizens*, Cambridge, Mass., MIT Press, 1973, p. XX.

impose adequate controls on the use of personal data.[6] Since the early 1970s, newspapers, magazines, and academic journals have been filled with hundreds of articles on the threats of automated data processing and the need for legal safeguards. The United States Congress has held hundreds of hearings on the subject in a few years time. More than 300 bills have been introduced. The literature of alarm was both a cause and a part of this call for legal development.

## 3. The Ideal of Privacy Guiding Legal Development

Almost everyone assumed that the problem of uncontrolled information power posed a threat to privacy. This apparent consensus is striking for it is widely recognized that the concept of privacy is vague.[7] Some even claim that the meaning of privacy varies from person to person.[8] Still, all the commentators agreed that privacy was the central value at stake and they all invoked the right to privacy to ground their claims for legal development.

For instance, the two most prominent representatives of the alarm literature, Westin and Miller, start their inquiries with a note on the vagueness of the concept of privacy. Westin expresses his surprise that a value so fundamental to society as privacy has been left so undefined.[9] Miller thinks the concept of privacy is 'exasperatingly vague and evanescent'.[10] The elusive nature of privacy did not stop these authors, however, from using it as the leading ideal in articulating the problem of uncontrolled information power and in formulating countermeasures. Both Westin and Miller refer to the ideal of privacy to criticize the technological developments.[11] In addition, they find in privacy a source of inspiration for the further development of law. What they try to do is

---

[6] For an overview, see Committee on the Judiciary, United States Senate, *Federal Data Banks and Constitutional Rights*, Washington, DC, U.S. Government Printing Office, 1974, pp. XII-XIII; Regan, *Legislating Privacy*, ch 3

[7] See W.A. Parent, 'Recent Work on the Concept of Privacy', *American Philosophical Quarterly* (1983/1984), 341-355; F.D. Schoeman (ed.), *Philosophical Dimensions of Privacy: An Anthology*, Cambridge, Cambridge University Press, 1984; J.R. Pennock and J.W. Chapman (eds.), *Nomos XIII: Privacy*, New York, Atherton Press, 1971.

[8] See J. Berman and D. Mulligan, 'The Internet and the Law: Privacy in the Digital Age. Work in Progress', *Nova Law Review* (1999), 549-582.

[9] Westin, *Privacy and Freedom*, p. 7.

[10] Miller, *The Assault on Privacy*, p. 25.

[11] Interestingly enough, the administrators who defended the use of technologies, often denounced these appeals to privacy as 'emotional' and 'unscientific' (Westin, *Privacy and Freedom*, p. 367). This may highlight another feature of the ideal-nature of the concept of privacy: emotive force.

restore a balance between privacy and the legitimate need for personal data. The other authors of the literature of alarm as well invoke the ideal of privacy, as the titles of their books show: *The Privacy Invaders*, *The Death of Privacy*, and *The Intruders: The Invasion of Privacy by Government and Industry*.[12]

Also the reports that various governmental and non-governmental organizations published on the subject, uniformly present the collection and use of personal data primarily as a violation of the right to privacy. The report *Records, Computers, and the Rights of Citizens* of the U.S. Department of Health, Education, and Welfare, for example, notes that 'concerns about computer-based record keeping usually centers on its implications for personal privacy, and understandably so'.[13] Another report *Federal Data Banks and Constitutional Rights* of the U.S. Senate, is, according to its introduction, '… essentially a study of privacy and how it has been eroded by governmental collection and dissemination of information about people'.[14] The academic journals, as well as the popular magazines and newspapers, without exception spoke of an invasion or even destruction of privacy. Still, no one was able to define the endangered right to privacy in terms that were more concrete than 'the right to be let alone' or 'the right to control the collection and dissemination of personal data'. Apparently, the notorious vagueness of the concept of privacy did not make it useless as a guiding ideal.

## 4. Legal Development Clarifying the Ideal of Privacy

It is important to note that the meaning of the concept of privacy as it was used in the context of data processing from the 1970s onwards, did not match completely the legal concept of privacy as it was recognized at that time. In other words, the ideal of privacy was reinterpreted in the light of the new technological and legal developments. Both the scope of the right to privacy and the level of protection gradually were adapted to the needs of the information society.

Until 1970, the main function of the legal right to privacy had been to guarantee the inviolability of a rather narrow sphere of private and domestic life. For instance, the international human rights documents that were adopted after World War II, all had formulated the right to privacy in terms of respect for the home, family life, and correspon-

---

[12] Brenton, *Privacy Invaders*; J.M. Rosenberg, *The Death of Privacy*, New York, Random House, 1969; Long, *Intruders*.

[13] HEW report *Records, Computers, and Rights of Citizens*, p. XX.

[14] Report *Federal Data Banks and Constitutional Rights*, p. IX.

dence.[15] Outside this sphere of private and domestic life, the right to privacy did not apply. The United States Supreme Court had found a right to privacy with a similar scope in the Amendments to the U.S. Constitution. In its interpretation, the Fourth Amendment protected primarily houses, telephone conversations, and other 'privacies of life' against unreasonable searches.[16] In addition, the Court had read a constitutional right to privacy in the 'penumbras' of several Amendments which guaranteed the inviolability of certain particularly private choices.[17] These choices fell primarily within the realm of family life, and included the decision whether to have a child or not, the choice of partner and the use of contraception.[18] So, the scope of the legal right to privacy traditionally had been restricted to a rather narrow private sphere of primarily the home, family life, and confidential communications.

The need for legal development, however, was not restricted to the protection of the traditional privacies of life. The uncontrolled flows of personal data were thought to be a problem independent of their relation to a private sphere. As indicated in section 1, the main concern was that personal data presented an instrument of power that could be used to the detriment of the individual. Whether personal data are susceptible to abuse is related to a number of factors, of which their private content is merely one. Information relating to relatively public features, such as one's political activities or one's ethnic background, can be just as vulnerable as information on the details of a person's intimate life. Besides, the object of the legal measures that were demanded in the

---

[15] See Art. 8 of the European Convention of Human Rights ('Everyone has the right to respect for his private and family life, his home and his correspondence'); Art. 17 of the International Covenant on Civil and Political Rights ('No one shall be subjected to arbitrary or unlawful interference with his privacy, family, home or correspondence'); Art. 12 of the Universal Declaration of Human Rights ('No one shall be subjected to arbitrary interference with his privacy, family, home or correspondence'); Art. 11 para. 2 of the American Convention of Human Rights ('No one may be the object of arbitrary or abusive interference with his private life, his family, his home, or his correspondence').

[16] The Fourth Amendment to the U.S. Constitution reads: 'The right of the people to be secure in their persons, houses, papers, and effects, against unreasonable searches and seizures, shall not be violated, and no warrants shall issue, but upon probable cause, supported by oath or affirmation, and particularly describing the place to be searched, and the persons or things to be seized'; telephone conversations were included in Katz v. United States, 389 U.S. 347, 351 (1967).

[17] Griswold v. Connecticut, 381 U.S. 479 (1965).

[18] Roe v. Wade, 410 U.S. 113 (1973); Zablocki v. Redhail, 434 U.S. 374 (1978); Eisenstadt v. Baird, 405 U.S. 438 (1972).

1970s was not to guarantee the inviolability or secrecy of a person's life. The advocates of 'data privacy' did not want to block the flows of personal data. Instead, they argued for a fair use of the data. The measures they proposed, therefore, were directed at safeguarding the transparency, legitimacy, and accuracy of the process. The code that the U.S. Department of Health published in 1973, for instance, laid down five principles of fair record-keeping:

– There must be no personal data record-keeping systems whose very existence is secret.

– There must be a way for an individual to find out what information about him is in a record and how it is used.

– There must be a way for an individual to prevent information about him that was obtained for one purpose from being used or made available for other purposes without his consent.

– There must be a way for an individual to correct or amend a record of identifiable information about him.

– Any organization creating, maintaining, using, or disseminating records of identifiable personal data must assure the reliability of the data for their intended use and must take precautions to prevent the misuse of the data.[19]

After the publication of this report, many similar codes of fair information practices have been formulated. In the U.S., these sets of principles can be found, for example, in the U.S. Senate report *Federal Databanks and Constitutional Rights*, in the preamble to the Privacy Act of 1974, and, more recently, in the National Information Infrastructure Privacy Principles, which were published in 1995 by a working group established by vice-president Gore.[20] In Europe, equivalent sets of principles have been adopted by the Council of Europe and the European Union.[21] These principles may differ in detail, but their main object is the same. First, they demand the legitimate, transparent, and accurate

---

[19] HEW report *Records, Computers, and Rights of Citizens*, pp. XX-XXI.

[20] Report *Federal Data Banks and Constitutional Rights* 1974, p. IX; Privacy Act of 1974, Pub. L. No. 93-579, 5 U.S.C. 552a; Privacy Working Group, Information Policy Committee, Information Infrastructure Task Force, *Privacy and the National Information Infrastructure, Principles for Providing and Using Personal Information*, <http://nii.nist.gov/>, under 'publications', June 1995.

[21] Council of Europe, Convention for the Protection of Individuals with regard to Automatic Processing of Personal Data, ETS no. 108, 28 January 1981; Directive 95/46/EC of the European Parliament and of the Council of 24 October 1995 on the protection of individuals with regard to the processing of personal data and on the free movement of such data, OJ L 281, 23 November 1995, pp. 31-50.

processing of personal data. Second, they safeguard the right of the individual to participate in the process. In short, these principles guarantee fair information practices.

Since the traditional right to privacy and the principles of fair information processing differed both in object and in scope, one would have expected that privacy would have been abandoned as a leading ideal in the context of data processing. This is not what has happened. As one commentator notes: 'Although fairness became the policy goal, the problem was still defined in terms of privacy and privacy continued to be utilized as a symbol in congressional and public discussions.'[22] Instead of relinquishing the concept of privacy, the meaning of privacy was adjusted to the needs of the information society. The authors of the HEW report *Records, Computers, and Rights of Citizens*, for instance, did note that dictionary definitions of privacy did not match completely with the values they saw threatened by uncontrolled record-keeping. However, from this fact they drew the conclusion that 'we must formulate a concept of privacy that is consistent with record-keeping'.[23] Thus, the meaning of privacy was modified in such a way that privacy could continue its role as a guiding ideal. In the HEW report, the modification is made explicitly. In most other documents, the changes remain implicit, but the result is the same. From the early 1970s onwards, respect for privacy in the context of data processing equals respect for the principles of fair information processing. In her overview of the legislative process in the U.S., Regan remarks, for instance, that 'the Code of Fair Information Practices provided both the meaning for the idea of privacy and the framework for subsequent policy formulation'.[24] Allen notes that the legislation in the field of data protection codifies the principles of fair information processing 'in the name of privacy'.[25] America's most prominent privacy advocate, Marc Rotenberg, concludes: 'It is generally understood that the challenge of privacy protection in the information age is the application and enforcement of Fair Information Practices.'[26] Some may note that the concept of privacy in

---

[22] Regan, *Legislating Privacy*, p. 77.

[23] HEW report *Records, Computers, and Rights of Citizens*, pp. 38-39.

[24] Regan, *Legislating Privacy*, p. 77.

[25] A.L. Allen, 'Constitutional Law and Privacy', in D.M. Patterson (ed.), *A Companion to the Philosophy of Law and Legal Theory*, Cambridge, Mass. [etc.], Blackwell's, 1996, pp. 139-155, at p. 139.

[26] M. Rotenberg, 'What Larry Doesn't Get: Fair Information Practices and the Architecture of Privacy', *Stanford Technology Law Review*, <http://stlr.stanford.edu/STLR/Working_Papers/00_Rotenberg_1>, 2000.

this sense is different from the classical right to privacy,[27] or that the term 'privacy' is a poor label for fair information practices,[28] but these critics have not prevented the ideal of privacy from continuing its leading role in the development of the law.

## 5. Evaluation

The orientation towards the ideal of privacy has had a substantial influence on the development of the law of data privacy. The main consequence of ideal-orientation has been a turn to abstraction. The focus on ideals has given the debate about the development of the law a relatively high level of abstraction. Instead of studying concrete rules, principles, and procedures for handling personal data and developing new rules on a piecemeal basis in response to particular practical problems, one grand theory of 'data privacy' was developed that was to apply to all uses of personal data.

The advantage of the more abstract approach that ideal orientation entails is that it brings together various subjects that would be treated separately in more concrete analyses. Abstraction from the particular context of a certain problem allows us to see connections between certain problems and to construct integrated solutions. As the editors to this book put it: ideals are 'a source of unity'.[29] Thus, by presenting every recording of personal data as a threat to the ideal of privacy, the various concerns relating to the processing of personal data were brought together under a single heading, namely 'privacy'.

Still, it is doubtful whether this rather abstract approach has been fruitful for the development of the law of data privacy. The processing of personal data can be unfair for numerous different reasons. These differences are easily obscured by the use of a single concept. The European Union Privacy Directive, for instance, treats both data relating to political activities and data relating to criminal activities as privacy-sensitive material.[30] The reasons why these two categories of personal

---

[27] See Paul M. Schwartz and Joel R. Reidenberg, *Data Privacy Law: A Study of United States Data Protection*, Charlottesville, Va., Michie, 1996, pp. 36-39.

[28] The Privacy Protection Study Commission, *Personal Privacy in an Information Society*, Washington, D.C., U.S. Government Printing Office, 1977, p. 21; J.R. Reidenberg, 'Setting Standards for Fair Information Practices in the U.S. Private Sector', *Iowa Law Review* (1995), 497-551, at p. 498; see also U.S. House Committee on Government Operations, *Health Security Act of 1994*, 103rd Congress, 2nd session, 1994, report 103-601, vol. 5, p. 83.

[29] See the Introduction to this volume.

[30] See Art. 8 paras. 1 and 5 of EU Directive 95/46/EG.

data have to be processed with extra care are completely different. With respect to political activities, the collection of data is problematic because it has a chilling effect on individual behaviour. Thus, governmental monitoring of an individual's statements in a public forum hinders free speech. Therefore personal data relating to political activities are considered 'special'. With respect to criminal activities, the problem is not the availability of personal data as such, but the use that is made of the personal data. Uses of criminal records that inhibit ex-convicts from building up a new life are considered unfair. The point of the protection of criminal records is to promote the rehabilitation of convicts who have served their sentence. These two cases show that privacy is invoked for completely different reasons. Sometimes the objective is to block the stream of data altogether, sometimes the objective is to direct the stream. In addition, there are cases in which the processing of personal data is unfair, even if the data are used for legitimate purposes. In such cases, the right to 'privacy' demands that the individual is given the opportunity to participate in the decision-making process by accessing and amending his data. For instance, the main object of the 'privacy rules' relating to credit reporting is to assure that the data are accurate and that the data subject gets the opportunity to correct the data. In this context, the meaning of 'data privacy protection' is again completely different from the protection of data relating to political activities or data relating to criminal records. These fundamental differences are obscured by the application of the ideal of privacy to all these cases. The neglect of these differences is the main source of the confusion surrounding the concept of privacy, which I mentioned in section 2. Given the rule of law, these confusions are unacceptable.

Moreover, the invocation of the ideal of privacy is often unnecessary and confusing since almost any problem with respect to data processing can be addressed on the basis of more concrete rules and principles. This can be illustrated on the basis of the three different uses of the concept of privacy that I discussed in the preceding section. The monitoring of political activities may conflict with the constitutional freedom of speech. In U.S. constitutional law, for instance, the monitoring of political activities is seen as a violation of the First Amendment rights to free speech and association.[31] This classification seems more apt to the problem than presenting it as an invasion of privacy, for the activities monitored are not private. On the contrary, political activities may be the most public activities there are. In addition, classification as a violation of the First Amendment underscores that the freedom at stake is a

---

[31]  See Talley v. California, 362 U.S. 60 (1960); McIntyre v. Ohio Elections Committee, 514 U.S. 334. (1995).

privileged liberty that deserves special protection in a democratic society. Reference to the general concept of privacy obscures that fact.

'Naming and shaming' of criminals may clash with the principle of *ne bis in idem*, the prohibition of unusual and cruel punishments, and, more generally, the right to get a second chance.[32] Again this classification seems more apt than the use of privacy. For the point of the protection of criminal records is, of course, not to let individuals freely commit crimes in private, but to promote rehabilitation.

The right to access and correct information that an organization uses to make serious decisions with respect to an individual and the right to participate in the process of decision making, is well established in almost every legal system as the principle of *audi et alteram partem* and the principle of open government. This principle has a basis in both U.S. constitutional law and the European Convention of Human Rights.[33] Thus, in 1959 the U.S. Supreme Court already declared, without any reference to the concept of privacy: 'Certain principles have remained relatively immutable in our jurisprudence. One of these is that where government action seriously injures an individual and the reasonableness of the action depends on fact findings, the evidence used to prove the Government's case must be disclosed to the individual so that he has an opportunity to show that it is untrue.'[34] This is exactly what the right of access and rectification in the context of data processing is about.

The focus on a rather abstract ideal of privacy has obscured many of these more concrete legal rules, principles, and procedures for controlling information power. So, orientation towards ideals may cause a neglect of well-established legal doctrines and, consequently, makes it harder to find solutions for practical legal problems. Given the fact that the orientation towards the ideal of privacy has obscured both the nature of the problems of data processing and the bases for solving them, one could argue that in this field the orientation towards ideals has got out of hand. The focus on the abstract ideal of privacy has unnecessarily distracted the legal developers from the specific context of the problem, and, consequently, made it harder to solve those problems in a pragmatic way.

---

[32] See A. Etzioni, *The Limits of Privacy*, New York, Basic Books, 1999, pp. 56-58.

[33] See Greene v. McElroy, 360 U.S. 474, 496 (1959); Art. 6 para. 3 of the European Convention on Human Rights.

[34] Greene v. McElroy, 360 U.S. 474, 496 (1959).

# 6. Conclusion

The text above will have made clear that with respect to the development of legal rules for the handling of personal data, the concept of privacy has functioned as an ideal in Van der Burg's sense. First, privacy is a relatively vague concept, which nonetheless has provided a point of orientation for future legal developments (section 3). Second, the meaning of the concept of privacy was not yet fully articulated in law, but open to further interpretation in the light of new legal and technological developments (section 4). These two points also make clear that ideals and legal developments may mutually influence each other. On the one hand, the ideal of privacy has functioned as a beacon for developments in the law. On the other hand, legal developments have altered the meaning of the ideal.

The case of data privacy also makes clear that an orientation towards ideals may not be fruitful for legal development. The focus on a relatively abstract concept, such as the ideal of privacy, clouds the specific context of a legal problem. Consequently, orientation towards ideals tends to obscure the particular nature of a problem and to cause a neglect of the various legal resources for solving the problem. Therefore, Van der Burg and Taekema's warning not to overstate the case for ideal orientation should be taken seriously. As they indicate, in many situations ideal orientation is 'completely out of place' since the main problem is often the disregard for basic rules.[35] If even a highly dynamic field such as the law of data privacy is such a situation in which ideal orientation is out of place, one could argue that, in general, legal developers should be wary of ideals and focus on concrete rules and principles instead.

# References

Allen, A.L., 'Constitutional Law and Privacy', in D.M. Patterson (ed.), *A Companion to the Philosophy of Law and Legal Theory*, Cambridge, Mass. [etc.], Blackwell's, 1996.

Berman, J., and D. Mulligan, 'The Internet and the Law: Privacy in the Digital Age. Work in Progress', *Nova Law Review* (1999), 549-582.

Brenton, M., *The Privacy Invaders*, New York, Coward-McCann, 1964.

Committee on the Judiciary, United States Senate, *Federal Data Banks and Constitutional Rights*, Washington, DC, U.S. Government Printing Office, 1974.

Etzioni, A., *The Limits of Privacy*, New York, Basic Books, 1999.

---

[35]   See their Introduction to this volume.

Foucault, M., *Discipline and Punish: The Birth of the Prison*, New York, Vintage Books, 1979.

Long, E.V., *The Intruders: The Invasion of Privacy by Government and Industry*, New York, Praeger, 1967.

Miller, A., *The Assault on Privacy*, Ann Arbor, The University of Michigan Press, 1971.

Packard, V., *The Naked Society*, New York, Pocket Books, 1964.

Parent, W.A., 'Recent Work on the Concept of Privacy', *American Philosophical Quarterly* (1983/1984), 341-355.

Pennock, J.R., and J.W. Chapman (eds.), *Nomos XIII: Privacy*, New York, Atherton Press, 1971.

Privacy Protection Study Commission, The, *Personal Privacy in an Information Society*, Washington, D.C., U.S. Government Printing Office, 1977.

Privacy Working Group, Information Policy Committee, Information Infrastructure Task Force, *Privacy and the National Information Infrastructure: Principles for Providing and Using Personal Information*, publications, <http://nii.nist.gov/>, June 1995.

Regan, P.M., *Legislating Privacy: Technology, Social Values, and Public Policy*, Chapel Hill & London, University of North Carolina Press, 1995.

Reidenberg, J.R., 'Setting Standards for Fair Information Practices in the U.S. Private Sector', *Iowa Law Review* (1995), 497-551.

Rosenberg, J.M., *The Death of Privacy*, New York, Random House, 1969.

Rotenberg, M., 'What Larry Doesn't Get: Fair Information Practices and the Architecture of Privacy', *Stanford Technology Law Review*, <http://stlr.stanford.edu/STLR/Working_Papers/00_Rotenberg_1>, 2000.

Schoeman, F.D., (ed.), *Philosophical Dimensions of Privacy: An Anthology*, Cambridge, Cambridge University Press, 1984.

Schwartz, Paul M., and Joel R. Reidenberg, *Data Privacy Law: A Study of United States Data Protection*, Charlottesville, Va., Michie, 1996.

U.S. Department of Health, Education, and Welfare, Secretary's Advisory Committee on Automated Personal Data Systems, *Records, Computers, and the Rights of Citizens*, Cambridge, Mass., MIT Press, 1973.

U.S. House Committee on Government Operations, *Health Security Act of 1994*, 103rd Congress, 2nd session, 1994, report 103-601, volume 5.

Westin, A.F., *Privacy and Freedom*, New York, Atheneum Press, 1967.

Westin, A.F., and M.A. Baker, *Databanks in a Free Society: Computers, Record-Keeping, and Privacy*, New York, Quadrangle Books, 1973.

# The Role of Ideals in Legal Development: Sustainable Development and the Conservation of Biological Diversity as Cases in Point

Jonathan VERSCHUUREN and Timon OUDENAARDEN

## 1. Introduction

Ideals, it is asserted in the Introduction to this book, are key elements in enabling development. Due to the fact that ideals can never be realised completely, a certain discrepancy always remains between the valuable state of affairs the ideal refers to and the current state of affairs, so that there is always room for improvement. Furthermore, ideals can 'provide points of orientation and inspiration for new directions'. Whenever we feel that our current legal system is no longer adequate for the ever-changing world around us, ideals can help us decide on the direction in which it could and should be developed. Ideals, therefore, not only make change possible, they also invite development and even serve as beacons that show us in which direction the development should go.

In this chapter, we will pursue in greater depth the question what role ideals have or can have in legal development, and in particular the extent to which ideals can provide guidance in this respect. Our focus will be on international environmental law and policy, more particularly on two specific ideals which for some time now have been predominant in debate and literature as well as in legal and policy documents in this field: the ideal of sustainable development and that of the conservation of biological diversity. We will examine whether these ideals have influenced developments in international environmental law and, if so, in what way.

## 2. Background

Although the rise of the sustainability concept in international environmental law is generally considered a fairly recent phenomenon, the concept builds on thoughts that go back a long time.[1] Swanson and Johnston trace it back to the 1893 Pacific Fur Seal Arbitration, when the United States claimed a right of protection over fur seals born within its jurisdiction against their taking and killing by British vessels outside US territory, and did so on the grounds that the seal stocks should be conserved for the benefit of humankind.[2] In economics, the concept of sustainability has been known and applied for a long time.[3] Nonetheless, it was not until the IUCN published its *World Conservation Strategy* (WCS) in 1980 that 'sustainable development' as such emerged as a central notion in an international semi-legal document.[4] Seven years later, the World Commission on Environment and Development (WCED, or Brundtland Commission) published its report *Our Common Future*, which centred on the concept of sustainable development. The WCED Report and the enormous attention it received worldwide gave sustainable development its position as a key concept in environmental law and policy. That it still holds this position today can be seen in numerous legal and political documents, most notably the UN Declaration of Rio de Janeiro, adopted during the 1992 United Nations Conference on Environment and Development (UNCED), which in its twenty-seven principles refers to 'sustainable development' twelve times.[5]

---

[1]  See C.V. Kidd, 'The Evolution of Sustainability', *Journal of Agricultural and Environmental Ethics* 1 (1992), 1-26.

[2]  T.M. Swanson and S. Johnston, *Global Environmental Problems and International Environmental Agreements: The Economics of International Institution Building,* Cheltenham, Edward Elgar, 1996, p. 236; on the Pacific Fur Seal Arbitration, see Ph. Sands, 'Turtles and Torturers: The Transformation of International Law', *New York University Journal of International Law and Politics* 33 (2001) 2, 527-560, at p. 529.

[3]  Pearce *et al.* use the term to describe a situation in which both the output of an economy and the resource base that provides that output are sustained over time; David Pearce *et al., Blueprint 3: Measuring Sustainable Development*, London, Earthscan, 1993, p. 3.

[4]  IUCN-UNEP-WWF, *World Conservation Strategy: Living Resource Conservation for Sustainable Development*, Gland, IUCN, 1980.

[5]  This includes one reference to 'international law in the field of sustainable development' (Principle 27). As regards the European Union, the 1992 Maastricht Treaty gave the promotion of 'harmonious, balanced and sustainable development of economic activities' a prominent place among the goals the Community should pursue (Art. 2 EC Treaty).

With regard to the conservation of biological diversity, similar remarks can be made. Some authors feel that, in retrospect, the international community can be said to have concerned itself with biodiversity conservation for a long time. Nature conservation laws – with regard to forestry, for instance – already existed thousands of years ago; and even international treaties intended to prevent natural resources from being overexploited have existed since the late nineteenth century.[6] It was not until the late 1960s and early 1970s, however, that the concept of what was then referred to as 'genetic diversity' began to find its way into international documents. UNESCO's Man and the Biosphere Programme published a report in 1971 which advocated the 'conservation of natural areas and of the genetic material they contain' through the establishment of nature reserves. Preservation of species as well as maintenance of genetic diversity are captured under this heading.[7] The Stockholm Action Plan, which was one of the results of the 1972 UN Conference on the Human Environment, also refers to the importance of conserving genetic diversity,[8] as does the 1980 *World Conservation Strategy* already mentioned. Since the United Nations Conference on Environment and Development, which was held in Rio de Janeiro in 1992, adopted the text of the Convention on Biological Diversity (CBD), this latter term has taken the place of 'genetic diversity' in debate and policy documents.[9] The CBD states the 'conservation of biological diversity' as its objective, along with 'the sustainable use of its components and the fair and equitable sharing of the benefits arising out of the utilization of genetic resources'.[10]

Bearing in mind the conception of ideals that is used in the introduction to this volume, it is plausible to regard both sustainable development and biodiversity conservation as ideals. Both represent states of affairs that are considered desirable. Moral considerations play an important role here; pleas for sustainability are most commonly based on the premise that using and managing the natural resources available to us in an unsustainable way would be unfair to the generations to come, whereas advocates of biodiversity conservation often derive arguments

---

[6] See, e.g., S. Lyster, *International Wildlife Law*, Cambridge, Grotius, 1985, p. xxi.

[7] International Co-Ordinating Council of the Programme on Man and the Biosphere, first session, Final Report, Paris, 1971, pp. 20-21.

[8] Recommendation 40(b).

[9] Nowadays, the phrase 'genetic diversity' is commonly used to refer to diversity within species and populations as opposed to diversity between species and diversity of ecosystems.

[10] Convention on Biological Diversity, Rio de Janeiro, 5 June 1992, IEL 992: 42, Art. 1 (text available at <http:// www.biodiv.org>).

either from the intrinsic value that other living creatures have or from the fact that diminishing the resource base would affect the possibilities and opportunities our children and grandchildren have to meet their needs.[11] That sustainable development and biodiversity conservation are generally seen as worthy causes that should be pursued can be seen when we look at the prominent place they have in documents, decisions, resolutions and policies by international organisations such as the UN, by national governments and by other non-governmental organisations at the national or international level. The MAB Programme Reports, the Stockholm Declaration, the *World Conservation Strategy*, the WCED Report, the Rio Declaration and the Biodiversity Convention are the most important examples, though many more documents could be mentioned here.

Although explicit reception is not a necessary condition for some-thing to be considered an ideal,[12] the fact that in the case of sustainable development and biodiversity conservation these ideals have been expli-citly formulated in legal documents makes it possible to study their con-sequences for legal practice more in detail.

Two other features of ideals, namely the fact that they usually cannot be realised completely and the fact that it is difficult to formulate them exactly, also seem to apply to sustainable development and biodiversity conservation. Notwithstanding the fact that the international community has agreed on the necessity to make development sustainable and to conserve biodiversity for decades, few people would maintain that these aims have now been realised completely, nor that there is the prospect of realising them in the near future. The differences that have existed over the years in terminology and in the exact phrasing of the thoughts we now tend to capture under the headings of sustainable development and biodiversity conservation, indicate that it has not been easy to find a formulation for either of these concepts that everybody involved could agree to.

---

[11] A wealth of literature exists on the question of the intrinsic value of non-human living organisms (particularly higher animals) as well as on intergenerational equity; for an anthology, see D. VanDeVeer and C. Pierce (eds.), *The Environmental Ethics and Policy Book*, Belmont, Cal., Wadsworth, 1998, esp. pp. 74-215 and 432-478.

[12] See the Introduction to this volume.

## 3. Enabling Development or Guiding Development?

Van der Burg and Taekema claim that ideals make legal development possible and that they may provide guidance with regard to the direction this development should take.[13] In contrast, we think that it would be wise to make a clear distinction between these two aspects, because, in our view, making a certain development possible and guiding it in a certain direction are completely different things. Furthermore, with regard to ideals, the same features that enable them to make legal development possible – in the sense that they facilitate discussions about the various possible ways of development – seem to reduce substantially the extent to which ideals can provide *guidance* to legal development. *Guiding* development is here taken to mean that the pursuit of a common ideal by two or more actors who are involved in law-making (such as members of a national legislature or – in the case of international law – representatives from States drafting a treaty or convention) indicates, to a certain extent at least, the kind of norms and regulations that are needed to reach the state of affairs aspired. It is precisely the two features of ideals mentioned last in the preceding section that give rise to doubts as to whether they really can guide legal development. Since they can never be captured entirely in one formulation and because they can never be completely realised, different interpretations of the same ideal may exist together with different actors, and these may even lead to different and sometimes conflicting ways of trying to realise the ideal in question. But if this is so, how can such an ideal guide legal development at the same time? If it is difficult or even impossible to reach an agreement on the exact formulation of an ideal or on its precise content, how then can we determine whether all the actors involved are actually striving towards the same objectives? And, if we cannot be sure about this, how can such an ideal indicate the direction that legal development should take? In short, it seems possible or even likely that ideals are *too* 'open-ended', or too vague, to guide the development of existing laws and regulations towards a common goal.

One may argue that, even if ideals cannot actually provide guidance to legal development in the sense in which this term is used here, at the very least they can indicate the direction such developments *should not* take. The idea is that it is easier to identify measures that are counterproductive if we want to reach a certain goal than it is to determine what actions are needed to bring it closer – more concretely, it is easier to determine what actions are harmful to sustainable development or biodiversity conservation than to identify what actions we should take to

---

[13]   *Ibid.*

bring us nearer to these goals. The problem here is that the profound differences of opinion that exist with regard to sustainability and biodiversity conservation concern not just the appropriate *means* by which these goals are to be reached, but also the exact meaning of the goals *themselves*. A state of affairs that is considered sustainable by some may very well be deemed unsustainable by others. Consequently, trying to agree on the unsustainable character of certain activities will not be much easier than reaching a consensus on the activities that contribute to sustainability.

Again, both of the ideals under discussion can be used to illustrate the problems that arise here. As for sustainable development, since the publication of the Brundtland Report many have commented on the concept's open and rather vague character, which some feel makes it impossible to determine exactly what its meaning is in more concrete environmental policy and law. Birnie and Boyle put it like this:

> It is clear, given the breadth of international endorsement for the concept, that few states would quarrel with the proposition that development should in principle be sustainable and that all natural resources should be managed in this way. What is lacking is any comparable consensus on the meaning of sustainable development, or how to give it concrete effect in individual cases.[14]

It is, for instance, equally possible, taking sustainable development as a starting point, to argue either in favour of a further growth of economic production or against it, depending on what view of sustainability one adheres to.[15] This lack of consensus on the concept's practical

---

[14] Patricia W. Birnie and Alan E. Boyle, *International Law and the Environment*, 2nd ed., Oxford [etc.], Oxford University Press, 2002, p. 95. Note that in these authors' view consensus is lacking both on the meaning of sustainable development and on 'how to give it concrete effect in individual cases'; that is to say, both on the best way to reach the goal of sustainability and on the goal itself, and its precise meaning.

[15] A common distinction in the literature is between strong and weak sustainability. Those who adhere to the weak sustainability concept feel that as long as we do not leave for next generations an overall capital stock that is smaller than it is today, we are meeting the demands of sustainability. In what form – man-made, human or natural – we pass on this capital is considered irrelevant. By contrast, advocates of the strong sustainability concept say we should keep intact either some or all of the natural resources that are present on earth today, because of the critical role they play in keeping the earth's ecological systems and life support processes, on which we depend for our existence, going. See Pearce *et al.*, *Blueprint 3*, pp. 15-21, and Wilfried Beckermann, '"Sustainable Development': Is It a Useful Concept?", in VanDeVeer and Pierce, *Environmental Ethics and Policy Book*, pp. 462-474, at p. 464. The weak sustainability concept would, therefore, be compatible with, or even call for, further economic growth; a perception of strong sustainability would not. The concept's

implications makes it vulnerable to criticisms saying that it leaves too much room for the actors involved to interpret it in the way that is the most convenient to them, and that therefore the apparent agreement on the importance of reaching sustainable development is meaningless. It has led some critics to draw the somewhat cynical conclusion that 'sustainable development' in practice simply means 'sustained growth'.[16] The fact that the WCED has provided a definition of sustainable development which is generally considered to be more or less authoritative has not been able to bring consensus on the concept's practical implications much closer. The Commission's conception of sustainable development reads:

> Sustainable development is development that meets the needs of the present without compromising the ability of future generations to meet their own needs.[17]

Since this definition leaves open the question how we are to determine what needs generations to come will have (it could, in fact, hardly do otherwise) and how they are to be weighed against our own when present and future needs conflict, it has been argued that it contains too many elements that leave room for subjective interpretation to be able to serve as a criterion to decide on environmental policies.[18]

---

practical implications are also dependent on whether one attaches more weight to ecological, economic or social aspects of sustainability – in terms of the WCED definition, whether ecological, economic or social 'needs and aspirations' are considered more important, and how the needs of the present are weighed against those of following generations.

[16] Bill Willers ('Sustainable Development: A New World Deception', *Conservation Biology* 8 (1994) 4, 1146-1148, at p. 1146) maintains that 'sustainable development is a code for "perpetual growth"'. According to Marc Pallemaerts ('International Environmental Law from Stockholm to Rio: Back to the Future?', in Ph. Sands (ed.), *Greening International Law*, London, Earthscan, 1993, pp. 1-19, at p. 14), 'the expression "sustainable development" is now more and more used interchangeably with, even equated with, the notion of "sustained growth"'. See also J.B. Callicott and K. Mumford, 'Ecological Sustainability as a Conservation Concept', *Conservation Biology* 11 (1997) 1, 32-40, at p. 34, who are not surprised that sustainable development has been interpreted to mean economic growth since, in their view, 'development' commonly denotes urbanisation, industrialisation of agriculture and an expanding market economy.

[17] *Our Common Future*, [s.l.], WCED, 1987, p. 43. Other definitions can be found in J. Pezzey, *Sustainable Development Concepts: An Economic Analysis*, Washington DC, The World Bank, 1992, pp. 55-61.

[18] '[S]uch a criterion is totally useless since "needs" are a subjective concept. People at different points in time, or in different income levels, or with different cultural or national backgrounds, will differ with respect to what "needs" they regard as impor-

Similar remarks can be made with regard to the conservation of bio-diversity. Although there is not a single definition of the term that is agreed upon, 'conservation' is not restricted to preserving some natural resource in its current state (the so-called 'hands-off approach'), but goes much further. The WCS definition of conservation serves as an example:

> Conservation is defined here as: the management of human use of the bio-sphere so that it may yield the greatest sustainable benefit to present genera-tions while maintaining its potential to meet the needs and aspirations of future generations. Thus conservation is positive, embracing preservation, maintenance, sustainable utilization, restoration, and enhancement of the natural environment.[19]

Instead of just requiring that we leave the resource in question alone, conservation therefore demands that we actively manage it, using it when needed, preserving its status quo when necessary, increasing and developing it when possible. When we ask *when* exactly we should do one or the other, however, the definition echoes the WCED's definition of sustainability, bringing all connected questions into the conservation concept.[20]

Apart from this, the biodiversity concept itself raises some other questions. Although popularly equated with the number of species that are represented within a given area, a quick glance at the definition the CBD provides in Article 2 reveals that this equation is not correct, or at least not complete. Biological diversity is described here as

> ... the variability among living organisms from all sources including, inter alia, terrestrial, marine and other aquatic ecosystems and the ecological

---

tant. Hence, the injunction to enable future generations to meet their needs does not provide any clear guidance as to what has to be preserved in order that future genera-tions may do so'; Beckermann in VanDe Veer and Pierce, *Environmental Ethics and Policy Book*, p. 464.

[19] See the IUCN's Statutes, which state that the 'conservation of nature and natural resources involves the preservation and management of the living world, the natural environment of humanity, and the earth's renewable natural resources on which rests the foundation of human civilization' (IEL 948: 75).

[20] The same holds when we examine the definition the Global Biodiversity Strategy (GBS) gives of biodiversity conservation: 'The management of human interactions with genes, species, and ecosystems so as to provide the maximum benefit to the pre-sent generation while maintaining their potential to meet the needs and aspirations of future generations, encompasses elements of saving, studying, and using biodiver-sity.' *Global Biodiversity Strategy: Guidelines for Action to Save, Study, and Use Earth's Biotic Wealth Sustainably and Equitably*, Washington DC, WRI/IUCN/ UNEP, 1992, p. 228.

complexes of which they are part; this includes diversity within species, between species and of ecosystems.[21]

This means that, apart from the species level, diversity can be described at the ecosystem level and at the level of genes, sub-species and populations as well. Moreover, in the literature the term 'diversity' is used to refer not only to sheer numbers (such as the number of different species present in a certain area), but also to other, more qualitative aspects, such as the rarity of a given species or the extent to which it is endemic.[22] If we want to know what measures will contribute most to the conservation of biodiversity, we need to know the particular level or aspect of biodiversity we should focus on; but the CBD definition does not tell us this, and neither do most of the other documents with regard to biodiversity conservation. It is not possible either to encapsulate the entire biodiversity concept, with all its aspects and different levels, in one single variable. Nonetheless, since we have only limited resources available to conduct research and plan and implement conservation measures, priorities should be set as to the particular species, populations, varieties or ecosystems we should focus on. Taken in itself and without further explanation, however, the biodiversity concept does not provide a clear criterion that we can use to set priorities in nature conservation; depending on the level and aspect of biodiversity one takes as a starting point, certain conservation measures can be supported as well as attacked as 'having a positive effect on biodiversity'.[23] As with sustainable development, the fact that this is so has provoked cynical responses.[24]

It seems, then, that both sustainable development and biodiversity conservation leave many questions unanswered and leave much room for subjective interpretation. Moreover, the fear expressed by critics that the open-ended character of the two phrases makes them vulnerable to abuse seems justified at least in part, precisely because both are gener-

---

[21] CBD, Art. 2. Strictly speaking, of course, variability is not a 'thing' that can be managed; it is the organisms, plants, animals, genes, populations, ecosystems, etc., themselves that must be conserved in order to conserve their variability. Thus, other definitions describe biodiversity as 'the totality of genes, species, and ecosystems' (GBS) giving the term a more 'material' meaning.

[22] See, e.g., E. Van der Maarel, *Biodiversity: From Babel to Biosphere Management*, Uppsala, Opulus Press, 1997.

[23] Flooding an area in order to create, e.g., a swamp or wetland, may enhance ecosystem diversity in the region while causing a number of species that were present there to disappear, thus reducing species richness.

[24] See, e.g., Gordon H. Rodda, 'How to Lie with Biodiversity', *Conservation Biology* 7 (1993) 4, 959-960.

ally regarded as ideals that everyone agrees should be pursued. A measure or argument presented by its proponent as a contribution to either sustainable development or biodiversity conservation therefore has a strong emotive prima facie appeal.

It appears therefore that the ideals of sustainability and biodiversity conservation can play a role in guiding the development of laws and regulations only to a limited extent. It seems fair to say that the fact that there are differences in interpretation may arouse lively discussions about which interpretation is the better, and in this way *facilitate* development; but if there is no consensus on the ideal's content and on the best way to reach it, it cannot really serve as a beacon indicating the direction legal development should take.

## 4. The Need for Flexibility

As already mentioned, the fact that the ideals discussed here are open to different, sometimes conflicting interpretations has given rise to criticism. Behind such criticism there seems to be the belief that the causes of making development sustainable and conserving biodiversity would have been better served if these ideals had been transformed somehow into clear, concrete, legally binding and enforceable rules. Thus, a global treaty defining the concepts of sustainable development and of biodiversity conservation in detail and containing specific, concrete and binding obligations for States with respect to the measures that need to be taken to reach the two objectives probably would have been applauded by these critics. The comments made in the literature on the use of non-binding principles and on the phenomenon of 'framework convention', discussed below in this chapter, are a case in point.

However, where international law – and especially international environmental or nature conservation law – is concerned, this assumption does not hold for a number of reasons. At a practical level, it is very difficult to get the international community to agree to precise and binding legal rules in today's world. Birnie and Boyle state that it is almost impossible to secure widespread consent to new rules, given the political, cultural and religious diversity of contemporary international society (and given the developmental diversity, we would add).[25] Treaties on environmental issues, therefore, cannot easily be concluded, nor does customary law evolve easily, at least not among a large number of states. Birnie and Boyle observe that treaties, although a more useful medium, either do not enter into force, or do so for only a limited number of parties which do not necessarily include those states whose

---

[25] Birnie and Boyle, *International Law and the Environment*, p. 24.

involvement is most vital to the achievement of their purposes, especially where modification of economically profitable conduct is required.[26]

Moreover, apart from being unfeasible in practice, the establishment of strict, concrete rules that apply globally is undesirable as well. The huge differences between nations worldwide with regard to economic, developmental, ecological, cultural and other circumstances call for different standards and regulations. Any worldwide regime for achieving sustainable development or biodiversity conservation will have to be flexible enough to take these differences into account. With regard to biodiversity conservation, after all, it is not only the general ideas on what 'biodiversity conservation' means that differ; it is also biodiversity *itself*. Each region or even each spot on earth has its own mix of plant and animal species or populations, many of which may be endemic or rare, and this particular mix is the result of specific ecological, climatological, geographical circumstances and their development over time. Moreover, the social, demographic, cultural and economic settings in which biological resources live and function differ widely as well. Hence, assessment of the measures that need to be taken to 'conserve biodiversity' from an ecological point of view can only take place if all local circumstances are taken into account; and the same applies with regard to the measures that can be taken from a socioeconomic perspective. After all, safeguarding the coral reefs off the coast of New Guinea requires actions much different from those that are needed to keep the wild hamster in the Netherlands from becoming extinct, and the resources available for these purposes and the extent to which nature conservation is considered a priority issue differ as well. A stricter common regulation and standard-setting for all components of biological diversity all over the world would therefore be undesirable as well as practically unfeasible; concrete measures can be planned and implemented much quicker and much more effectively at a national, regional or local level.[27]

---

[26] *Ibid.*, p. 25.

[27] Cf. Kiss's discussion of the merits of the framework approach in international environmental law: 'This technique broadly consists in the gradual introduction of standards governing a specific matter which needs to be regulated. This characteristic, moreover, corresponds to many other aspects of the innovative side of international environmental law, including the fact that this new branch of international law, which has only been in existence for just over twenty years, takes account of the passage of time. It can also serve, if need be, to adapt universal rules to regional or even local situations' (A. Kiss, 'Framework Conventions: A Legal Technique for International Environmental Protection', in *Symposium on the United Nations Conference on Environment and Development (UNCED), the Convention on Biological*

With regard to sustainable development, the same holds true, *mutatis mutandis*; what constitutes 'development' and what is needed to achieve it varies along with the social, economic, geographical and other circumstances a country is in, as is the case with 'sustainability'. Also, we can observe a trend in which businesses and NGOs and/or local communities discuss the relationship between economy and ecology at the local level, without government interference. This trend of cooperative approaches has been enabled by the concept of sustainable development: instead of having to deal with fixed government-set standards, businesses and NGOs now negotiate how sustainable development should be achieved in a specific situation.

Any legal system that addresses these two issues therefore needs to be flexible enough to be able to take local or regional circumstances into account. Apart from that, since these circumstances evolve and change over time, it has to be able to adapt to these changes as well – the more so because scientific knowledge on the functioning of ecosystems and the environment develops rapidly as well.

In the remainder of this chapter, we will examine in what ways the ideals of sustainable development and biodiversity conservation, respectively, have been given legal shape. In our view, these two ways represent two different – although interconnected – systems that in fact do leave room for flexibility, as we will try to show. First, in section 5, we will have a closer look at the ideal of sustainable development. We will start by showing the influence of this ideal on international law, especially through legal principles (5.1), followed by a study of the role of these principles in national environmental law (5.2). In section 6, we will show the consequences of the ideal of biodiversity conservation for international law on nature conservation.

---

*Diversity and the Bern Convention: The Next Steps*, Strasbourg, Council of Europe Publishing, 1995, pp. 107-112, at p. 108). See also the Council of Europe's *Framework Convention for the Protection of National Minorities*, ETS no. 157, the Explanatory Report to which states that: 'In view of the range of different situations and problems to be resolved, a choice was made for a framework Convention which contains mostly programme-type provisions setting out objectives which the Parties undertake to pursue. These provisions, which will not be directly applicable, leave the States concerned a measure of discretion in the implementation of the objectives which they have undertaken to achieve, thus enabling them to take particular circumstances into account.' Available at the Council of Europe's Treaties website <http://conventions.coe.int>.

# 5. Giving Legal Shape to the Ideal of Sustainable Development

## 5.1 *Sustainable Development and the Role of Legal Principles*

By 1992, when the UNCED took place in Rio de Janeiro, sustainable development had become an ideal that no one could ignore.[28] All the documents signed at the Rio Conference state, in one way or another, that everything that had been agreed on was necessary in order to achieve sustainable development. The Rio Declaration on Environment and Development, which was concluded during the UNCED as well, states in Principle 1:

> Human beings are at the centre of concerns for sustainable development. They are entitled to a healthy and productive life in harmony with nature.[29]

Interestingly, many principles in this Declaration explicitly refer to the ideal of sustainable development, as do preambular provisions and binding articles of many international treaties, such as the UN Framework Convention on Climate Change and the 1997 Kyoto Protocol.[30]

At the European level, the ideal of sustainable development is explicitly mentioned in various EC directives. In their preambles, directives very often state that the provisions are necessary to promote 'sustainable development'. The Council Directive concerning Integrated Pollution Prevention and Control (IPPC) gives concrete rules on permits for certain branches of industry.[31] Certain installations, in, for instance the energy, mineral, metal or chemical industries, can only be operated after a permit has been granted. The permit must include requirements ensuring that a high level of protection is given to the environment as a whole. The ultimate goal is to promote sustainable development.[32]

---

[28] See, on earlier international documents on sustainable development, section 2 of this contribution.

[29] UN Doc. A/CONF. 151/26/REV. 1/Vol. 1 (1992), reprinted in (1992) 31 ILM 876.

[30] E.g., Art. 2 of the Kyoto Protocol reads: 'Each Party included in Annex I, in achieving its quantified emission limitation and reduction commitments under Article 3, in order to promote sustainable development, shall: (a) ...'; FCCC/CP/1997/7/Add. 1, reprinted in (1998) 37 ILM 22.

[31] Council Directive 96/61/EC of 24 September 1996 concerning Integrated Pollution Prevention and Control, [1996] OJ L 257/26.

[32] The Preamble states, under no. 9: 'Whereas this Directive... lays down the measures necessary to implement integrated pollution prevention and control in order to achieve a high level of protection for the environment as a whole; whereas application of the principle of sustainable development will be promoted by an integrated

One may even argue that the introduction of the ideal of sustainable development has stimulated the use of legal principles. For a vague ideal such as sustainable development, to be used in a legal context, the ideal has to be made more concrete through legal principles. From a more theoretical point of view, principles can be seen as the link between ideals and duties, between the morality of aspiration and the morality of duty, between values and rules.[33] Selznick argues that 'normative systems' (i.e., law, or more precisely, principles and rules) are oriented towards ideals, and that these normative systems can only be understood if the ideal is understood as well.[34] A first step to make the ideal more concrete is the formulation of (legal) principles, and, in order to apply these principles, certain (even more concrete) rules have to be developed. Principles can be part of written, formal law, can be part of legislation and treaties and can, together with more concrete rules (or in combination with such rules), impose duties on the state or on individuals. On the other hand, principles themselves do not comprise enforceable legal duties.[35] They do, however, shed more light on the (moral) targets of legislative rules and thus form the link between the morality of aspiration and the morality of duty. Principles are a necessary medium for ideals to find their way into concrete rules. They can be used to bridge the gap between the morality of duty and the morality of aspiration.

When we take a closer look at international environmental law, we can indeed observe that the 1992 Rio Declaration has given an enormous boost to the role of environmental legal principles in international and European law. This becomes obvious when comparing environmental treaties before and after Rio, and when looking into international

---

approach to pollution control; ...' Note that the word 'principle' is used here to denote the ideal of sustainable development.

[33] Neil MacCormick, 'Law as Institutional Fact', *Law Quarterly Review* 90 (1974), 102-129, at p. 127; Philip Selznick, *The Moral Commonwealth: Social Theory and the Promise of Community*, Berkeley, Cal., University of California Press, 1992, p. 439.

[34] Philip Selznick, 'Sociology and Natural Law', *Natural Law Forum* 6 (1961), 84-108, at p. 87.

[35] It should be acknowledged, however, that this distinction is not a very strict one: there is a sliding scale with a theoretical abstract and indeterminate principle on one end and a very concrete, highly practical rule on the other. See Aulis Aarnio, 'Taking Rules Seriously', in Werner Maihofer and Gerhard Sprenger (eds.), *Law and the States in Modern Times*, Stuttgart, Steiner, 1990, pp. 180-192, at p. 184.

case law.[36] If we take the precautionary principle as an example, we can see that, after 1992, this principle, albeit in different formulations, is included in almost every treaty that has been drafted since. Examples of these are the Convention on Biodiversity[37] and the Biosafety Protocol[38], the Framework Convention on Climate Change[39], the Convention for the Protection of the Marine Environment of the North-East Atlantic[40] and a series of other conventions on the protection of water[41] as well as the 2001 Convention on Persistent Organic Pollutants.[42] As far as case law is concerned, all international tribunals and courts that have been discussed on various occasions had to deal with the principle. What we see here is that some courts consider it a binding principle (European Court of Justice),[43] while others do not think this so yet (WTO Appellate Body).[44] Within the International Court of Justice, the majority still refuse to adopt the view that the precautionary principle is a principle of customary law, although there is a growing number of dissenting opinions on this issue.[45]

In most countries where environmental principles have been codified, this has been done in relationship to the overall goal of aiming for sustainable development as well. In Australia, the statutory principles

---

[36] See Jonathan Verschuuren, *Principles of Environmental Law: The Ideal of Sustainable Development and the Role of Principles of International, European and National Environmental Law*, Baden-Baden, Nomos, 2003, pp. 106-107.

[37] (1992) 31 ILM 818: Preamble.

[38] Cartagena Protocol on Biosafety, Montreal, 29 January 2000, IEL 992: 42/A, Art. 1. The text of the Protocol can also be found at the Convention on Biodiversity website <http://www.biodiv.org/biosafety>.

[39] (1992) 31 ILM 851: Art. 3(3).

[40] (1992) 31 ILM 1069: Art. 2(2)(a).

[41] Art. 3(2) of the Convention on the Protection of the Marine Environment of the Baltic Sea Area, Art. 2(5) of the Convention on the Protection and Use of Transboundary Watercourses and International Lakes, Art. 3(2) of the 1994 Convention on the Protection of the Meuse River and Art. 3(1) of the 1996 Protocol to the 1972 Convention on the Prevention of Marine Pollution by Dumping Wastes and Other Matter.

[42] (2001) 40 ILM 531: Art. 1.

[43] E.g., cases C-284/95 and C-341/95, *Safety Hi-Tech/S&T* and *Bettati/Safety Hi-Tech*. See extensively on these cases Michael Doherty, 'The Status of the Principles of EC Environmental Law: Gianni Bettati against Safety Hi-Tech', *Journal of Environmental Law* 11 (1999) 2, 354-386.

[44] E.g. the *Beef hormones* case between the EC and the US: WTO Appelate Body 16 January 1998, WTO Doc. AB-1997-4, WT/DS48/AB/R.

[45] See, e.g., the dissenting opinions of judges Weeramantry, Koroma and Palmer in the *2nd Nuclear Test Case*, ICJ 22 September 1995, [1995] ICJ Rep. 359, 379 and 412 respectively.

have been laid down as 'principles of ecologically sustainable development',[46] while in Belgium[47] and in Finland[48] sustainable development has been formulated as an over-all goal for environmental policy; environmental policy must be carried out through the application of legal principles. In the Netherlands, the government has announced that the codification of principles will contribute to sustainable development.[49] All these examples show that principles are put in the perspective of sustainable development; they have to be applied to reach the higher goal of sustainable development.

## 5.2 Adopting Environmental Principles Enhances Environmental Law

So far, we have argued that applying legal principles is necessary to attain the ideal of sustainable development. But how exactly do environmental principles contribute to sustainable development? What are the advantages of the use of principles in international environmental law? Although many are sceptical on the role of such general principles,[50] we will show that adopting environmental principles at the international level actually enhances national environmental law throughout the world. We have seven arguments:

1. Principles enhance the normative power of statutory rules.
2. Principles help to define open or unclear statutory rules.
3. Principles increase legal certainty and enhance the legitimacy of decision-making.
4. Principles form the basis of new statutory rules.
5. Principles give guidance to self-regulation.
6. Principles create flexibility in the law.
7. Principles stimulate the integration of environmental considerations into other policy fields.

---

[46] Section 3A of the Environment Protection and Biodiversity Conservation Act 1999, Act No. 91, 1999.

[47] Art. 1.2.1, § 1, of the Flemish Decree on General Provisions concerning Environmental Policy, June 1995.

[48] Section 1 of the Environmental Protection Act, No. 86/2000, February 2000.

[49] Fourth National Environmental Policy Plan, *Kamerstukken II*, 2000/01, 27 801, No. 1, p. 69.

[50] E.g., Gary Lawson, 'A Farewell to Principles', *Iowa Law Review* 82 (1997) 2, 893-903.

*1. Principles enhance the normative power of statutory rules*

In many countries, modern environmental law consists of one or more framework Acts, together with a vast amount of very detailed (delegated) rules in administrative orders, administrative guidelines, policy plans, licences, etc. Framework legislation usually consists of procedural rules. Substantive statutory rules, for instance, on the level of environmental protection that should be reached, are mostly put in a rather general wording in statutes, to be elaborated in more detail in individual licences. Article 8.11, paragraph 3, of the Dutch Environmental Protection Act, for instance, states that a licence must be subject to any provisions '... that are necessary to protect the environment'. No further clues as to what is 'necessary' are given.

The reasons for this style of regulation are the technical complexity of environmental problems, the fact that environmental effects may deviate with the natural circumstances at a certain location, the rapidly changing insights in environmental problems as well as the ever-changing technological means to reduce negative effects on the environment. It is therefore quite understandable that the legislature feels restricted in formulating procedural or general rules in framework Acts and leaves the more substantive rules to constantly changing guidelines or delegated regulations.

Modern legislators often decide to include environmental legal principles in framework Acts to enhance the normative power of these Acts. Indeed, when read in combination with environmental legal principles, 'open' rules get a more substantive meaning. The right to environmental protection, laid down in the Belgian Constitution, applied in combination with the standstill principle of the Flemish Decree on Environmental Policy, becomes a strong right: relaxation of existing environmental standards is not permitted.[51]

At the international level, it is the same with modern treaties. Framework conventions have to be elaborated in protocols, manuals, guidelines, etc., the Framework Convention on Climate Change being a good example. In the 2000 Biosafety Protocol, the precautionary principle, as laid down in the 1992 Biodiversity Convention, has been taken as a normative starting point for further rules on biosafety.

*2. Principles help to define open or unclear statutory rules*

Enhancing the normative power of statutory rules also means that these rules can be applied more easily in concrete cases by the competent administrative authorities. This probably is the most important

---

[51] Council of State, 29 April 1999, *Tijdschrift voor milieurecht* 8 (1999) 4, 301.

function principles have in daily legal practice. Administrative authorities use principles to interpret open or unclear rules, for instance in case the applicable rule leaves ample room for discretion, in the case of conflicting rules or in case the situation was not foreseen by the legislator. The latter is a particularly relevant function of the precautionary principle. Cases on 'new risks', like the risks involved in radiation from mobile phone installations, have to be decided upon by competent authorities using existing legislation that may not yet have been adapted to such new and as yet unknown risks.[52]

Obviously, this function is extremely important for the judiciary as well. The European Court of Justice solved the conflict between the provisions in the EC Treaty on the free movement of goods and the EC Directive on Waste by interpreting EC law through the principles of self-sufficiency and proximity.[53] The same Court applied the precautionary principle and the prevention principle to define an unclear rule in the Directive concerning the storage of waste.[54]

National courts do the same thing. Since the Australian National Park and Wildlife Act was not entirely clear concerning the question whether a permit could be granted for the construction of a road, the New South Wales Land and Environment Court in the famous *Leatch v. National Park and Wildlife Service* case tested the decision against the precautionary principle to find an answer.[55] A Dutch Court did the same when testing a decision to allow the discharge of a certain chemical for which no concrete emission standards existed.[56]

### 3. Principles increase legal certainty and enhance the legitimacy of decision-making

Principles increase legal certainty and enhance the legitimacy of decision-making in two ways. Firstly, they more or less oblige a government to motivate a decision in the light of the relevant principles. Secondly, this decision, including its motivation, can be tested in court. Courts do test against these principles. Both contribute to a certain predictability of governmental and judicial decisions, and thus to an increase in legal certainty. This is important because environmental law

---

[52] E.g., the Belgian Council of State, 9 November 2000, No. 90.730.

[53] Case C-2/90, *Commission v. Belgium*, ECJ 9 July 1992, [1992] ECR I-4431.

[54] Joint cases C-175/98 and C-177/98, *Lirussi* and *Bizzaro*, ECJ 5 October 1999, [1999] ECR I-6881.

[55] (1993) 81 LGERA 270.

[56] Administrative Law Division Council of State, 12 May 2000, *Milieu en Recht* 27 (2000) 9, 231.

usually consists of general and procedural rules on the one hand, and a large body of rapidly changing technical norms on the other hand.

In 1999, when there was a discussion on the amount of a certain species of fish that could be caught without endangering the species, and legislation was not clear about the extent of the data to be produced to decide on fishing permits, the precautionary principle helped the Australian Government to underpin its decision on the distribution of fishing permits.[57] When the European Commission wanted to develop new, far-reaching legal instruments on environmental liability, it referred to the polluter pays principle to show that new measures were justified.[58]

Testing regulations and decisions against legal principles also enhances legitimacy: The courts see to it that governmental authorities apply basic environmental principles. There are many cases in which courts were asked to test a certain regulation against one or more environmental legal principles, such as the *Safety Hi-Tech/S&T* and *Bettati/ Safety Hi-Tech* cases before the European Court of Justice,[59] and a case on state taxes imposed on packaging waste in Germany.[60]

*4. Principles form the basis of new statutory rules*

Principles not only influence existing statutory rules, thus instructing governments, courts and citizens how to apply these rules; they also give guidance to rulemakers, as they form the basis for new statutory rules. When the basic principles of environmental law are codified in legislation, legislators are obliged to reflect on these principles every time new legislation is prepared. After all, new legislation has to be consistent with the principles; this can even be tested in court (at least in countries where legislation can be reviewed). The same goes for policies.

Considering the fact that environmental legislation is very often of a rather technical nature, reacting to a new problem or to new technologies that have been developed, reflecting on the basics is not a bad thing to do: it leads to a systematisation of statutory rules and makes it difficult simply to depend on *ad hoc* solutions. New rules must be justified by the principles, as these principles have been laid down as the basic goals of environmental law; they provide the legislator with a focal point.

---

[57] *Dixon and Ors and Australian Fisheries Management Authority*, [1999] *AATA* 1024 (21 December 1999).

[58] White Paper on Environmental Liability, COM(2000)66, pp. 11-12.

[59] Supra, footnote 43.

[60] *BVerfGE* 98, 106 (121).

Although it is not always easy to find out whether legislators actually considered the principles when drafting new legislation, the EC legislator often refers to the relevant principles in preambular recitals of directives. At a national level too, it is sometimes obvious from explanatory statements that principles did play a role, as was the case, for instance, with the precautionary principle and the 1998 Nature Protection Act in the Netherlands.[61] Still, it seems that things can be improved here: in our view, legislators have to consider explicitly and systematically new statutory rules and new policies in the light of existing principles. Of course, it would help when courts regularly test regulations against principles. Thus, the growing case law of the European Court of Justice may force EC legislators to be more consistent and precise in this respect.

## 5. Principles give guidance to self-regulation

Principles not only help to systematise government regulations, they also do so with the growing number of non-governmental or collaborative rules and standards. In fact, modern environmental law consists of a complex set of governmental and non-governmental rules and standards, all of which may originate either nationally or internationally, thus making the situation even more complex than before. Therefore, the need for systematisation is great.

The growing number of companies that develop and apply private environmental rules (such as environmental agreements, contracts, partnerships with NGOs and/or local communities, standards for environmental management systems), individually or through their organisations, in many countries lead to a declining role for command-and-control regulation.[62]

Self-regulation and regulatory reform, i.e. less regulation and enforcement of the command-and-control type, stress the need for the codification of principles. With fewer administrative rules, or more general rules (to allow businesses to apply their own standards, such as ISO14001), there is a greater need for guidance through principles. Also, principles may form the basis for agreements with industry and give some direction as to how industry should develop its own standards

---

[61] *Kamerstukken II*, 1996/97, 23 580, No. 11, p. 10. Cf. extensively Wybe Douma, 'The Precautionary Principle in the Netherlands', in Tim O'Riordan, James Cameron and Andrew Jordan (eds.), *Reinterpreting the Precautionary Principle*, London, Cameron May, 2001, pp. 163-181, at pp. 164-169.

[62] Eric W. Orts and Kurt Deketelaere, 'Introduction: Environmental Contracts and Regulatory Innovation', in Eric W. Orts and Kurt Deketelaere (eds.), *Environmental Contracts*, London, Kluwer Law International, 2001, pp. 1-35, at p. 2.

and rules. Especially in situations where industry or individual companies have to negotiate with NGOs or local communities, principles provide a common ground, a basis for further negotiations.[63] In the Netherlands, this is one of the main reasons to propose the codification of principles in the Environmental Management Act.

The latter implies that businesses have to adopt these principles as well, as it is not possible for the legislature to *force* industry to apply principles, except maybe in cases where the government is involved in self-regulation (for instance, when the authorities themselves are a party to an environmental contract).[64] However, not only international business organisations draft declarations with important environmental principles, individual companies too adhere to principles in their corporate environmental statements or guidelines. A certain pedagogical effect can be observed: businesses will have to consider their actions and policies in the light of the principles they have formulated in their corporate guidelines.[65]

Again, this function will be further strengthened when courts apply principles in (civil) cases involving companies and individual citizens or NGOs. Principles may help courts to define what are generally accepted standards, or to determine the scope of the right to the use of property among citizens (like in the Belgian case on the installation of antennas for mobile communications in residential areas in relation to the precautionary principle).[66] Environmental principles thus become general principles of law.

## 6. Principles create flexibility in the law

One of the main reasons for regulatory reform initiatives is to create more flexibility in environmental law. Companies should be allowed to change production methods or installations more easily, without expensive and time-consuming administrative procedures. Also, standard

---

[63] This would further ensure a more solid role for the public involved, amending Mank's proposals for a statute to implement 'responsible reform'; Bradford C. Mank, 'The Environmental Protection Agency's Project XL and Other Regulatory Reform Initiatives: The Need for Legislative Authorization', *Ecology Law Quarterly* 25 (1998) 1, 1-88, at p. 70.

[64] Jason Scott Johnston, 'The Law and Economics of Environmental Contracts', in Orts and Deketelaere, *Environmental Contracts*, pp. 271-304, at p. 288.

[65] Nash sees these 'pedagogical effects' as a result of the 'polluter pays' principle; Jonathan Remy Nash, 'Too Much Market? Conflict between Tradable Pollution Allowances and the "Polluter Pays" Principle', *Harvard Environmental Law Review* 24 (2000) 2, 465-535, at p. 479.

[66] Civil Court Ostend, 29 June 2000, [2000-01] AJT 197.

command-and-control instruments do not stimulate companies to go beyond what is written down in a licence, because doing so would only incur unilateral costs and competitive disadvantages.[67] Companies therefore tend to stick to their old, more polluting installations, rather than adapt to new technologies. Introducing market-based instruments and relying more on negotiation and persuasion to stimulate companies' own initiatives seems to be more effective in this respect.[68]

Principles come into the picture of regulatory reform not only to give guidance to self-regulation by industry and to (other) collaborative approaches (see above); they also *create* flexibility, in the sense that they are, by their nature, flexible norms: norms of a general and open character, leaving much freedom, to be applied in practice through general rules. Rulemakers can therefore limit themselves to making less detailed rules, which, in combination with a set of legal principles, offer a high level of protection to the environment, to be elaborated in collaborative approaches in which command-and-control elements are coupled with self-regulatory or market-based instruments.[69] Strasser even showed that prevention can only be achieved when moving towards company innovations, away from traditional pollution control.[70] This leads to the conclusion that the prevention principle can only be aimed for when introducing regulatory reform, which, in turn, implies the codification of principles, such as the prevention principle itself!

## 7. *Principles stimulate the integration of environmental considerations into other policy fields*

In Belgium and the Netherlands, one of the reasons to codify environmental legal principles in environmental legislation is to stimulate the integration of environmental considerations into other policy fields, i.e. other than the policy field of environmental protection. The integration of environmental objectives into all decision-making processes is considered to be a legal principle itself, a principle that has been laid down in various international documents, such as the Rio Declaration (Principle 4) and the EC Treaty (Article 6). Integrating environmental

---

[67] Jonathan Golub, 'Introduction and Overview', in Jonathan Golub (ed.), *New Instruments for Environmental Policy in the EU*, London [etc.], Routledge, 1998, pp. 1-29, at p. 4.

[68] Golub, 'Introduction', p. 6.

[69] An OECD study shows that a mix of instruments is most effective; Peter Börkey, Matthieu Glachant, Jean-Philippe Barde and François Lévêque, *Voluntary Approaches for Environmental Policy: An Assessment*, Paris, OECD, 1999.

[70] Kurt Strasser, 'Preventing Pollution', *Fordham Environmental Law Journal* VIII (1996) 1, 1-57, at p. 56.

objectives into decisions regarding traffic and transport, spatial planning, energy, agriculture and technology, however, appears to be difficult in practice, because of conflicting interests. It is thought that principles are less threatening for other policy fields, because of their general wording and because of the fact that they are not directly legally binding, but only through the application of legal rules. Therefore, they leave enough room to give equal attention to all interests at stake. Interestingly, the above-mentioned Belgian case law shows that the integration of the precautionary principle into telecommunications decisions and decisions on the use of property does indeed take place.

## 6. Giving Legal Shape to the Ideal of Biodiversity Conservation: The Convention on Biological Diversity

In the preceding section it was argued that the ideal of sustainable development was at the basis of the Rio Declaration and thus influenced environmental law through the Declaration's principles. The ideal of biodiversity conservation, however, was given a somewhat different legal shape, viz. a central position as an overall objective of the UN Convention on Biological Diversity. In fact, the ideal has been elaborated in various provisions of the Convention. In the present section we take a closer look at the Convention, and we will try to show that its specific characteristics have made it a useful and effective framework for further development and clarification of the ideals of biodiversity conservation.

In its 1987 report *Our Common Future*, the WCED expressed its concern about the alarming rate at which species and ecosystems were disappearing, and suggested that governments investigate the prospect of agreeing to a 'Species Convention' to address the problem.[71] Taking the hint, the United Nations Environment Programme set up a group of experts that was given the task of 'investigating the desirability and possible form of an umbrella convention to rationalize current activities in this field'.[72] After UNEP had concluded that the drafting of an additional legal instrument of some sort, 'possibly in the form of a framework convention', was in fact desirable,[73] formal negotiations were commenced, and these led eventually to the adoption in May 1992 of the

---

[71] *Our Common Future*, p. 162; the WCED in its turn referred to work already done by the IUCN, which as early as 1984 had advocated the drafting of a global agreement on conservation of the world's wild genetic resources (IUCN-GA Res. 16/24, November 1984).

[72] UNEP GC Decision 14/26, 17 June 1987.

[73] UNEP GC Decision 15/34, 25 May 1989.

UN Convention on Biological Diversity. The negotiating process, however, was not an easy one, dominated as it was by controversies between different groups of nations – especially between the developed and the developing countries.[74] Since a draft convention had to be ready for signature before the UN Conference on Environment and Development in Rio de Janeiro, which started 4 June 1992, there was a strong pressure on the delegates to reach consensus before that date; however, disagreement on many issues turned out to be too strong to reach consensus, and the final draft consequently shows traces of compromise in many respects.

The Biodiversity Convention has been referred to as a 'Framework Convention', which means that the Convention itself contains provisions that are either of a formal and procedural nature, or that impose only rather vague and general obligations upon the parties. An example of the latter category can be found in Article 8(a), which states that the parties are to '[e]stablish a system of protected areas or areas where special measures need to be taken to conserve biological diversity', but does not specify how many of these areas should be established, how large they should be, what locations would be suitable, what level of protection would be needed, etc. Similarly, the same article states in section (d) that each Contracting Party is to '[p]romote the protection of ecosystems, natural habitats and the maintenance of viable populations of species in natural surroundings'. Again, in the Article itself nothing is said about the way in which this protection or maintenance is to take place. Moreover, since the provisions of Article 8 and most other Articles apply only 'as far as possible and as appropriate' and, in the end, it is the Contracting Party itself that decides to what extent application is in fact possible and appropriate, this kind of provisions leaves much room for interpretation by the party concerned.

Conventions of this kind usually provoke sceptic, or at best mixed, responses. Most authors, and perhaps lawyers in general, intuitively prefer clear, unambiguous and binding rules and standards to vague ones that can be interpreted in different and sometimes conflicting ways and that can (at least theoretically) be ignored by the addressees if they want to.[75] Thus, with regard to the Biodiversity Convention, Boyle concludes in line with objections raised by the United States that

---

[74] See Veit Koester, 'The Biodiversity Convention Negotiation Process and Some Comments on the Outcome', *Environmental Policy and Law* 27 (1997) 3, 175-191, at p. 181.

[75] With regard to the UN Framework Convention on Climate Change, Bodansky e.g. remarks that 'continuing disagreements about the magnitude of the threat [i.e., global warming] and the costliness of response measures have thus far prevented the nego-

[the Convention's] central obligations of conservation and sustainable use are weak, potentially contradictory and may prove difficult to operate in practice. Moreover, the heavily qualified wording of the Convention's central articles, including the frequent use of the words 'as far as possible' and 'appropriate' leaves open to question how far the parties are in reality committed to anything. It will not be clear for some time whether the Convention provides a viable framework for real progress or is merely an exercise in political symbolism.[76]

However, as we noted before, not only would it have been extremely difficult to get 180 countries to agree on specific and concrete obligations,[77] it would not have been desirable either. Laying down such rules in the Convention itself would have made it impossible to take all relevant local circumstances into account, or to adapt the measures to be taken to changes in those circumstances. With this in mind, the fact that the CBD is drafted as a framework convention can be appraised more positively.

Two other features of the CBD are of importance here. The first is that, as we mentioned before, the ideal of the conservation of biological diversity has been incorporated into the objectives of the CBD. Article 1 of the Convention reads as follows:

> The objectives of this Convention, to be pursued in accordance with its relevant provisions, are the conservation of biological diversity, the sustainable use of its components and the fair and equitable sharing of the benefits arising out of the utilization of genetic resources...

---

tiation of an international agreement requiring specific actions to mitigate global warming. Instead, the most that could be achieved in the [UNFCCC] was to establish a regime for addressing the climate change problem in the future – a regime involving national planning, continued scientific research and assessments, and a legal and institutional framework to facilitate the adoption of international control measures if they are ultimately deemed necessary.' The phrase 'the most that could be achieved' indicates that, in the author's view, an agreement 'requiring specific actions' would have constituted a better outcome. Daniel Bodansky, 'Managing Climate Change', *Yearbook of International Environmental Law* 1 (1993), pp. 60-74, at p. 60.

[76]   Alan E. Boyle, 'The Rio Convention on Biological Diversity', in Michael Bowman and Catherine Redgwell (eds.), *International Law and the Conservation of Biological Diversity*, London, Kluwer Law International, 1996, pp. 33-49, at p. 49.

[77]   Burhenne-Guilmin and Casey-Lefkowitz argue that probably the only alternative to using qualifiers such as 'as far as possible or appropriate' in the Convention's obligations would have been weakening the obligation itself; F. Burhenne-Guilmin and S. Casey-Lefkowitz, 'The Convention on Biological Diversity: A Hard Won Global Achievement', *Yearbook of International Environmental Law* 1 (1993), pp. 43-59, at p. 51.

In spite of the somewhat fuzzy and open-ended character of the phrase 'conservation of biological diversity' referred to above, by incorporating it as an overall objective in Article 1 the drafters of the Convention gave it a key role in the interpretation of the remainder of the Convention's provisions. Apart from the text of the Article itself, which states that the Convention's objectives must be pursued and that this should be done 'in accordance with its relevant provisions', a legal basis for this role can be found in Article 31 of the Vienna Convention on the Law of Treaties, which states that any treaty '... shall be interpreted... in the light of its object and purpose'.[78] Furthermore, reference to the aim of biodiversity conservation is made not only in the CBD's objectives, but also in a considerable number of the Convention's provisions.[79] This way of drafting makes it clear that even if the Parties have considerable room for interpreting the Convention's provisions in the way which suits them best, in the end all actions and measures taken under the CBD should be aimed at conserving biodiversity. Thus, the ideal of biodiversity conservation provides the background against which the Convention's Articles should be read.

The second feature of the CBD worth mentioning is that, as is typical for framework conventions, it contains a number of Articles of a more formal and procedural nature, whose importance should not be overlooked. Especially relevant in this respect are Articles 23 (establishing a Conference of the Parties or COP), 24 (establishing a Secretariat), 25 (establishing the Subsidiary Body on Scientific, Technical and Technological Advice or SBSTTA), 26 (putting an obligation on all Parties to report to the COP on the measures they have taken for the implementation of the Convention) and 28 (which provides for the adoption by the COP of Protocols). These provisions set up a structure within which further debate and more substantive decision-making can take place. An example of the results this approach may lead to is the Cartagena Biosafety Protocol, based on Article 28 of the CBD, which was concluded in January 2000.[80] Starting from the Convention text, which in Article 19(3) states that the Parties are to consider 'the need for and modalities of a protocol' with regard to the safe handling and use of genetically modified organisms (GMOs), the Cartagena Protocol provides for fairly detailed regulations that must be observed when GMOs are moved from one Party to another, including an 'advance informed agreement procedure'. This way, one aspect of biodiversity conservation that could be

---

[78]   Vienna, 23 May 1969, 1155 UNTS 331, Art. 31(1).

[79]   See, e.g., Arts. 5, 6, 7(a) and (c), 8(a), (c), (g), (i), (j), (l) and (m), 9(a) (b), 10, 11, 12, 13 and 14.

[80]   See, supra, section 5.1.

regulated in a uniform manner and on which agreement could be reached was translated into more concrete rules.

A central role in this process of implementing and clarifying the Convention's objectives and through them the ideal of biodiversity conservation is played by the COP. According to Article 23, the COP meets at regular intervals – during its first meeting it was decided that the COP was to meet every two years[81] – and has as its main task to keep the implementation of the Convention under review. Apart from adopting protocols – the Cartagena Biosafety Protocol was signed by the COP – and amending protocols or the Convention itself, the COP considers the national reports handed in by the Parties, reviews technical and scientific advice provided by the SBSTTA and lays down guidelines for its activities, co-ordinates efforts taken under the CBD with actions taken under other relevant Conventions, and considers and undertakes 'any additional action that may be required for the achievement of the purposes of [the CBD] in the light of experience gained in its opera-tion'.[82] Over the last ten years, the COP has discussed almost all of the Convention's provisions and developed guidelines on its implementa-tion with regard to many different subjects. Although these guidelines are not legally binding, they are considered authoritative because they are the result of consensus among the Parties.

Two examples (out of many) can be given here of the way the COP elaborated the Convention's provisions. Article 7 calls, among other things, for the identification and monitoring by the Parties of compo-nents of biodiversity that are 'important for its conservation and sustain-able use', and for the identification of processes and activities which may have 'significant adverse impacts' on biodiversity. The COP, and the SBSTTA under its supervision, have addressed the question of how this identification and monitoring should take place, with particular focus on the role that biodiversity indicators could have in these proc-esses. In 1997, the SBSTTA published a paper entitled 'Recommenda-tions for a Core Set of Indicators of Biological Diversity',[83] in which the notion of a Natural Capital Index (NCI) was examined. This NCI com-prises several aspects of biological diversity such as species richness, rarity and endemism, as well as the quantity of area of a certain type (e.g., forests, wetlands, etc.) which are compared with the ecological

---

[81]   Rules of Procedure, adopted by the COP in Decision I/1 (annex), Rule 4.

[82]   Art. 23(4)(i).

[83]   UNEP/CBD/SBSTTA/3/9, published in the *Handbook of the Convention on Biologi-cal Diversity*. The Handbook is available from the CBD website <http://www.biodiv.org>.

quality and quantity at an earlier point in time (say 50 or 100 years earlier) and expressed as a percentage. This way, the NCI can be used to indicate the ecological quality of a given area or region, to identify trends in ecosystem quality and quantity and to assess the effectiveness of the measures taken by the Parties to implement the Convention's provisions.[84] Another example is the way in which the COP has given effect to Article 8(h), which states that Parties should prevent the introduction of 'alien species which threaten ecosystems, habitats or species'. During its fifth meeting, it proposed a set of fifteen guiding principles to the Parties that should be observed when dealing with alien species; among these are the precautionary principle and the ecosystem approach, as well as principles pertaining to border control and quarantaine measures, risk assessment prior to a decision to introduce alien species into the environment, etc.

These three examples, the Biosafety Protocol and the work done with respect to Articles 7 and 8(h), show how, starting from the objective of conserving biodiversity, the COP and other institutions set up by the Convention such as the SBSTTA help Parties implement the CBD's obligations and help give a more concrete meaning to provisions which in themselves are rather open-ended. In the Protocol, one particular aspect of biodiversity conservation was singled out and was made the object of common regulation. The development of Articles 7 and 8(h) show how the institutional and procedural framework provided by the CBD may lead to more concrete norms and principles that still allow regulation and standard-setting in accordance with local circumstances, problems and possibilities. In this way, as was the case with sustainable development, the ideal of biodiversity conservation affects legal development in an indirect way. Whereas sustainable development influenced developments in environmental policy and law mainly through the principles adopted at the UNCED, the CBD framework convention has been an intermediary through which biodiversity conservation has been given more concrete implementation.

## 7. Conclusion

What role can ideals play with regard to legal development? Can they provide guidance? If so, in what way and under what circumstances? And do ideals make development possible or even stimulate it, as Van der Burg and Taekema claim? These are the main questions that

---

[84]  See also UNEP/CBD/SBSTTA/5/12, para. 51. On the concept of an NCI, see the report by B. ten Brink, 'Biodiversity Indicators for the OECD Environmental Outlook and Strategy: A Feasibility Study', Bilthoven, RIVM, 2000.

we addressed in this chapter, using the ideals of sustainable development and of biodiversity conservation as cases in point. With regard to
these two ideals, we tried to show that it is illusory to think that, taken
by themselves, they can 'guide' legal development in the sense that
agreement on their importance immediately leads to agreement on the
legal and other measures that are required for their implementation.
Both sustainable development and biodiversity conservation in themselves leave too much room for interpretation for us to be able to indicate the concrete actions that would be necessary to bring these ideals
closer, or even to serve as a criterion by which to assess which measures
might adversely affect their pursuit.

By contrast, these two ideals have proved very effective in stimulating development in international law (and, indirectly, in national law as
well). In our view, it is precisely those characteristics that make them
ineffective in guiding legal development that make these ideals highly
suitable as catalysts for debate and discussion and in this way stimulate
legal development. These two features – the fact that they provide
guidance to legal development only to a very limited extent but at the
same time constitute strong factors in enabling such a development – in
our view represent two sides of the same coin.

However, we have argued that this lack of 'guiding capacity' should
not necessarily be considered a drawback. The two ideals at hand cannot
be implemented in a globally uniform way, nor should they. Instead,
their implementation should take place taking into account all the relevant local and regional environmental, economic, social and cultural
circumstances. The ways in which the two ideals have been incorporated
into international law – as the background notion which was at the basis
of the Rio Declaration principles and the overall objective of the CBD,
respectively – is fully in line with these requirements. Moreover, the
frameworks provided by the Declaration's principles, by its Articles and
by COP decisions have played an important role in clarifying and implementing the ideals of sustainable development and biodiversity
conservation, as the examples given in sections 5 and 6 show.

The question to what extent our findings concerning the two ideals
under discussion here can be transposed to other ideals and other settings cannot be answered easily. Ideals may take many different shapes,
ranging from very abstract and general notions like 'justice' or 'equity'
to ideas that are applicable in a specific setting only or that concern only
a limited number of people. Typical for sustainable development and
biodiversity conservation is that they are both part of the vocabulary of
today's international legal system, which means that all states, many
international organisations (both governmental and non-governmental)

and even private enterprises and 'ordinary people' have their own roles and responsibilities in the process of implementing them, and all look upon these ideals from their own perspective. This, of course, makes it extremely difficult to find a way of translating the ideal into measures and activities that everyone agrees to. However, as we have tried to show, if given the proper legal form, even such highly abstract and multi-faceted ideals can facilitate discussions and bring about major changes in international law – changes, by the way, that are still taking place today, and will probably continue to do so in the next decades.

## References

Aarnio, Aulis, 'Taking Rules Seriously', in Werner Maihofer and Gerhard Sprenger (eds.), *Law and the States in Modern Times*, Stuttgart, Steiner, 1990, pp. 180-192.

Beckermann, Wilfried, '"Sustainable Development": Is It a Useful Concept?', in D. VanDeVeer, and C. Pierce (eds.), *The Environmental Ethics and Policy Book*, Belmont, Cal., Wadsworth, 1998, pp. 462-474.

Birnie, Patricia W., and Alan E. Boyle, *International Law and the Environment*, 2nd ed., Oxford [etc.], Oxford University Press, 2002.

Bodansky, Daniel, 'Managing Climate Change', *Yearbook of International Environmental Law* 1 (1993), 60-74.

Börkey, Peter, Matthieu Glachant, Jean-Philippe Barde and François Lévêque, *Voluntary Approaches for Environmental Policy: An Assessment*, Paris, OECD, 1999.

Boyle, Alan E., 'The Rio Convention on Biological Diversity', in Michael Bowman and Catherine Redgwell (eds.), *International Law and the Conservation of Biological Diversity*, London, Kluwer Law International, 1996, pp. 33-49.

Burhenne-Guilmin, F., and S. Casey-Lefkowitz, 'The Convention on Biological Diversity: A Hard Won Global Achievement', *Yearbook of International Environmental Law* 1 (1993), 43-59.

Callicott, J.B., and K. Mumford, 'Ecological Sustainability as a Conservation Concept', *Conservation Biology* 11 (1997) 1, 32-40.

Doherty, Michael, 'The Status of the Principles of EC Environmental Law: Gianni Bettati against Safety Hi-Tech', *Journal of Environmental Law* 11 (1999) 2, 354-386.

Douma, Wybe, 'The Precautionary Principle in the Netherlands', in Tim O'Riordan, James Cameron and Andrew Jordan (eds.), *Reinterpreting the Precautionary Principle*, London, Cameron May, 2001, pp. 163-181.

*Global Biodiversity Strategy: Guidelines for Action to Save, Study, and Use Earth's Biotic Wealth Sustainably and Equitably*, Washington DC, WRI/IUCN/UNEP, 1992.

Golub, Jonathan, 'Introduction and Overview', in Jonathan Golub (ed.), *New Instruments for Environmental Policy in the EU*, London [etc.], Routledge, 1998, pp. 1-29.

Johnston, Jason Scott, 'The Law and Economics of Environmental Contracts', in Eric W. Orts and Kurt Deketelaere (eds.), *Environmental Contracts*, London, Kluwer Law International, 2001, pp. 271-304.

Kidd, C.V., 'The Evolution of Sustainability', *Journal of Agricultural and Environmental Ethics* 1 (1992), 1-26.

Kiss, A., 'Framework Conventions: A Legal Technique for International Environmental Protection', in *Symposium on the United Nations Conference on Environment and Development (UNCED), the Convention on Biological Diversity and the Bern Convention: The Next Steps*, Strasbourg, Council of Europe Publishing, 1995, pp. 107-112.

Koester, Veit, 'The Biodiversity Convention Negotiation Process and Some Comments on the Outcome', *Environmental Policy and Law* 27 (1997) 3, 175-191.

Lawson, Gary, 'A Farewell to Principles', *Iowa Law Review* 82 (1997) 2, 893-903.

Lyster, S., *International Wildlife Law*, Cambridge, Grotius, 1985.

MacCormick, Neil, 'Law as Institutional Fact', *Law Quarterly Review* 90 (1974), 102-129.

Mank, Bradford C., 'The Environmental Protection Agency's Project XL and Other Regulatory Reform Initiatives: The Need for Legislative Authorization', *Ecology Law Quarterly* 25 (1998) 1, 1-88.

Nash, Jonathan Remy, 'Too Much Market? Conflict between Tradable Pollution Allowances and the "Polluter Pays" Principle', *Harvard Environmental Law Review* 24 (2000) 2, 465-535.

Orts, Eric W., and Kurt Deketelaere, 'Introduction: Environmental Contracts and Regulatory Innovation', in Eric W. Orts and Kurt Deketelaere (eds.), *Environmental Contracts*, London, Kluwer Law International, 2001, pp. 1-35.

*Our Common Future*, [s.l.], World Commission on Environment and Development, 1987.

Pallemaerts, Marc, 'International Environmental Law from Stockholm to Rio: Back to the Future?', in Ph. Sands (ed.), *Greening International Law*, London, Earthscan, 1993, pp. 1-19.

Pearce, David, *et al.*, *Blueprint 3: Measuring Sustainable Development*, London, Earthscan, 1993.

Pezzey, J., *Sustainable Development Concepts: An Economic Analysis*, Washington DC, The World Bank, 1992.

Rodda, Gordon H., 'How to Lie with Biodiversity', *Conservation Biology* 7 (1993) 4, 959-960.

Sands, Ph. (ed.), *Greening International Law*, London, Earthscan, 1993.

————, 'Turtles and Torturers: The Transformation of International Law', *New York University Journal of International Law and Politics* 33 (2001) 2, 527-560.

Selznick, Philip, *The Moral Commonwealth: Social Theory and the Promise of Community*, Berkeley, Cal., University of California Press, 1992.

————, 'Sociology and Natural Law', *Natural Law Forum* 6 (1961), 84-108.

Strasser, Kurt, 'Preventing Pollution', *Fordham Environmental Law Journal* VIII (1996) 1, 1-57.

Swanson, T.M., and S. Johnston, *Global Environmental Problems and International Environmental Agreements: The Economics of International Institution Building*, Cheltenham, Edward Elgar, 1996.

Ten Brink, B., 'Biodiversity Indicators for the OECD Environmental Outlook and Strategy: A Feasibility Study', Bilthoven, RIVM, 2000.

Van der Maarel, E., *Biodiversity: From Babel to Biosphere Management*, Uppsala, Opulus Press, 1997.

VanDeVeer, D., and C. Pierce (eds.), *The Environmental Ethics and Policy Book*, Belmont Cal., Wadsworth, 1998.

Verschuuren, Jonathan, *Principles of Environmental Law: The Ideal of Sustainable Development and the Role of Principles of International, European and National Environmental Law*, Baden-Baden, Nomos, 2003.

Willers, Bill, 'Sustainable Development: A New World Deception', *Conservation Biology* 8 (1994) 4, 1146-1148.

# Subject Index

# Author Index

# List of Contributors

All contributors are former participants of the PIONIER-research programme on the importance of ideals.

**Peter Blok** works as an attorney in Amsterdam. He wrote his dissertation on privacy, published as *Het recht op privacy* (Boom Juridische Uitgevers 2002).

**Wouter de Been** is a Ph.D. candidate at the University of Tilburg. His dissertation on American Legal Realism and pragmatism is to be completed in 2004.

**Marc Hertogh** is Associate Professor of Socio-Legal Studies at Tilburg University. His current research interests include: empirical studies of the rule of law, legal consciousness, dispute resolution, and Eugen Ehrlich. He is the editor (with Simon Halliday) of *Judicial Review & Bureaucratic Impact: International and Interdisciplinary Perspectives* (Cambridge Studies in Law and Society) (to be published by Cambridge University Press 2004).

**Timon Oudenaarden** works as a legislative advisor at the Dutch Council of State. His dissertation on biodiversity in national and international law is to be completed in 2004.

**Roland Pierik** is Assistant Professor of Political Theory and Jurisprudence at Tilburg University. His research interests are contemporary political theory, especially liberal egalitarianism in plural and multicultural societies, and issues of global justice. He wrote a dissertation on Dworkinian egalitarian political theory in relation to multicultural difference (2000).

**Caroline Raat** works as a legal advisor at the Rijnland District Water Control Board. Her dissertation on the rule of law in private organisations with a public responsibility is to be completed in 2004.

**Sanne Taekema** is Assistant Professor of Jurisprudence at Tilburg University. She writes on legal theory, pragmatism, the role of values in law, and law and literature. Her book *The Concept of Ideals in Legal Theory* was published by Kluwer in 2003.

**Bert van den Brink** is Research Fellow of the Royal Netherlands Academy of Arts and Sciences, and Assistant Professor of Social and Political Philosophy at Utrecht University. His research interests and publications are in the fields of contemporary social and political philosophy and critical social theory. Among his publications are *The Tragedy of Liberalism* (SUNY Press 2000) and (co-edited with Willem van Reijen) *Bürgergesellschaft, Recht und Demokratie* (Suhrkamp 1995).

**Wibren van der Burg** is Professor of Jurisprudence at Tilburg University; from 1996 until 2002, he was the director of the research program *The Importance of Ideals in Law, Morality and Politics*. He writes on law and ethics, methods of ethics, communicative legislation, interactionist approaches to law, and political philosophy. He published four books in Dutch, and co-edited *Rediscovering Fuller* (Amsterdam University Press 1999) and *Reflective Equilibrium* (Kluwer 1998).

**Jonathan Verschuuren** is Professor of European and International Environmental Law at Tilburg University. He published seven books in Dutch, and one in English, entitled *Principles of Environmental Law* (Nomos 2003). He is a member of the Commission on Environmental Law of the IUCN (World Conservation Union).

**Willem Witteveen** is Professor of Jurisprudence at Tilburg University. Presently he is also a member of the Upper House of the Parliament of the Netherlands. His current research interests are communicative legislation, the political theory of the rule of law, the rhetorical tradition, and law and literature. Among his publications are five books in Dutch; he also co-edited *Rediscovering Fuller* (Amsterdam University Press 1999).

# "Philosophy & Politics"

Open to thinkers from all countries and cultures who are not limiting their efforts to understand the processes of social institutions, but are raising questions about their goals and meaning, this series hopes to contribute to a renewal of political philosophy. Beyond the different disciplines of social sciences, ideological commitments and the limits of "national schools", philosophy is bound to pursue its universal enquiry on human wisdom in a world chaotically pushed towards greater unity.

*Series directed by Gabriel Fragnière*

## Series Titles

*The Importance of Ideals. Debating Their Relevance in Law, Morality, and Politics*, Wibren VAN DER BURG & Sanne TAEKEMA (eds.), No. 10, 274 p., 2004, ISBN 90-5201-226-1

*Social Sciences and Political Change. Promoting Innovative Research in Post-Socialist Countries*, Robin CASSLING & Gabriel FRAGNIÈRE (eds.), No. 9, 297 p., 2003, ISBN 90-5201-168-0

*Working-Class Women in Academia. A Philosophical Inquiry*, Claudia LEEB, No. 8 (forthcoming), ISBN 90-5201-979-7

*L'autonomie éthique. Débat démocratique et vérité*, Giuseppe G. NASTRI, No. 7, 2002, 200 p., ISBN 90-5201-972-X

*Plus est en l'homme. Le personnalisme vécu comme humanisme radical*, Vincent TRIEST, No. 6, 2000, 214 p., ISBN 90-5201-922-3

*Enlightenment and Genocide, the Contradictions of Modernity*, James KAYE & Bo STRÅTH (eds.), No. 5, 2000, 278 p., ISBN 90-5201-919-3

*Les défis du nationalisme moderne. Québec, Catalogne, Écosse*, Michael KEATING, No. 4, 1997, 298 p., ISBN 90-5201-705-0

*Pour une philosophie de l'opinion et de la citoyenneté. Essai européen de mémoire et de stratégie sophistiques*, Henri WIBAULT, No. 3, 1996, 389 p., ISBN 90-5201-514-7

*L'obligation morale et l'éthique de la prospérité*, Gabriel FRAGNIÈRE, No. 2, 1993, 270 p., ISBN 90-5201-304-7

*L'État providence. Un débat philosophique / The Welfare State. A Philosophical Debate*, Guus (A.)J.M. VAN WEERS (ed.), No. 1, 1986, 164 p., ISBN 90-70776-12-X

**Peter Lang—The website**

Discover the general website of the Peter Lang publishing group:

**www.peterlang.net**

You will find

– an online bookshop of currently about 21,000 titles from the entire publishing
  group, which allows quick and easy ordering
– all books published since 1992
– an overview of our journals and series
– contact forms for new authors and customers
– information about the activities of each publishing house

Come and browse! We look forward to your visit!